MEDIEVAL & ENGLISH & THEATRE

VOLUME FORTY-FOUR (2022)

MEDIEVAL & ENGLISH THEATRE

VOLUME FORTY-FOUR (2022)

Executive Editor: Meg Twycross
General Editors: Sarah Carpenter, Elisabeth Dutton, & Gordon Kipling

D. S. BREWER

Medieval English Theatre is an international refereed journal publishing articles on medieval and early Tudor theatre and pageantry in all its aspects (not confined to England), together with articles and records of modern survivals or equivalents. Most issues are illustrated. Contributions to be considered for future volumes are welcomed: see end of this volume and website for further information:
<www.medievalenglishtheatre.co.uk>.

© *Medieval English Theatre* and contributors (2023)

All Rights Reserved. Except as permitted under current legislation, no part of this work may be photocopied, stored in a retrieval system, published, performed in public, adapted, broadcast, transmitted, recorded or reproduced in any form or by any means, without the prior permission of the copyright owner

First published 2023
D. S. Brewer, Cambridge

ISBN 978 1 84384 649 9
ISSN 0143–3784

D. S. Brewer is an imprint of Boydell & Brewer Ltd
PO Box 9, Woodbridge, Suffolk IP12 3DF, UK
and of Boydell & Brewer Inc.
668 Mt Hope Avenue, Rochester, NY 14620–2731
website: www.boydellandbrewer.com

A catalogue record for this title is available from the British Library

The publisher has no responsibility for the continued existence or accuracy of URLs for external or third-party internet websites referred to in this book, and does not guarantee that any content on such websites is, or will remain, accurate or appropriate

MEDIEVAL & ENGLISH & THEATRE

VOLUME FORTY-FOUR (2022)

CONTENTS

List of Illustrations	vi
Notes on Cover Image and Online Links	vii
List of Common Abbreviations	viii
Editorial	1

Nadia T. van Pelt
    John Blanke's Wages: No Business Like Show Business   3

Pamela M. King
    Perpetually Editing Towneley: A Speculative Textual Note on Mrs Noah's 'Stafford Blue'   36

Ben Parsons and Bas Jongenelen
    Understanding the Blanket-Toss in Medieval Drama: The Case of *Een Cluijt van Lijsgen en Jan Lichthart*   48

Ernst Gerhardt
    Alimentary Address and the Management of Appetite and Hunger in *Jacob and Esau*   91

Elisabeth Dutton and Olivia Robinson
    Last Supper, First Communion: Some Staging Challenges in N. Town and the Huy Nuns' Play based on Deguileville's *Pèlerinage de la vie humaine*   124

Editorial Board	161
Submission of Articles	162

ILLUSTRATIONS

Ben Parsons and Bas Jongenelen: 'Understanding the Blanket-Toss'

FIG. 1	The *Vuilen Bruidegom* being tossed in a blanket in the *Ommegang* of St Rumbold of 1775: detail from commemorative booklet, BL 1482 d. 1(1)	57
FIG. 2	Valentijn van der Lantscroon *Opsinjoorke* (1645); Museum Hof van Busleyden, Mechelen	58

Elisabeth Dutton and Olivia Robinson: 'Last Supper, First Communion'

FIG. 1	Fra Angelico *The Last Supper*; Florence: Museo San Marco, fresco 1437–1446	134
FIG. 2	'Moses', accompanied by Grace Dieu, distributes wafers to kneeling pilgrims; BNF MS Français 1577 (1345–1377) fol. 7r detail, Deguileville *Pèlerinage de la vie humaine*	141
FIG. 3	Moses and Grace Dieu at table with three others, from Bodleian Library MS Douce 300 (c.1400) fol. 13v; Deguileville *Pèlerinage de la vie humaine*	147
FIG. 4	The Bleeding Host of Dijon, from BNF MS lat 1156A (before 1480) fol. 22r; Heures de René d'Anjou	149
FIG. 5	*The Hospitality of Abraham and the Sacrifice of Isaac*; Ravenna: San Vitale, mosaic, 546–556	150
FIG. 6	Charity (Sylvia Wiederkehr), instructed by Wisdom (Elisa Pagliaro) prepares the *relief* for pilgrims; from the Medieval Convent Drama Project film	152
FIG. 7	Maître d'Antoine Rolin *The Bleeding Scrip*; Bibliothèque de Genève, Ms. fr. 182 #1 (after 1465) fol. 45r; prose version of Deguileville's *Pèlerinage*	157

Full credit details are provided in the captions to the images in the text. The editors, contributors, and publisher are grateful to all the institutions and persons for permission to reproduce the materials in which they hold copyright. Every effort has been made to trace the copyright holders; apologies are offered for any omission, and the publisher will be pleased to add any necessary acknowledgement in subsequent editions.

NOTES

Cover Image

'Shawm band with sackbut player', detail from Master of the Retable of Santa Auta *Encontro de Santa Úrsula e do Princípe Conan* ('Meeting of Saint Ursula and Prince Conan'), left panel interior of the *Retábulo de Santa Auta* ('Retable of St Auta') (1522–1525), © Museu Nacional de Arte Antiga, Rua das Janelas Verdes, 1249-017, Lisbon, Portugal. Inventory number 1462-A. Oil on oak panel. Photographer Luísa Oliveira (2018). Reproduced by kind permission of the Direção-Geral do Património Cultural/Arquivo de Documentação Fotográfica (DGPC/ADF).

The painting was originally made for the Convento da Madre de Deus ('Convent of the Mother of God'), Xabregas, Lisbon, which was founded in 1509 by Queen Leonor (Eleanora) of Viseu, widow of John II of Portugal and sister of King Manuel I. St Auta was one of the eleven thousand virgins martyred with St Ursula at Cologne. Her relics were sent to Dom Manuel I by their cousin the Emperor Maximilian in 1517, and enshrined in the chapel built in the convent by Leonor.

Online Links

An active list of all the URLs referred to in the current volume is posted on the METh website at <www.medievalenglishtheatre.co.uk/urlsvol44.html>. This enables the reader to view coloured images and link to video, as well as giving access where possible to online texts and articles.

COMMON ABBREVIATIONS

AND	*Anglo-Norman Dictionary Online* edited William Rothwell, David Trotter, Geert De Wilde, and others, Aberystwyth University, 2005– <https://anglo-norman.net>
DMLBS	*A Dictionary of Medieval Latin from British Sources* edited R.E. Latham, D.R. Howlett, and R.K. Ashdowne (British Academy: Oxford, 1975–2013): available online via subscribing libraries or from <http://logeion.uchicago.edu> (search by headword)
EETS	*Early English Text Society*
	ES *Extra Series*
	OS *Ordinary Series*
	SS *Special Series*
HMC	Historical Manuscripts Commission
Letters and Papers	*Letters and Papers, Foreign and Domestic, of the Reign of Henry VIII* edited J.S. Brewer, James Gairdner, and R.H. Brodie (London: HMSO by Longman, Green, Longman, Roberts & Green, 1862–1932); online at <https://www.british-history.ac.uk/search/series/letters-papers-hen8>
MED	*Middle English Dictionary*: online version © 2001, the Regents of the University of Michigan <https://quod-lib-umich-edu> available via subscribing libraries
NRS	National Records of Scotland
ODNB	*Oxford Dictionary of National Biography*: online version (Oxford UP, 2004–) at <https://www.oxforddnb.com/> available via subscribing libraries
OED	*Oxford English Dictionary*: online version © 2019 Oxford University Press <www.oed.com> available via subscribing libraries

PL	*Patrologia Latina* edited J.-P. Migne, 221 vols (Paris: Migne, then Garnier, 1844–91). Online at <https://catalog.hathitrust.org/Record/007035196>
REED	*Records of Early English Drama*
STS	*Scottish Text Society*
TNA	The National Archives

EDITORIAL

The forty-fourth meeting of *Medieval English Theatre* in 2022 was the third held online, as COVID restrictions continued. The conference took the theme of *Editing and Adapting*, being held in memory of Peter Happé and Martial Rose, two recently lost eminent scholars of medieval theatre, especially in the fields of editing and modern performance. Hosted by Jodi-Anne George from Dundee, the meeting was generously enabled by Clare Egan when the pandemic struck down its host. A tribute having been offered to Peter Happé last year, the day opened with a memorial from Phil Butterworth, recalling Martial Rose's influential and groundbreaking production of 'The Wakefield Plays' at Bretton Hall (1958) and at the Mermaid Theatre in London in the early 1960s, and sharing vivid extracts from his correspondence.

Several papers addressed early and recent issues in the editing of texts of medieval theatre. Meg Twycross gave a wide-ranging account of the problems confronting would-be editors in the late seventeenth and the eighteenth centuries, from lack of access to the manuscripts to an anti-Catholic mindset that inevitably distorted their narrative. Garrett Epp brought home the importance of modern editors' sensitivity to performance, as well as text, in supplying stage directions for early playscripts, while Diana Wyatt opened up the very different editorial techniques needed to unpack the theatrical implications of the record evidence gathered by the REED project. Pamela King offered an insight into the importance of detail in editing as she explored the potentially revealing meanings in just two words of the Towneley *Noah*.

On adaptation, Bart Ramakers and Elsa Strietman reported on a major project to stage a fascinating Dutch *tafelspel*, and the fundamental questions it poses about engaging modern audiences with historically based performance. Eleanor Bloomfield and Tom Straszewski each considered modern adaptations of York plays, Eleanor addressing the revivals since 1951 that engage the plays with contemporary concerns, and Strasz the *bricolage* shaping of a site-specific production of the plays of Our Lady for the church of All Saints, North Street, York. Hilariously visual – and thought-provoking – entertainment was provided by Jeffery Stoyanoff's 'TikTok-ing The Fall'.

The papers in this volume take forward a number of rich, often interlocking, strands and themes that have been developing in recent

EDITORIAL

Medieval English Theatre issues and conference meetings. Nadia van Pelt's timely and topical paper presents the first in-depth scholarly investigation into the employment by Henry VII and Henry VIII of the now-famous Black Tudor trumpeter John Blanke. While nuancing our understanding of the international nature of court entertainment, it continues the royal theme that dominated the last volume. Pamela King's discussion of 'Stafford Blue' reveals a new insight into a local reference in the Towneley *Noah*, contributing to current scholarship by helping to point towards a mid-sixteenth-century date for the play. In 'Understanding the Blanket Toss', Ben Parsons and Bas Jongenelen provide a translation of a spirited Dutch *rederijkers* play: a lively farce that combines traditional horseplay and stereotypes with a surprisingly sympathetic interest in problems of domestic abuse. The paper also adds to our understanding of Towneley, this time the *Second Shepherds' Play*, as the action climaxes with the drunken protagonist, like Mak, being tossed in a blanket. The wide-ranging exploration of contemporary blanket-tossing practices in Europe in their introduction throws revealing light on the social context of what today still remains the most widely known medieval English play. Ernst Gerhardt's essay on the Tudor interlude *The History of Jacob and Esau*, arising from the 2020 *METh* meeting on *Consumption*, addresses the play's pervasive interest in food, used as a means of both persuasion and control between characters. Close analysis of its foodstuffs not only heightens our understanding of the interlude's play on contemporary feasting but suggests a Shrovetide context for its performance that it shares with the very different Dutch farce. Another essay that had its genesis at the *Consumption* meeting is Elisabeth Dutton and Olivia Robinson's consideration of the complexities of staging the Eucharist. This explores the choreography and props through which the bread of Passover, the Last Supper, and the Mass could be evoked, layered, and shared in performances in which the audiences' experiences of theatre and of communion overlap and inform each other. Such questions may well be explored more variously in the next *METh* meeting in 2023, which addresses *Bodies and Embodiment*.

JOHN BLANKE'S WAGES
No Business Like Show Business

Nadia T. van Pelt

John Blanke (also spelled 'Blak' or 'Banke'), a Tudor court trumpeter of African descent, participated in some of the key ceremonial events of the early Tudor period. He was granted mourning livery for the funeral of Henry VII on 9 May 1509,[1] was issued with 'scarlet' as one of the nine 'Kyngs Trompyttes' for the coronation of Henry VIII on 24 June six weeks later,[2] and rode in the opening and closing processions at the two-day tournament organised in honour of the birth of the second Tudor's first son Henry, Duke of Cornwall, on 12–13 February 1511. This event is commemorated visually in the Westminster Tournament Roll, where a black musician appears as one of a group of six royal trumpeters, and has been identified, originally by Sydney Anglo, with Blanke.[3] Blanke's established position as one of the king's servants is underscored by his receiving 'a gown of violet cloth, a bonnet and a hat' as a marriage gift from the king on 14 January 1512.[4] The records also appear to reveal that

---

1 TNA LC 2/1 fol. 126; calendared in *Letters and Papers 1* 14 (#20, 11 May 1509); online at <http://www.british-history.ac.uk/letters-papers-hen8/vol1/pp8–24>. See *Records of English Court Music* edited Andrew Ashbee, 9 vols (Aldershot: Scolar Press, 1993) 7 25.

2 TNA LC 9/50 fol. 207v; calendared in *Letters and Papers 1* 42–3 (#82, 24 June 1509); online at <http://www.british-history.ac.uk/letters-papers-hen8/vol1/pp36–55>. See *English Court Music* edited Ashbee 7 29. Here the musician's name is spelled 'Banke'.

3 London: College of Arms MS Westminster Tournament Roll, 1511; from the workshop of Garter King of Arms Sir Thomas Wriothesley. Sydney Anglo was the first to identify the black trumpeter with John Blanke: 'The Court Festivals of Henry VII: A Study Based Upon the Account Books of John Heron, Treasurer of the Chamber' *Bulletin of John Rylands Library 43* (1960/1961) 12–45, at 42 and note 3. The identification is repeated by Miranda Kaufmann in *Black Tudors* (London: Oneworld, 2017) and 'John Blanke (fl. 1507–1512)' *ODNB*; at <https://doi.org/10.1093/ref:odnb/107145>.

4 TNA E101/417/6 #50; image online at <http://aalt.law.uh.edu/AALT7/E101/E101no417/E101no417no6/IMG_0161.htm>. Calendared in *Letters and Papers 1* 505 #1025; online at <http://www.british-history.ac.uk/letters-papers-hen8/vol1/pp502–510>; referred to in *Dress at the Court of King Henry VIII* edited Maria Hayward (Leeds: Maney, 2007) 231. The original is very worn and in places illegible; most studies depend on the *Letters and Papers* version.

following the death of his – presumably Italian[5] – colleague Dominic Justinian, John Blanke (in this document called Blake) formally petitioned Henry VIII to request permission to take on Justinian's position, and with that, to ask for a raise in wages.[6] Like the majority of petitions, this one was not dated; they rarely are. But Dominic Justinian was last seen in the records on 24 June 1509, when he was listed as one of the trumpet players present at Henry VIII's coronation.[7] And, given that, as we will see below, Blanke asked to be paid in arrears for work done in lieu of the deceased from 'the furste day of Decembre last passed', this day in the year 1509 could be considered a theoretical *terminus post quem* for Blanke's request.

Blanke's petition pleads that 'his wag*es* nowe and as yet is not sufficient to maynteigne and kepe hym to doo y*our* grace lyke s*er*uice as other y*our* Trompeto*ur*s doo',[8] suggesting a discrepancy between the other trumpet players' wages and his own. The petition reads in full:

> To the king o*ur* souue*r*ain lorde
>
> In moost humble wise besecheth y*our* highnes y*our* true and faithfull s*er*uaunte John Blake oon of y*our* Trompeto*ur*s That where as his wag*es* [sic] nowe and as yet is not sufficient to maynteigne and kepe hym to doo y*our* grace lyke s*er*uice as other y*our* Trompeto*ur*s doo It may therfo*re* please y*our* highnes in consideraci*on* of the true & faithfull s*er*uice Whiche y*our* s*er*u*a*nt daile doeth vnto y*our* grace and so during his lyf entendeth to doo To yeue and graunte vnto hym the same Rowme of Trompeto*ur* whiche Domynyc Decessed late had / To haue and enioye the said

---

5   Theodor Dumitrescu *The Early Tudor Court and International Musical Relations* (Aldershot: Ashgate, 2007) 68: 'A name such as "Dominic Justinian" … surely points to Italian origins'.

6   TNA E101/417/2 #105; image online at <http://aalt.law.uh.edu/AALT7/E101/E101no417/E101no417no2/IMG_0158.htm>. Transcribed (slightly inaccurately) in Kaufmann *Black Tudors* 21.

7   TNA CL 2/1 fol. 126r. Calendared in *Letters and Papers 1* 42-3 #82; online at <http://www.british-history.ac.uk/letters-papers-hen8/vol1/pp36-55>. The record lists 'The King's trumpets': 'Mr. Peter, marshal of the Trumpets, Jaket, Franke, John de Cecill, Domynyk, Audryan, Christopher, John Broun, John Banke, John Hert, Thomas Wrethe, John Frere, John Scarlett, John Strett, Robert Wrethe'. This list is also transcribed in *English Court Music* edited Ashbee 7 29.

8   TNA E101/417/2 #105. See note 6.

Rowme to *your* said *seru*ant from the furste day of Decembre last passed During *your* moost graci*ous* pleas*our with* the wag*es* of xvjd by the day And that this bill signed *with your* moost gracious hand may be sufficient warrant and discharge vnto John heron Tresourer of *your* Chambre for the payment of the said wag*es* accordingly And he shall dailie pray to god for the p*reseru*aci*on* of *your* moost noble and royall estate longe to endure.[9]

The king's signature at the top left-hand side of the document is the standard official authorisation to Heron 'for the payment of the said wag*es* accordingly'. And, indeed, all the documents in E101/417/2 are signed in this way.

John Blanke's origins are not known, and we cannot – at this moment – firmly situate him in a context prior to his showing up in the English court records. He may have been English, or perhaps, as some scholars have speculated, Continental European, or African.[10] In recent years, a focus of interest in the trumpet player has intensified, to the extent that – to borrow the words of Michael Ohajuru – 'John Blanke has become the poster boy for the Black presence in Tudor England'.[11] This interest in the court musician was in part raised through *The John Blanke Project*, which is described on its webpage as 'an art and archive project *celebrating* John

9 TNA E101/417/2 #105. See note 6.
10 Imtiaz Habib *Black Lives in the English Archives, 1500–1677: Imprints of the Invisible* (London: Routledge, 2008) 39: 'he was very likely a surviving member of the Spanish princess's entourage'. Habib based his claim on K.J.P. Lowe 'Stereotyping Black Africans' in *Black Africans in Renaissance Europe* edited T.F. Earle and K.J.P. Lowe (Cambridge UP, 2005) 17–47, at 39. Some scholars take a less certain tone and allow for the *possibility* that John Blanke was part of Katherine of Aragon's retinue, e.g. Tess Knighton 'Instruments, Instrumental Music and Instrumentalists' in *Companion to Music in the Age of the Catholic Monarchs* edited Tess Knighton (Leiden: Brill, 2017) 116. Others leave open a variety of possibilities for John Blanke's heritage. See, for example, Peter Fryer *Staying Power: The History of Black People in Britain* (London: Pluto Press, 2018) 4: 'Whether he [John Blanke] came straight from Africa or from Scotland – or, indeed, as is quite possible, from Spain or Portugal – is not recorded'; Miranda Kaufmann, 'John Blanke (*fl.* 1507–1512)' in *ODNB*, at <https://doi.org/10.1093/ref:odnb/107145>: 'Blanke may have come from Spain, Portugal, or Italy, all of which had growing African populations at this time'.
11 Michael I. Ohajuru 'Insights into John Blanke's Image from The John Blanke Project' in *The Tudors: Passion, Power, and Politics* edited Charlotte Bolland (London: National Portrait Gallery, 2022) 26–8, at 26.

Blanke, the Black trumpeter to the courts of Henry VII and Henry VIII, the first person of African descent in British history for whom we have both an image and a record' [*emphasis mine*].[12] Yet, without undermining the importance of the project or the celebration of the historical performer, Onyeka Nubia warns on the project webpage: 'be careful of superstardom. By making John Blanke an exception we marginalise and make strange his existence. Exceptionalism can help us keep our prejudices.' From the point of view of the black presence in sixteenth-century England, indeed, John Blanke was not unique. During this time many other persons of African descent lived in England, as Onyeka has observed, some of whom 'may have had a greater impact on that society than Blanke did'.[13]

Current scholarship has set out to fill a gap and redress a balance by studying the lives of persons of African descent in Tudor England more widely and intensively. The branch that takes the life and career of John Blanke as its focus could benefit from a closer study of the original documentary material to provide a context that enables scholars to look beyond the trumpet player's 'poster boy' status to give a fuller and more balanced understanding of the professional career of this instrumentalist as a member of the royal household and his place in the high-achieving and international community of musicians in the service of Henry VIII.[14] In the current essay I seek to contribute to the discussion by exploring how John Blanke's petition to Henry VIII relates to the evidence of trumpet players' wages generally and to other musicians' petitions, within the contexts of the early Tudor court. As I will show, the financial evidence from the Tudor Chamber Books,[15] which record in detail the

---

12 Michael Ohajuru 'About the John Blanke Project' in *The John Blanke Project*; at <https://www.johnblanke.com/about-copy.html>.

13 Onyeka Nubia 'The Author of *Blackamoores: Africans in Tudor England*' in *The John Blanke Project*; at <https://www.johnblanke.com/onyeka.html>.

14 For recent work on John Blanke, see also Michael Ohajuru 'The John Blanke Project' in *Britain's Black Past* edited Gretchen H. Gerzina (Liverpool UP, 2020) 7-25; and *The John Blanke Project* website at: <https://www.johnblanke.com>; Michelle L. Beer *Queenship at the Renaissance Courts of Britain* (Royal Historical Society Studies in History NS 101; Woodbridge: Boydell and Brewer for the Royal Historical Society, 2018) 94; Nadia T. van Pelt 'John Blanke's Hat in the Westminster Tournament Roll' *Notes & Queries 68: 4* (2021) 387-9; online at <https://doi.org/10.1093/notesj/gjab156>, downloadable as <gjab156.pdf>.

15 *The Chamber Books of Henry VII and Henry VIII, 1485-1521* edited M.M. Condon, S.P. Harper, L. Liddy, S. Cunningham, and J. Ross (Collaborative Project

Court's monthly (and sometimes weekly) expenditure, enables the researcher to create a continuous payment history. The other manuscript collections in which petitions and warrants are filed are the source of the documents that are usually quoted as examples of John Blanke's uniqueness; but, seen in context, it becomes plain that, for example, the grant of a wedding garment was nothing out of the ordinary, and the terms in which he makes his requests are standard formulae drafted by a clerk. Taken all in all, the records suggest that John Blanke was not remunerated differently from other trumpet players working in the same professional context or treated either favourably or disadvantageously compared with other court musicians. In other words, professionally speaking, he was not 'marginalised'.

The second part of this essay is concerned with the financial implications of John Blanke's petition, for which, as a starting point, I address the question posed by Miranda Kaufmann in *Black Tudors*: 'what did Blanke want, or need, that 8d a day would not cover? Like other court servants, he had his livery, board, and lodging paid for by the king.' As possible explanations for Blanke's request she put forward that 'when the court travelled, servants often had to pay for their own accommodation and transport', and that 'perhaps Blanke wanted to buy more expensive clothing'.[16] In the current contribution I consider this question in relation to both the purchasing power connected to wages received by a trumpet player at court and the additional costs of living and sources of income that should be considered alongside registered wages. Finally, gifts of clothing as an additional perk for royal servants, including musicians, are considered. As such, I provide a context to facilitate a better understanding of John Blanke's petition.

I

John Blanke the trumpet player is first seen in the payment records by name in December 1507:[17] 'Item to John blanke the blacke Trumpet

---

    between The University of Winchester, The National Archives and The Digital Humanities Institute at the University of Sheffield); online at <https://www.tudorchamberbooks.org/>.

16 Kaufmann *Black Tudors* 22.

17 Sean Cunningham has recently discovered a record in the National Archives from June 1488, which mentions a 'John Blank' who worked as a footman for King Henry VII; Sean Cunningham 'Are the 1507 John Blanke (sic) Trumpeter and

for his moneth wag*es* of Nouembre last passed at viij d the Day _ xx s'.[18] Later that month, when the remunerations for December were registered, 'the wag*es* of the vij Trumpett*es*' – that is, the established trumpet players – comprised £14 (if divided equally, 40s per person), and Blanke was mentioned separately from them: 'wag*es* of þe blake Trumpet xx s' (20s), showing that the newcomer earned half of the established trumpet players' salaries.[19] Entries separating John Blanke from the other trumpet players continued to be recorded up to and including November 1508: 'Item for the wag*es* of the vij Trumpett*es* xiiij li | Item for the blake Trumpett*es* wag*es* xx s'.[20] Then, in January 1508/9, eight trumpet players were jointly paid a sum of £16 for their month's wages for December 1508.[21] At this point in time, 'the blake Trumpett' is no longer mentioned separately.

1488 John Blank (sic) Footman one and the same person?' in *The John Blanke Project*; at <https://www.johnblanke.com/sean-cunningham.html>. Although we cannot be certain that this was the same person as John Blanke the trumpet player, the source *might* refer to him, and, as Cunningham notes, 'An earlier date and a different job calls for some re-evaluation of John's life story'. At the other end of the time scale, in 1543 there was a John Blank, stranger (foreigner) living in St Peter's Parish in the Liberty of the Tower: *Returns of Aliens Dwelling in the City and Suburbs of London from the Reign of Henry VIII to that of James I: Part III 1598–1625; Additions 1522–1595* edited R.E.G. Kirk and Ernest F. Kirk (Huguenot Society of London 10: 3; Aberdeen: The Society, 1907) 314. He was worth only £3 in goods. 'Blank' was also by no means an uncommon surname at the time for persons who were not of African descent. There was a prosperous alderman and haberdasher called Thomas Blank, net worth £1000, living in St Leonard's Parish, Bridge Ward in 1541; *Two Tudor Subsidy Rolls for the City of London, 1541 and 1582* edited R.D. Lang (London: London Record Society, 1993); online at <http://www.british-history.ac.uk/london-record-soc/vol29/pp29–33>.

18   TNA E36/214 #109; transcribed in 'E36/214 fol. 109r (Payments) 1507' in *Chamber Books* at <https://www.dhi.ac.uk/chamber-books/folio/E36_214_fo_109r.xml>. Image online at <https://www.nationalarchives.gov.uk/wp-content/uploads/2019/02/E-36_214-f109_7-December-1507.jpg>.

19   'E36/214 fol. 113r (Payments) 1507' in *Chamber Books* at <https://www.dhi.ac.uk/chamber-books/folio/E36_214_fo_113r.xml>.

20   'E36/214 fol. 152r (Payments) 1508' in *Chamber Books* at <https://www.dhi.ac.uk/chamber-books/folio/E36_214_fo_152r.xml>.

21   'Item for the wag*es* of the viij Trumpett*es* xvj li'; 'E36/214 fol. 155v (Payments) 1508' in *Chamber Books* at <https://www.dhi.ac.uk/chamber-books/folio/E36_214_fo_155v.xml>.

Based on this information, the researchers of the Tudor Chamber Books project suggested that John Blanke 'served his probation in 1507 and graduated onto full pay in 1508'. They noted that 'The value placed on the expertise of the Shakbusshes and trumpeters was reflected in the £2 per month salary they received after completing a year-long probation period, during which they received half wages'.[22] This sounds like a neatly organised custom, but, given that the English records concerned with musicians' payments are limited in number and, to borrow Andrew Ashbee's words, the 'continuity of places is often impossible to determine since records giving all names are sparse',[23] it may be that their suggestions invite further investigation. The use of full- and half-wages is indeed suggested in the records for the reign of Henry VII by the two levels of payment for trumpet players, which show 20s (8d a day) or 40s (16d a day) per month respectively. In the reign of Henry VIII the lower rate goes up from 8d to 12d a day, which produces roughly 30s a month, depending on the number of days in each month.[24]

An additional point to make regarding the 'year-long probation period' that was suggested as customary is that, for some trumpet players who did start on half-pay, it is uncertain how long this period lasted. For example, when John de Cecil (also spelled 'de Cecely' or 'Dececill')[25] was first mentioned in the payment records by name on 4 June 1502, he was registered as receiving 20s: 'Item for John de Cecely the trumpet wag*es* xx s', a rough approximation of 8d a day.[26] In January 1506

---

22   Margaret Condon, Samantha Harper, and James Ross 'The Chamber Books of Henry VII and Henry VIII, 1485–1521: An Analysis of the Books and a Study of Henry VII and his Life at Court' in *Tudor Chamber Books* (online pdf) 35 and note 204, at <https://www.tudorchamberbooks.org/wp-content/uploads/sites/11/2020/12/Chamber-books-Analysis-and-Synopsis.pdf>.

23   David Lasocki and Andrew Ashbee with Peter Holman and Fiona Kisby *A Biographical Dictionary of English Court Musicians, 1485–1714* 2 vols (London: Routledge, 1998) 1695 (continuous numbering).

24   See, for example, 'BL Add MS 21481 fol. 17v (Payments) 1509' in *Chamber Books* at <https://www.dhi.ac.uk/chamber-books/folio/LL_BL_AddMS_21481_fo017v.xml>, which will be addressed below.

25   As the name indicates, he was very probably a native 'of Sicily', as I will discuss in greater detail in my forthcoming book with Oxford University Press.

26   'E101/415/3 fol. 97v (Payments) 1502' in *Chamber Books* at <https://www.dhi.ac.uk/chamber-books/folio/E101_415_3_fo_097v.xml>. If as usual this was payment in arrears for the month of May, it was only an approximation of 8d a

de Cecil and four colleagues were paid wages for December 1505, adding up to a group total of £10, and thus presumably 40s each if the money was shared equally between them: 'Item to Jaques Trumpet. Thomas Freman. John Broune. John Dececill & Franke for their moneth wag*es* of Decembre last passed x li'.[27] From this it would follow that, sometime between 1502 and 1506, de Cecil had 'graduated', to use the word of the Tudor Chamber Books' editors, to full payment. If a formal probationary period with a fixed time-frame of a year was indeed a custom at court, this is – due to the sparseness of the documentation – unfortunately not proven in the case of John de Cecil. The overall number of the trumpeters is cited – nine until June 1504, then eight from September 1504 – but not who they were.

Indeed, a more pragmatic custom appears logical in which young or inexperienced trumpet players at first earned half wages for an unspecified amount of time and could, when a position or 'room' opened, apply for the post and its accompanying wages.[28] However, this probationary period was not inevitable. A new trumpet player did not necessarily start on half wages. For example, Thomas Gardener joined the group of trumpet players in 1510 and immediately earned the full 16d a day: 'Item to oone Thomas Garden*er* opon a war*a*unt signed to be in the Rowme of a Trumpet with the wag*es* of xvj d by the day begynnyng the xvjth day of July C s'.[29]

Several other examples of musicians petitioning for a 'room' or position and stepping directly into full pay can be found. Baltazar Robert,[30] for example, requested the 'Rowme of oon of y*our* mynstrelles ca[l]led a Taberet', with wages of 8d a day.[31] The king endorsed the request and the tabaret [*a small drum*] player's wages for December 1509

day; it should have been 20s 8d, but the 8d a day seems to have been levelled out at a notional 20s a month, unlike in the following reign.

27 'E36/214 fol. 13v (Payments) 1506' in *Chamber Books* at <https://www.dhi.ac.uk/chamber-books/folio/E36_214_fo_013v.xml>.

28 For the meaning of *room* as 'An office, function, appointment; a post, situation, employment', see *OED* sv room 10a, 11.

29 'BL Add Ms 21481 fol. 42v (Payments) 1510' in *Chamber Books* at <https://www.dhi.ac.uk/chamber-books/folio/LL_BL_AddMS_21481_fo042v.xml>.

30 For Robert and taberet players, see Dumitrescu *Early Tudor Court* 98–101.

31 TNA E101/417/12 #48; image online at <http://aalt.law.uh.edu/AALT7/E101/E101no417/E101no417no12/IMG_0507.htm>. See *English Court Music* edited Ashbee 7 407.

are mentioned in the Chamber Book accounts: 'Item for Baltazar Rob*er*t a taberet wag*es* xx s viij d'.[32]

An undated petition, estimated by Andrew Ashbee as 'early Henry VIII', shows a request 'in consideracion of the good and true s*er*uice which y*our* daily bedman Antony Etfeld entendith to doo vnto y*our* highnesse during his lif To geue and grauntE vnto hym the Rowme of oon of youre Trumpeto*ur*s with the wag*es* of sixtene pens by the day' to be paid 'in like man*er* and at suche termes [*due dates*] as other of the same trompettes ben vsely payed'.[33] The king endorsed the request, and a payment record from May 1510 expressly refers to Etfeld's wages paid out 'opon his war*a*unt', it reads:

Item for vij Trumpettes moneth wag*es* xiiij li

Item for oone Anthony Etfeld wag*es* opon his war*a*unt xl s

Item for vj other Trumpett*es* moneth wag*es* ix li vj s.[34]

Etfeld's wages match those of the 'vij Trumpettes' who together earned £14 – that is, 40s per month each if these wages were distributed equally between the seven performers. The payment directly below Etfeld's shows that he is joining the higher-paid trumpet players who earned (the equivalent of) 16d a day each, not the ones who are, confusingly, referred to as 'other Trumpett*es*', and earn 12d a day. He makes it plain in his petition that he is asking to be 'oon of youre [i.e. the king's] Trumpeto*ur*s', and to be paid 'in like man*er* and at suche termes as other of the same trompettes ben vsely payed', *same* meaning the king's trumpeters. The 'other Trumpettes' appear to have been Henry's household trumpeters when he was Prince of Wales, and their names appear in the main records as 'Trumpets' at the funeral of Henry VII.[35] They are first recorded as one group with the former king's trumpeters in the records for the

---

32 'BL Add MS 21481 fol. 19v (Payments) 1509' in *Chamber Books* at <https://www.dhi.ac.uk/chamber-books/folio/LL_BL_AddMS_21481_fo019v.xml>.

33 TNA E101/417/2 #100; image online at <http://aalt.law.uh.edu/AALT7/E101/E101no417/E101no417no2/IMG_0153.htm>. See *English Court Music* edited Ashbee 7 408.

34 'E36/215 fol. 61 (Payments) 1510' in *Chamber Books* at <https://www.dhi.ac.uk/chamber-books/folio/LL_E36_215_p061.xml>.

35 See note 1. Note that at the funeral the 'King's Trumpets' are presented separately from the 'Trumpets'; the former group is listed between the 'Minstrels of the

coronation.³⁶ Over the next few years they are gradually absorbed into the higher paid group.³⁷

A further example can be found in Henry VIII's endorsing a petition of Jenyn Marcasyn and Marquas Lorydon, minstrels 'vnto your derrest wif the Quene', for the wages of 8d a day, 'like as other your mynstrelles haue and doo receyue', to be paid monthly by Heron, the Treasurer of the Privy Chamber 'from the furst daye of Nouembre the first yere of youre most noble Reigne'.³⁸ These wages were promptly paid, as testified by the account books for November 1509: 'Item for Jenyn Marcasyn wag*es* opon a war*a*unt xx s | Item for Marcus Loriden wag*es* opon a war*a*unt xx s'.³⁹

The 'other' trumpet players from May 1510, earning the lesser amount of 12d, did so as a consequence of yet another successful petition that had previously been endorsed by the king. In a collective petition the trumpet players John Hert, Thomas Wray, John Scarlet, John Frere, John Strutt, and Robert Wrey asked for a fee of 12d a day each, to be paid monthly during pleasure, backdated to 24 June 1509 (the date of the coronation), providing as an argument the formulaic 'in consideraci*o*n of the true and ffaithfull seruice. Whiche ... yo*ur* trumpt*es* hertofore hath done and during their lyves they entendith to do to yo*ur* highnes'.⁴⁰ The wages of 12d a day were paid out retroactively in November of that year:

Chamber' and 'The King's Falconers', the latter group is listed behind a 'groom', a 'hosier', and a 'ferrour'.

36 See note 2.
37 *English Court Music* edited Ashbee 7 ix. The process was slower and more complex than this suggests.
38 TNA E101/417/12 # 47; image online at <http://aalt.law.uh.edu/AALT7/E101/E101no417/E101no417n012/IMG_0506.htm>. See *English Court Music* edited Ashbee 7 407.
39 'BL Add MS 21481 fol. 17v (Payments) 1509' in *Chamber Books* at <https://www.dhi.ac.uk/chamber-books/folio/LL_BL_AddMS_21481_f0017v.xml>. Marcasyn and Loriden first appear as minstrels to Elizabeth of York, wife of Henry VII; see Dumitrescu *Early Tudor Court* 103 and Richard Rastall 'The Minstrels of the English Royal Households, 25 Edward I–1 Henry VIII: An Inventory' *Royal Musical Association Research Chronicles 4* (1964) 1–41, at 37–8; online at contributing libraries via <https://www.jstor.org/stable/25093657>.
40 TNA E101/417/2 #59; image online at <http://aalt.law.uh.edu/AALT7/E101/E101no417/E101no417n02/IMG_0102.htm>. See *English Court Music* edited Ashbee 7 408.

> Item to John Hert your Trumpet opon a waraunt signed for his wages at xij d the day by the space of v monethes & vj days. that is to say from the xxiiijth day of Juyn anno primo R[egni] Regis Henrici viij^{ui}. vnto the last day of Nouembre next ensuyng vij li xix s
>
> Item to Thomas Wrey a nother Trumpet vpon the same waraunt for lyke wages by þe said space vij li xix s
>
> Item to John Scarlet a nother Trumpet opon the same waraunt for lyke wages by þe said space vij li xix s
>
> John Freer a nother Trumpet opon the same waraunte for lyke wages by the said space vij li xix s
>
> Item to John Strute a nother Trumpet opon the same waraunt for lyke wages by þe said space vij li xix s
>
> Item to Robert Wrey a nother Trumpet opon the same waraunt for lyke wages by þe said space vij li xix s.[41]

Another group petition (not extant) can be dated February 1510/11, after which fifteen royal trumpet players were rewarded with a one-off extra remuneration in line with their participation in the festivities held at Westminster in honour of Henry VIII's first-born son. In other words, they were remunerated for their work at the jousts shown in the Great Tournament Roll, in which John Blanke was visually represented. The accountant recorded:

> Item to the kinges 15 Trumpettes oppon theyr warnnte signed for thir duetyes belonging to their office of Auncientie apperteignyng for the Justes holden at Westmynster the 12th day of February last passed. £26. 13s. 4d.[42]

Considering that only roughly two weeks had passed since the festivities, this extra payment had been swiftly processed, and the 'warnnte' does not seem to have been more than a formality needed to set this in motion.

A number of these petitions cluster around the time of the death of Henry VII and the accession of Henry VIII in 1509. This naturally led to

---

41   'BL Add MS 21481 fol. 17v (Payments) 1509' in *Chamber Books* at <https://www.dhi.ac.uk/chamber-books/folio/LL_BL_AddMS_21481_fo017v.xml>.

42   *English Court Music* edited Ashbee 7 196.

some reorganisation of the household, and it seems to have been a period of uncertainty during which a highly experienced musician sometimes appears to apply for his previous position. The wait[43] and bagpipe player William Kechin received a back-payment in October 1511 'opon a warraunte' detailing the following:

> Item to William Kechyn backpype wayte opon a warraunte signed from the furst day of July last past by the space of iiij monethes that is to say. July. August. Septembre. & Octobre. at iiij d the day xlj s.[44]

The words 'opon a warraunte' generally invite further scrutiny of the accounts, and indeed, the payment follows a petition in consideration of service done to Henry VII, and to be done to his successor, for 'the Rowme of Waite with your good grace whiche he had with the said late kyng your fader', from 1 July 1511.[45] It reads in full:

> To the kyng our souuerain Lord
>
> Please it your highnesse of your most noble and habundaunt grace in consideracion of the true and faithfull seruice whiche your humble subgiett William kechyn hertofore hathe doon vnto the late kyng your fader of most famous memory and so duryng his lyff entendeth to do vnto your good grace / To geve and graunte vnto hym the Rowme of Waite with your good grace whiche he had with the said late kyng your fader whoes soule god pardon With the wages of iiijd by the daye / To be had and yerely perceyved[46] monthly from the first day of July the thride yere of

---

43 For the office of *wait* or watchman, see *The Household of Edward IV: The Black Book and the Ordinance of 1478* edited A.R. Myers (Manchester UP, 1959) 132; also *OED* sv *wait*. See also Richard Rastall 'Secular Musicians in Late Medieval England' (PhD thesis: University of Manchester, 1968) <https://townwaits.org.uk/rastall-thesis/>, chapter 5 'Haut and Bas Minstrelsy', section 'Pipers, Wayts and Vigilatores' 155–63. Richard Rastall's valuable book, with Andrew Taylor, *Minstrels and Minstrelsy in Late Medieval England* (Woodbridge: Boydell Press) unfortunately appeared too late to be taken into account in writing this essay.

44 'E36/215 fol. 145 (Payments) 1511' in *Chamber Books* at <https://www.dhi.ac.uk/chamber-books/folio/LL_E36_215_p145.xml>.

45 *English Court Music* edited Ashbee 7 409.

46 For *perceyve* meaning *receive*, see *OED* sv *perceive v.* 8a.

*y*our most noble Reigne dury*n*g *y*our most gracious please*r* by the hand*es* of the tresourer of *y*our Chambre for the tyme beyng / And that this byll signed w*ith* y*our* most gracious hand may be sufficient Warrant and comaundme*n*t vnto the tresourer of *y*our said Cha*m*bre for the contentacion of the said wag*es* in ma*n*e*r* and fou*r*me as it is a bove rehersed accordingly / And he shall dailly pray to god for the blessed p*r*eservacion of your most noble and Royall Estate.[47]

Unfortunately, however, the Chamber Book accounts of Henry VII do not appear to yield an entry that mentions William Kechin by name or even a regular payment to 'the Wait'; these start only in the next reign, in November 1511, after his backdated four months' pay. In August 1496, a payment of 3s 4d was made 'to one that pleyeth on the bagpip',[48] but this sounds like a casual entertainer's payment. From his petition, we have to assume that William Kechin had already served Henry VII in 'the Rowme of Waite', but there is no record of it.

John Blanke appears to have been in a situation similar to Kechin's, albeit with a subtle but important difference: where the latter applied for the job he had previously held within the *last reign*, Blanke applied for his current job. From this follows that both petitions contain explanations detailing the particularities of the petitioners' respective situations, needed by the accountants once the petition had been turned into a warrant through the king's signature. This is why they appear to be more elaborate than the petitions written in applications for a new 'room', such as those drawn up for Baltazar Robert or Anthony Etfield. Similarities between the petitions, however, exceed their differences. Indeed, in what follows I show how very similar John Blanke's petition is to Kechin's, as well as to the straightforward applications for new jobs, in terms of their structure, level of formality, and the formulaic nature of the language used.[49]

---

47 TNA E101/417/2 # 106, image online at <http://aalt.law.uh.edu/AALT7/E101/E101no417/E101no417no2/IMG_0159.htm>.

48 'E101/414/6 fol. 41r (Payments) 1496' in *Chamber Books* at <https://www.dhi.ac.uk/chamber-books/folio/E101_414_6_fo_041r.xml>.

49 In what follows, William Kechyn's petition refers to TNA E101/417/2 Part 2 #106 (pencilled 104); image online at <http://aalt.law.uh.edu/AALT7/E101/E101no417/E101no417no2/IMG_0159.htm>. Baltazar Robert's petition refers to TNA E101/417/12 #48; image online at <http://aalt.law.uh.edu/AALT7/E101/

First of all, the extant petitions open with an address to the king. Both Blanke's and Kechin's petitions open with, 'To the king our souuerain lorde'. A variation on this theme can be found in the petitions of Etfield and the minstrel Pety John Cokeryn, which open with, 'To the kinges most noble grace'.

Then follows a highly formulaic construction – subject to small additions or changes depending on the situation at hand – in which the petitioner is introduced and the king is asked to favourably consider said petition on the basis of good service done in the past and the promise of the intention to keep providing good service during the petitioner's lifetime. The standard phrase is found in Cokeryn's petition: 'in consideracion of the faithfull seruice whiche your humble seruaunt Pety John Cokerin oon of your Mynstrelles hath Doon vnto youre good grace and soo During his lif entendeth to doo'. But for the newcomer Etfeld previous service could not be mentioned, so only the *intention* to serve in the future is presented, as we have already seen in the above: 'in consideracion of the good and true seruice which your daily bedman Antony Etfeld entendith to doo vnto your highnesse during his lif'.

In Kechin's petition the standard phrase is altered to communicate that Kechin had already served under Henry VII, and the promise of future good service is made, in line with custom, as well as to highlight the wish to serve the son as he had the father:

> in consideracion of the true and faithfull seruice whiche your humble subgiett William kechyn hertofore hathe doon vnto the late kyng your fader of most famous memory and so duryng his lyff entendeth to do vnto your good grace.

The formulaic sentence was subtly but overtly tailored to express John Blanke's situation in which the applicant was already doing the job petitioned for: 'It may therfore please your highnes in consideracion of the true & faithfull seruice Whiche your seruant daile doeth vnto your

E101no417/E101no417n012/IMG_0507.htm>. Antony Etfield's petition refers to TNA E101/417/2 #100 (pencilled 98); image online at <http://aalt.law.uh.edu/AALT7/E101/E101n0417/E101n0417n02/IMG_0153.htm>. Pety John Cokeryn's petition refers to TNA E101/417/2 #113 (#111 pencilled top right); image online at <http://aalt.law.uh.edu/AALT7/E101/E101n0417/E101n0417n02/IMG_0168.htm>. Jenyn Marcasyn and Marquas Lorydon's petition refers to TNA E101/417/12 # 47; image online at <http://aalt.law.uh.edu/AALT7/E101/E101n0417/E101n0417n012/IMG_0506.htm>.

grace and so during his lyf entendeth to doo'. The words 'daile doeth' are crucial here – they clarify for the accountant why retroactive payment as addressed further on in the petition is required – and stand out to the reader accustomed to the usual formula.

Next followed the main objective of the document: the asking for a specific 'room' or position and specifying the wages that the applicant wanted to earn. This again represented practical information necessary for the accountants, to be followed up on once the king's signature turned the petition into a warrant. To exemplify, Kechin petitions, 'To geve and graunte vnto hym the Rowme of Waite w*ith* y*our* good grace whiche he had w*ith* the said late kyng y*our* fader whoes soule god p*ar*don'. Baltazar Robert more generally petitioned for 'the Rowme of oon of your mynst[rell*es* called?] a Taberet w*ith* the wages of eight pens sterling by the day'. And Anthony Etfield's petition requested, 'To geue and graunte vnto hym the Rowme of oon of youre Trumpeto*ur*s with the wag*es* of sixtene pens by the day'.

John Blanke, like Kechin, asks for a specific 'room' – 'the same Rowme of Trompeto*ur* whiche Domynyc Decessed late had' – and pointedly requests the benefits of the petition along with the chance to perform the role, as seen in the phrase 'To haue and *enioye* the said Rowme' (*emphasis mine*). This may suggest that he already is occupying the 'room' but is currently not enjoying its monetary fruits. He then asks for payment in arrears, from which we can gather that he had started taking on the late Dominic's duties from 'the furste day of Decembre last passed', and that this petition sought to formalise his occupying Dominic's position, as well as reimbursing him for a job already done. As we have seen in the above example of the 'other' Trumpet players, John Hert, Thomas Wrethe, John Frere, John Scarlett, John Strett, and Robert Wrethe, this was not unusual.

Then followed a formulaic line that confirmed the procedure that turned the petition into a warrant. For example, Etfield's petition reads, 'And that this bill signed with y*our* moost gr*a*ciouse hande may bee sufficient warrant and c*om*maundement vnto John heron tresourer of y*our* Chambre'. We see a very similar statement in John Blanke's petition: 'And that this bill signed w*ith* y*our* moost graci*ou*s hand may be sufficient warrant and discharge vnto John heron Tresourer of y*our* Chambre for the payment of the said wag*es* accordingly'.

Petitions of this type typically end on a prayer for the king. Blanke's is completely formulaic: 'And he shall dailie pray to god for the p*re*ser*u*aci*on* of y*our* moost noble and royall estate longe to endure'. By comparison,

Etfield's reads: 'And he shall pray for y*our* moost noble and Royall estate'. Pety John Cokeryn's ends with: ' And he shall eu*er* praye to god for your most noble and Royall estate', and the joint petition by Jenyn Marcasyn and Marquas Lorydon concludes in the promise, 'And they shall eu*er* pray to god for your most noble and Royall estate'.

As observed, John Blanke's petition includes elements that may at first glance strike readers as less formulaic, and in previous work suggestions have been made that John Blanke's 'own voice' can be heard coming through.[50] We have already seen that the lion's share of the document follows standard formulae,[51] but it may be observed also that the aspects of the letter that do not appear to run parallel to the other petitions referred to in the above are more formal than may be suspected. First of all, the opening of the petition, in which the 'true and faithfull s*er*uaunte' is typically introduced by name, shows that in John Blanke's case his current position is pointedly given behind his name ('John Blake oon of y*our* Trompeto*urs*'). This additional bit of information seems a practical addition to the formula to help both the king, and the accountant (once the petition had become a warrant), to 'place' the trumpet player in the group of the King's Trumpeters. This has a function similar to the information added to Cokerin's name in his petition: 'y*our* humble s*er*uau*n*t Pety John Cokerin oon of your Mynstrell*es*'.

The statement in Blanke's petition, 'That where as his wag*es* [sic] nowe and as yet is not sufficient to maynteigne and kepe hym to doo y*our* grace lyke s*er*uice as other y*our* Trompeto*urs* doo', may at first read as an anomaly within the wider body of petitions, as it can be read as a complaint about his wages. Previous scholarship has suggested that the warrant at this point implies that the current pay does not enable him to pay for his lifestyle.[52] However, the main point of the sentence seems to be to preserve his equality with his fellow-trumpeters. A similar request to be paid like other musicians of a particular type or status can be found

---

50   Kaufmann *Black Tudors* 21.

51   Kaufmann acknowledges but downplays the formulaic nature of the petition by calling it 'somewhat formulaic'; Kaufmann *Black Tudors* 21.

52   Kaufmann *Black Tudors* 22: 'There also seems to be some rivalry with the other trumpeters: he wants to live in the same style as his peers and claims that his previous wage of 8d a day was insufficient for this.' Below I will also show that the '8d a day' that Kaufmann refers to here is unlikely to have been the pay that John Blanke received at the time of the petition.

in other petitions. For example, we see in Jenyn Marcasyn and Marquas Lorydon's joint petition the request 'to bee paide ... Like as other your mynstrel*les* haue and do p*er*ceyue'. It is also very much in line with Etfield's specified wish to be taken on 'in like man*er* and at suche termes as other of the same trompettes ben vsely payed'.

John Blanke's petition and its endorsement by the king thus sit in a tradition of many such warrants and approvals, and do not seem to be out of the ordinary within the context of the Tudor court. There is something odd, however, in Blanke's petitioning for higher wages when, as we have seen, the financial records of January 1508/09 have suggested that he was already included in the group of eight trumpet players who had shared £16 for December 1508.[53] If this was the case, then why would he ask to be raised to £2 after Dominic Justinian's death? Here it is worth comparing the payments of wages for December 1509 and January 1509/10. From April 1509 the group of king's trumpeters had risen from eight to nine. In December 1509 the wages were listed: 'Item for the ix Trumpet*tes* moneth wag*es* xviij li | Item for the vj other Trumpet*tes* moneth wag*es* ix li vj s'.[54] It turns out that the wages of January 1509/10 reflect a reduction in the number of these trumpet players (from nine to eight), whereas the group of other trumpet players remains constant in size (six): 'Item for the viij Trumpet*tes* moneth wag*es* xvj li | Item for the vj Trumpet*tes* moneth wag*es* ix li vj s'.[55] If this is indicative of the gap the death of Dominic Justinian left in the group of players, it does not provide evidence of why Blanke would want to take Justinian's place if he was already one of the king's trumpet players belonging to the higher-paid group – *unless* he had at that moment not belonged to the higher-paid group.

In November 1509 John Hert and his colleagues in the lower-paid group, as seen in the above, were firmly established by the accountant as trumpet players earning 12d a day. Until that moment, they can thus confidently be taken to represent the group of six players. It is not impossible that, sometime between November 1509 and January 1509/10, John Blanke's position and that of one of the six were reversed, and that

---

53 'E36/214 fol. 155v (Payments) 1508' in *Chamber Books* at <https://www.dhi.ac.uk/chamber-books/folio/E36_214_fo_155v.xml>. See note 21.

54 'E36/215 folio 38 (Payments), 1509' in *Chamber Books* at <https://www.dhi.ac.uk/chamber-books/folio/LL_E36_215_p038.xml>.

55 'E36/215 folio 45 (Payments), 1510' in *Chamber Books* at <https://www.dhi.ac.uk/chamber-books/folio/LL_E36_215_p045.xml>.

Blanke then saw an opportunity to return to his previous status and its accompanying wages upon the death of Dominic.

However, there is no evidence in the records to suggest that John Blanke had been dropped back to lower wages, at this or any other point after December 1508, or to explain the apparent contradiction that he was asking for wages he was already receiving. It may well be that the petition was simply designed to correct an accounting mistake or to put on record an administrative clarification of his existing wages at a time of uncertainty.

It is significant that this odd situation, implied by the petition read alongside the financial records, occurred in the months directly following the change of king. We have seen in the petition of William Kechin that existing personnel might experience a disadvantage at a change of reigns, as not all appointments would be automatically continued by the new monarch. Indeed, in theory, all appointments made by the king came to an end when he died. Practically speaking, however, dismissing all staff would have been highly impractical. Indeed, we see court servants, including musicians, being taken on by the next king, and sometimes even serving several monarchs. Think, for example, of the trumpet player John de Peler, who pops up in the household of Edward IV, then serves Richard III, and whose name appears as one of the sackbut or shawms players of Henry VII, continuing in this instrument group for Henry VIII in 1509.[56] Likewise, whether or not there was an interruption in his wages, John Blanke remained one of the trumpet players in service of the new king Henry VIII.

II

To give a fuller context to John Blanke's petition, it may be helpful to consider the broader implications of income and expenditure for a court trumpeter at this period. As suggested above, trumpet players' wages at the start of Henry VIII's new reign were set at either 12d or 16d a day. What did these wages, translated as 30s or 40s a month, mean in terms of purchasing power? The National Archives' currency converter offers an approximate estimate of what a specific amount would have bought a person. This suggests, for example, that between 1500 and 1510 a monthly payment of 20s (or £1, starting wages for some trumpeters under Henry

---

56 Rastall 'The Minstrels of the English Royal Households' at 32, 34, 36, and 40.

VII) would have provided a buyer with enough money to purchase two cows, nine stones of wool, or two quarters of wheat.[57] During the same decade £2 could buy a person one horse or five cows, but this amount could also represent eighteen stones of wool or five quarters of wheat. After John Blanke's petition had been turned into a warrant by the king's signature one month's work for him represented sixty-six days of labour by a skilled tradesman.[58] But the relative wealth of a court musician was not solely determined by the wages they earned along with the court benefits of board, lodging, and livery, nor can the expenses made by court musicians be generalised in the way that previous research has done.[59] In what follows I address both the additional income that could be generated alongside the formal wages found in the Chamber books and the additional costs of living that some musicians would have faced if they took up residence in the City.

As can be seen from the records, musical high-achievers from different nations found their way to the Tudor court to take up individual positions, and both Henry VII and Henry VIII also patronised musical ensembles that were distinctly international in make-up.[60] Thus we see that the sackbut and shawm ensemble referred to by Dumitrescu as the 'first ensemble', performing during the late fifteenth century and into the first decade of the sixteenth century, comprised musicians from a number of places, although Low Country musicians appear to dominate.[61] From 1516 to the 1530s the Flemish 'Olde Sagbuttes' played at court, and they were followed, between the 1520s and the 1540s, by the Italian 'Newe Sagbuttes'. The Venetian Bassanos joined in the 1530s.

57 TNA 'Currency Converter' at <https://www.nationalarchives.gov.uk/currency-converter/>. The TNA Currency Converter provides the same general indication of the historical value of this amount for both 1500 and 1510.

58 Robert C. Braddock has pointed out that one cannot directly compare the wealth accumulated through the wages of an 'ordinary workman' outside the context of the court with servants working within that context, as 'ordinary workmen could work only about three hundred days a year and were paid accordingly, while the servants in the Royal Household were paid for three hundred and sixty-five days whether they had been in attendance or not'. See Robert C. Braddock 'The Rewards of Office-Holding in Tudor England' *Journal of British Studies 14: 2* (1975) 29–47, at 33.

59 See e.g. Kaufmann *Black Tudors* 22.

60 Dumitrescu *Early Tudor Court* 74.

61 For the following examples see Dumitrescu *Early Tudor Court* 68–75.

Fiona Kisby has shown that some of these performers occupied residences away from court.[62] Using as evidence Alien Subsidies and testamentary requests for burial, wills, parish registers, and churchwardens' accounts, Kisby's study concluded that the royal musicians for whom residentiary evidence can be found in the records between roughly 1520 and 1600 'appear to have lived in the eastern parts of the City [of London], in particular Portsoken and Tower Ward'. She reports, 'there was a relatively high degree of clustering in certain areas within these, notably in the parish of St Olave Hart Street, All Hallows Barking by the Tower and the precinct of Holy Trinity Minories'.[63] Examples from Kisby's evidence show that one of the Flemish 'Olde Sagbuttes', Claise Forceville, also recorded as 'Nicholas Forcyvall', lived in St Olave, Southwark in 1535.[64] Peregrine Simon, who was one of the 'Newe Sagbuttes', stayed in Bishopsgate Ward, specifically in the parish of St Botolph without Bishopsgate in 1541.[65] The chamber minstrel Possant Bonitamps lived in Langborne Ward in the years 1508–13,[66] and the trumpet player Jaquet de la Now resided in Tower Ward in 1521, as we learn from the will of Elizabeth, his wife.[67] Tower Ward was also the place of choice of the aforementioned tabor player Baltazar Robert, who can be located there in 1538,[68] as can the Low-Country lute player Philip van Wilder in 1524 and between 1534 and 1552. Later, members of the Bassano family would keep residence there.[69]

---

62   Fiona Kisby 'Royal Minstrels in the City and Suburbs of Early Tudor London: Professional Activities and Private Interests' *Early Music 25: 2* (1997) 199–219.
63   Kisby 'Royal Minstrels in the City' 208.
64   Kisby 'Royal Minstrels in the City' 210. For Forceville, see Dumitrescu *Early Tudor Court* 74.
65   For the identification of Peregrine Simon as one of the Italian 'Newe Sagbuttes' see Dumitrescu *Early Tudor Court* 74; Kisby 'Royal Minstrels in the City' 210.
66   Identified by Dumitrescu as a 'foreign musician': *Early Tudor Court* 231.
67   Kisby 'Royal Minstrels in the City' 211.
68   Identified by Dumitrescu as a 'foreign musician': *Early Tudor Court* 231, 233.
69   Kisby 'Royal Minstrels in the City' 201, 211–12; Dumitrescu *Early Tudor Court* 74. The *Returns of Aliens* for 1567 describes Tower Ward inhabitants 'Anthonnye Bassanio' and 'Augustyne Bassanio' as 'Italions', 'the quenes ma^ties music[i]ons' and as 'denisens' (in other words, they have been naturalised as English): *Returns of aliens dwelling in the city and suburbs of London from the reign of Henry VIII. to that of James I* edited R.E.G. Kirk and Ernest F. Kirk, 4 vols (Aberdeen: 1900–8) *I* 340. For a detailed study of the Bassano family and their lives in England see

The harper William More, who started employment at court in 1515 and appears to have worked there still in 1557, was, as Kisby suggests, 'resident in Westminster'.[70] However, he may not have started out his musical career living in property there; the extant documentary evidence places him in the city relatively late in his career, in 1540-2, as evidenced from a 'testamentary request for burial', and later again (or still) in 1570.[71] Alien subsidy records for Alhallows Barking parish list as resident one 'Anthon. Basam [*Bassani*] Italian, and Heleyn his wife, and five children, all born there; he is a musician to the queen'.[72] The Bassani presumably held property and had a servant, as a 1569 Lay Subsidies certificate that registered 'persons within the Warde of the Tower had no goods, chattels, lands, or tenements within the Ward' does not mention the Bassani themselves but does mention 'Augustine, servaunt to the Basanyes'.[73]

As seen in the example of Jaquet de la Now and Anthony Bassani and his wife Heleyn, marriage and potentially family life may have been a good reason for musicians to rent or buy a place where they could live outside of the court. This would have been practical, given that, when provided with lodging at court, the king's servants would have been expected to sleep among their peers, often on 'straw and russhes', as suggested by the Black Book of Edward IV.[74] This presumably would not have been conducive to marital life.

Even if most of the evidence put forward by Kisby, by virtue of the source types on which she had to rely, is somewhat later than the first two decades of the sixteenth century that are of interest in the current study, her work does highlight two important things. First of all, the combined facts that many court musicians were foreign, and that they 'clustered' – to use Kisby's observation – in parts of East London where they could live relatively independently away from the court within the means of their budgets, provides an interesting context for understanding the lifestyles and levels of comfort attainable to court musicians beyond that

    David Lasocki and Roger Prior *The Bassanos: Venetian Musicians and Instrument Makers in England, 1531–1665* (London: Routledge, 2016).
70   Kisby 'Royal Minstrels in the City' 212.
71   Kisby 'Royal Minstrels in the City' 212.
72   *Returns of Aliens 10, Part I* 391.
73   *Returns of Aliens 10, Part I* 394.
74   *The Household of Edward IV: The Black Book and the Ordinance of 1478* edited A.R. Myers (Manchester UP, 1959) e.g. at 115.

which is known through their registered wages. Secondly, the evidence provides a glimpse of the way in which musicians aspiring to married life and perhaps a family may have sought to combine their careers with their private lives.

However, residing in the city, as Kisby suggests, clearly also had professional advantages.[75] She notes, 'It is possible that minstrels augmented their court salaries by playing privately at venues outside the royal household whose locations may have been a powerful determinant in their choice of lodgings'.[76] She furthermore speculates that 'The many taverns of the river front in the south-eastern corner of the City probably provided suitable opportunities for such work.'[77]

Trumpet players represented a specialised branch of musicians who are likely to have sought out different gigs than the royal minstrels as ways to boost their incomes. Simon Polson's recent doctoral research provides a valuable insight into 'the King's trumpeters' being engaged to play for the mayor's and sheriffs' processions in London. He writes, 'From 1475 and to the end of the period, the archival documents record payments either to the King's trumpeters, with their marshal or sergeant, or to an undescribed band of trumpeters, also with a leader. Probably these were always royal trumpeters, though the records only occasionally articulate it'.[78] Evidence found by Polson includes, for example, the Goldsmiths' Wardens' Accounts and Court Minutes of 1482, which specify that £3 was paid 'to the marshal of the king's trumpeters and eight other trumpeters'.[79] And in 1509 the Drapers' Wardens' Accounts record a payment to twelve trumpet players (including for their hats) for participation in the Sheriffs' procession.[80] A slightly later example shows that in 1518 the Skinners' Receipts and Payments again include a payment to 'Fraunces Knyff, marshal of the king's trumpeters, for 12 trumpeters for the livery and 10 trumpeters for the Bachelors, with costs'.[81] This

---

75 Kisby 'Royal Minstrels in the City' 212.
76 Kisby 'Royal Minstrels in the City' 212–13.
77 Kisby 'Royal Minstrels in the City' 213.
78 Simon Polson 'Musicians and Commoners in Late Medieval London' (PhD thesis: University of Maryland, 2020) 100.
79 Polson 'Musicians and Commoners' 295.
80 Polson 'Musicians and Commoners' 314.
81 Polson 'Musicians and Commoners' 297.

evidence shows that the king's trumpeters participated in these civic events before John Blanke joined them, and that these engagements continued while John Blanke was part of the group, and after.

The city also provided further opportunities for lucrative businesses, which court musicians could exploit based on licences given out as favours from the king. For example, in 1511 the French lute player Giles Duwes, sometimes referred to as 'the King's servant' and at others as an 'alien', was on different occasions provided with a licence 'to import … Gascon wine'.[82] A licence 'to export six hundred sacks of wool' was given to William Crane, a 'gentleman of the Chapel', in October 1512.[83] 'The King's Trumpeters' James de la Noa (above spelled as 'Jaquet de la Now',[84] resident of Tower Ward) and John de Cecil (here again spelled in a different way as 'John de Cicilia') were delivered a licence 'to import 400 butts of Malvesyes' in May 1514.[85] In the same year, a generous licence was granted to the lute player John Petrus of Bressa 'to retain in his hands for four years the customs on goods exported and imported by him within 18 months after 1 June 1514, to the amount of 1000 marks in custom'.[86] A licence delivered on 22 January 1518/19 to the same player, now referred to as 'John Piero of Brescia', granted him the right to 'import 400 tuns of Toulouse woad or Gascon wine'.[87] The organ player Benedict de Opiciis (Benedictus de Opiciis) was licenced 'to export 1000 quarters of wheat, not to exceed 6s. 8d. the quarter' in January 1516/17.[88] A late example, of 1555, shows that a Robert Richemond, who was a gentleman of the Chapel, was even given a licence 'to keep a tavern within the town of Barking'.[89] The musicians mentioned – apart from the two gentlemen of the Chapel – had in common that none of them were English. Duwes was French,

---

82 *English Court Music* edited Ashbee 7 36; on this occasion '100 tuns'. On 30 September 1514 he was given a licence to 'import 200 tuns of Gascon wine'; *English Court Music* edited Ashbee 7 44. On 14 June 1515 he was again given a licence 'to import 200 tuns of Gascon wine'; *English Court Music* edited Ashbee 7 47.
83 *English Court Music* edited Ashbee 7 39.
84 Kisby 'Royal Minstrels in the City' 212.
85 *English Court Music* edited Ashbee 7 43.
86 *English Court Music* edited Ashbee 7 43.
87 *English Court Music* edited Ashbee 7 52.
88 *English Court Music* edited Ashbee 7 49.
89 *English Court Music* edited Ashbee 7 137.

Benedict de Opiciis had previously worked in the Low Countries,[90] John Piero (or 'Zuan Piero') was associated with the courts of 'Mantua and Ferrara, keeping personal contact with Isabella and Alfonso d'Este',[91] and John de Cecil was Spanish and had worked for Philip the Handsome in the Burgundian Netherlands.[92] Dumitrescu identifies Jacques or James de Lanoa as an international musical performer but does not specify a 'previous location' or heritage.[93] It is possible that the licences may have been given to talented musicians as a form of reward, or as an incentive for them to keep providing their services at the English court, given the mobility of high-achieving musicians at the time, but this is a conjecture; the explicit individual motivations for the provision of each licence have not been uncovered if they were ever recorded.

Evidence from the records shows, furthermore, that musicians could at times be found to have had other means of an income through additional positions, either at courtly residences or at satellite courts – that is, great houses that stood in close connection to the king's court, such as those of the royal children, or even the houses of high dignitaries. For example, the aforementioned French lute player Giles Duwes had also served as French teacher to Henry VII's children and, as Ashbee observes, 'following his accession Henry VIII granted Duwes the office of Keeper of the King's Library at Richmond'.[94] But less obviously glamorous positions can also be found to have been given to musical servants. Think, for example, of the grant given out in 1524 to a John Gilmyn and his son, John, of a position as 'keeper, auditor and doorward' of Bristol Castle, which provided 'a grant of the Castle close and 2d. a day as doorward'.[95] The document records that the post was 'formerly held by Gilmyn the elder, then serjeant [*marshal*] of the King's minstrels', a position to which

---

90 Dumitrescu *Early Tudor Court* 8.
91 Dumitrescu *Early Tudor Court* 83.
92 G. van Doorslaer 'La chapelle musicale de Philippe le Beau' *Revue belge d'archeologie et d'histoire de l'art 4* (1934) 21–57, at 39.
93 Dumitrescu *Early Tudor Court* 232.
94 Andrew Ashbee 'Groomed for Service: Musicians in the Privy Chamber at the English Court, c.1495–1558' *Early Music 25: 2* (1997) 185–97, at 188.
95 *English Court Music* edited Ashbee 7 60; *Letters and Papers Henry VII* 4.1 464, #27.

he had been appointed in 1514.[96] This is, thus, another post that was understood to have been held alongside other musical duties.

Wages aside, there were additional remunerations that court musicians could look forward to receiving on numerous occasions. *Records of Early English Drama* reveal that the trumpeters played and were subsequently rewarded in various places across the country.[97] For example, the Exeter Receivers' Account Rolls of 1495–6 record a payment of 6s 8d to *Mimis domini Regis*. They specifically mention that these are the King's Trumpeters: *videlicet lez Trumpettes*.[98] The standard gratuity to the king's trumpets seems to be have been 6s 8d, half a mark.[99] However, some places added wine and sometimes a meal. For example, the Sandwich Treasurer's Accounts of 1507–8 record that they 'paid to my lord prin*ces* [Henry Prince of Wales] Trumpiters for a reward and for a Galon of wyne iiij s. and paid for a Galon of wyne spent aft*er*ward upon theym viij d. and paid for their supp*er* the same night and for their horsmet ij s.'[100]

Musicians and other entertainers often received rewards from persons other than their patrons for services rendered. That it would have been a breach of decorum *not* to tip the musicians is testified by Sir Robert Wingfield's exasperated letter to the Lords of the Council in April 1515; having been sent on a foreign mission he had run completely out of

---

96 *English Court Music* edited Ashbee 7 44–5. Gilmyn, who had been a 'yeoman of the Crown in Henry VII's time', had initially held this grant along with an old colleague, John Williams, who had also served under Henry VII. The fact that the grant was being renewed to Gilmyn the elder and his son John, an usher of the chamber, 'in survivorship' may suggest that John Williams was now dead.

97 REED *Patrons and Performances* website, <https://library2.utm.utoronto.ca/otra/reed/>. To search by patron, go to <https://library2.utm.utoronto.ca/otra/reed/patrons-list>; to search for King's Trumpeters: <https://library2.utm.utoronto.ca/otra/reed/troupe-list/K?page=2>. The trumpeters, unlike the minstrels in general, usually seem to be accompanying the king: see e.g. the marginal notes for Canterbury 1513 'Rewardes gevyn to the kyngys seruantys when he went into ffraunce' and 'Rewardes gevyn to the kynges seruantes when he cam out of ffraunce'; *REED: Kent* edited James M. Gibson (University of Toronto Press, 2002) 109 and 110. These included his trumpeters, together with the heralds and pursuivants: all got a flat rate of 6s 8d.

98 *REED: Devon* edited John M. Wasson (University of Toronto Press, 1986) *1* 112.

99 E.g. Sandwich 1497/8, 6s 8d; *REED: Kent* 831, Canterbury 15–30 June 1513, 6s 8d; *REED: Kent* 109.

100 *REED: Kent* 833.

funds, but was complaining about his housing in 'this city [*Augsburg*], the dearest in all Almayne', where 'His lodgings cost 3*s.* 4*d.* sterling a day, and he must give rewards to trumpeters, minstrels and fools.'[101]

The custom of rewarding musicians patronised by others can be seen to have been honoured all the way up to the highest echelons. For example, the household book of Katharine Countess of Devon (1479–1527) records her spending 10s paying 'a harper and a tumbler with the King's servants', and, on a later occasion, 5s 'to minstrels of the King, Cardinal, and lord Daubney'.[102] The *Privy Purse Expenses* of the Princess Mary (1516–1558) show that she gave New Year's gifts to the king's servants, including, on 1 January 1542/3 10s for 'the Trompettes', 10s for 'the Players', 10s for 'the newe Sagbuttes', 5s for the 'Dromslades', 3s 9d for 'the Welshe mynstrels', 10s for 'the Flutes', 5s for 'Yevan and his fellowe', 2s 6d for 'Haunce the luter', the same amount for 'the northe luter', 10s for 'the recorders', and 5s for 'More the harper'.[103] But Mary also dutifully rewarded the musicians belonging to other households who played for her at other times in the year.[104]

The king would also remunerate the musicians in the trains of other rulers, visiting ambassadors, and dignitaries. For example, when in the twelfth year of his reign (July 1520) Henry met Charles V in Calais after the spectacular diplomatic festival of the Field of Cloth of Gold, he paid a 'Reward to the officers of the Emperor's household, 100*l*. ... To the Emperor's minstrels, 20*l.*; to his trumpets, 10*l.*'[105] These customs were shared internationally, and when, on 9 October 1514, Mary Tudor married the French king Louis XII, Sanuto reports that

---

101 *Letters and Papers* 2:1 93, #294 (3 April 1515); online at <http://www.british-history.ac.uk/letters-papers-hen8/vol2/pp89–104>. Also *Letters and Papers* 2:1 181 #684 at Vienna: 'To reward the exceeding number of trumpets, tamboryns and other minstrels of all the kings and princes will make a great hole in his purse'.

102 *Letters and Papers* 4 340, #771 (24 October 1524); online at <http://www.british-history.ac.uk/letters-papers-hen8/vol4/pp332–346>.

103 *English Court Music* edited Ashbee 7 378.

104 For example, in June 1543, she made a payment 'to my lady Anne of Cleves servauntes at Richemount the 12th Daye of June', which included 30s 'to the mynstrels'. *English Court Music* edited Ashbee 7 379.

105 'The King's Book of Payments, 1520' in *Letters and Papers* 3 1539–1543, online at <http://www.british-history.ac.uk/letters-papers-hen8/vol3/pp1539–1543>.

to each of the eight trumpeters who came with the Queen from England, the King caused 150 crowns to be given. Monseigneur d'Angouleme gave them each 50; and 'Madame' as many more; all the other French princes gave them something.[106]

As part of extending his hospitality to the foreign visitors, and 'to avoid putting the English ... to expense', the French king 'prohibited his trumpeters, fifers, musicians, singers, and all others, at the peril of their lives, from going to play or sing in their [the English visitors'] dwellings as mendicants'.[107] The French king's prohibition underscores once more how engrained was the custom to reward royal musicians belonging to another person's entourage, as well as how eager musicians were to make use of opportunities to earn some extra money in potentially lucrative contexts such as those of international encounters and festive cheer.

Finally, occasional, one-off gifts of clothing, presented to them on special occasions, represented a perk for royal servants including musicians. I have already mentioned the wedding present that John Blanke received, 'a gown of violet cloth &c., including a bonnet and a hat, "to be taken of our gift against his marriage"' through the king's warrant to the Great Wardrobe on 14 January 1511/1512.[108] It would appear that these garments were not the 'unprecedented wedding gifts from the National Treasury' that has been claimed.[109] Maria Hayward has contextualised these marriage gifts from the king by noting that, 'On 26 December 1510 John Hette (Hethe), yeoman almoner of the chamber, was given broad cloth for a gown "to be taken of our gift and reward to

---

106 *Calendar of State Papers Relating to English Affairs in the Archives of Venice* edited Rawdon Brown and others, 38 vols (London: 1864–1947) 2 211–12; # 511 (2 November 1514); online at <http://www.british-history.ac.uk/cal-state-papers/venice/vol2/pp202–213>. This example is also quoted in Dumitrescu *Early Tudor Court* 38.

107 *Calendar of State Papers Venice 2* 212 (2 November 1514).

108 TNA E101/417/6 #50; image online at <http://aalt.law.uh.edu/AALT7/E101/E101no417/E101no417no6/IMG_0161.htm>. Calendared in *Letters and Papers 1* 505 #1025 (14 January 1512); online at <http://www.british-history.ac.uk/letters-papers-hen8/vol1/pp502–510>. See note 4.

109 Robin Walker 'A Black Man with a Trumpet: Changing Perceptions' in <https://www.johnblanke.com/robin-walker1.html>; see also the longer version at <https://www.johnblanke.com/robin-walker.html>. He cites Onyeka Nubia *Blackamoores: Africans in Tudor England, Their Presence, Status and Origins* (London: Narrative Eye, 2013) as his source.

the marriage of our said servant"'.[110] She observes that 'other examples include a gown of violet cloth containing 4 broad yards (3.6m), furred with black Irish lamb, and tawny camlet for a jacket for Richard Mayre, one of the yeomen of the Ewery, on 12 January 1512', and that 'his bride was also given 3 broad yards (2.7m) of violet cloth for her gown'.[111] The warrant for Richard Mayre as a whole reads:

[Signed] Henry R

By the king

We wol and charge you that vnto o*ur* wellbiloued *ser*ua*n*t Richard Mayer oon of the yeomen of our Ewery or to the bringer herof in his name ye delyu*e*re or do to be delyu*e*red for his weddyng apparayll a gown cloth of violet conteynyng foure brode yardes and asmoche blak Irisshe lamb as wol suffice to furre the same / It*em* thre yard*es* of blak sat[in?] for a dublet w*ith* lynyng sufficient to the same Item eight yard*es* of tawney chamlet for a jaquet It*em* a bonet / And for his wif we wol that ye delyu*e*re vnto the bringer herof thre brode yard*es* of violet cloth for hir gowne and that [this] shalbe yo*ur* sufficient warraunt and descharge in that behalf. Yeuen vnder o*ur* Signet at o*ur* mano*ur* of Grenewich the xij^th day of January the thyrd yere of o*ur* Reigne

To our trusty and welbeloued
sir Andrew Windsor knight
keper of o*ur* grete wardrobe

The king's warrant issued to present Mayer with his wedding present is almost identical to the warrant written to supply John Blanke with his, except that Mayer's wife is included in his warrant. This suggests that she was also a member of the Household. By implication, John Blanke appears to have married someone outside the Household. Given that the warrant for Blanke's gift is very worn and in places illegible, most studies

---

110   Hayward *Dress at the Court of King Henry VIII* 231.
111   Hayward *Dress at the Court of King Henry VIII* 231. For the original document, see TNA E101/417/6 #57, filed a few documents later: image online at <http://aalt.law.uh.edu/AALT7/E101/E101no417/E101no417no6/IMG_0169.htm>, calendared *Letters and Papers 1: 1509–1514* 504 #1023.

depend on the *Letters and Papers* version, but by transcribing it here I hope to show how very formulaic is the language used, the order of the words, and, indeed, the contents of the parcels about to be delivered. The two warrants were written out only two days apart,[112] and seem to be calling on the same bale of violet cloth. The legible parts of John Blanke's wedding gift warrant read:

[Signed] Henry R [*but almost disappeared*]

By the kyng

We wol and charge you that vnto o*ur se*r*ua*unt John Blak[e] our Trompeter ye deliuer thes[e] p*ar*celles folowing Item[?] [for a] g[owne?] of violet clothe conteyning iiij brode[?] yard*es*[?] to be f[ur?]ed *with* spanysshe buge I[tem?] … … … … … vjs viijd Jtem a dublet of velwet[?] conteynyng … … … … … … … … … … … p[air?] of s[carl?]et [hose?] I[t*em*] a [bonet and a Hatte?]: to be takyn of o*ur* gift ayenst[?] his mariage[?] And these o*ur* letres shalbe yo*ur* sufficient warraunt and descharge [for the same?] Yeuen vnder o*ur* Signet at o*ur* mano*ur* at Grenewich the xiiij[th] daye of januarie the thrid[?] y[*ear of our*][113] Reigne.

> To our trusty and welbeloued
> *se*r*ua*u*n*t *sir* Andrewe Windesor
> knight keper of o*ur* greate
> wardrobe[114]

The examples of the two warrants clearly indicate that this kind of gift represented a routine exercise. Furthermore, the warrant detailing Mayer's gift may be used to fill in the blanks to better understand the warrant detailing John Blanke's wedding gift.

Wedding gifts of clothing were given out on multiple occasions. Anita Hewerdine also gives examples of Yeomen of the Guard who received gifts

---

112 The dates on both documents are not easy to read. TNA E101/417/6 #57 reads 12 or 7 January 3 Henry VIII (so January 1511/12). TNA E101/417/6 #50, which is very rubbed, reads 14 January (also 1511/12).

113 This is under a paper seal-holder.

114 TNA E101/417/6 #50; image online at <http://aalt.law.uh.edu/AALT7/E101/E101no417/E101no417n06/IMG_0161.htm>.

of clothing or dress lengths 'towards [their] marriage'.[115] These include William Wynnesbury,[116] who is well known as Henry's Lord of Misrule. His colleague James Gartside, who married six years later, seems to have received a cash payment of ten marks (£6 13s 4d) in lieu.[117] Judging from the two Yeomen's Chamber Accounts entries, that was the accepted going rate for the expected value of the cloth. A wedding present at this rate seems to have been so standard that in 1516 John Basshe, the master of the Greyhounds, actually asks for his ten marks in cash.[118]

Other apparently individual issues of clothing given to musicians look as if they could have been livery, such as when in December 1511 'blynde Dikke, *our* harper' was provided with 'a gowne of tawny conteynyng four brode yer*des* furred w*ith* blakke Irishe lambe And thre yer*des* of blakke saten for a doublet', as per the king's warrant under his signet.[119] In October 1511 James Worsley and his wife were delivered from the Great Wardrobe materials to furnish themselves with matching livery in luxurious fabrics. James was provided with 'sixtene yer*des*[120] of Russet damaske for a gowne and asmoche blakke bogy as shall suffice to furre the same gowne'. The gown was to be worn with 'a Jaquet' for which he was given 'eight yer*des* of tawny velvet' and 'a furre therunto of white bogy'. 'Thre yer*des* of Crymesyn sateyn for a doublet' were also provided. Mrs Worsley was to be dressed to match her husband. The

---

115   Anita Hewerdine *The Yeomen of the Guard and the Early Tudors: The Formation of a Royal Bodyguard* (London: I.B. Tauris, 2012) 26.
116   BL Additional MS 21481 fol. 32r, 16 June 1510: William Wynnesbury, Yeoman of the King's Guard; 'item to william wynnesbury opon a waraunt signed for his clothing & his wyffes for his mariage vj li xiij s iiij d'; in *Chamber Books* at <https://www.dhi.ac.uk/chamber-books/folio/LL_BL_AddMS_21481_fo032r.xml>.
117   BL Additional MS 21481 fol. 239r, 2 November 1516 (nearest written date), James Gartside, Yeoman of the King's Guard: 'item to jamys gartside oone of the yomen of the kinges garde opon a warraunt by way of the kinges rewarde towardes his mariage vj li xiij s iiij d'; in *Chamber Books* at <https://www.dhi.ac.uk/chamber-books/folio/LL_BL_AddMS_21481_fo239r.xml>.
118   TNA E101/417/2 #155; 1 June 1516, John Basshe, keeper of the greyhounds: petition 'To geue and grante vnto hym by waye of your moost gracious Rewarde / towardes his mariage the s*omm*e of ten m*a*rkes sterling*es*'. Image online at <http://aalt.law.uh.edu/AALT7/E101/E101no417/E101no417no2/IMG_0225.htm>.
119   *English Court Music* edited Ashbee 7 37. TNA 417/6/#73; image online at <http://aalt.law.uh.edu/AALT7/E101/E101no417/E101no417no6/IMG_0187.htm>.
120   The damask will have been narrow in width – these were not 'broad' yards.

Great Wardrobe warrant for delivery specifies 'sixtene yerdes of russet damaske for a gowne for his wif'. She was also to have 'nyne yerdes of tawny sateyn for a kyrtill'. Her outfit could be completed with 'two yerdes of Crymesyn velvet for bynding of the said gowne' and 'asmoche whit Cotton as shall suffice to lyne the said gowne'.[121]

Since the Great Wardrobe existed to provide livery of clothes for the household, they bought in material for stock, so had ample amounts to hand out.[122] The Wardrobe were used to sudden bulk demands. On 31 October 1511 the king issued a warrant for

> asmoche white and grene Clothe as shal suffice for oon hundred Jaquettes with half slevys and basys for oure garde / And asmoche crymson clothe of golde of tyssue as shall suffice for the bordering of the same.[123]

As Hayward explains,

> clothes in the Tudor livery colours of green and white were most frequently given to soldiers, sailors, trumpeters and, on occasion, heralds. In contrast, liveries in one colour, frequently black but also often in russet and tawny, were given to members of the chamber and privy chamber.[124]

So did John Blanke want to buy more expensive clothes? Who knows. The Great Wardrobe provided best-quality garments for the court and its servants as 'livery', and this was part of the expected wages. The items that John Blanke is recorded to have received *aside from* his wedding costume, such as the four yards of 'mourning liveries' for the funeral of Henry VII[125] and the four and a half yards of red livery for the coronation of Henry VIII and Katherine of Aragon,[126] equal those of the other trumpet

---

121 TNA E101/417/6 #89; image online at <http://aalt.law.uh.edu/AALT7/E101/E101no417/E101no417no6/IMG_0204.htm>.

122 See Andrew Windsor's document files TNA E101/417/3, E101/416/7, E101/418/1, online at <http://aalt.law.uh.edu/HouseholdH8.html>.

123 TNA 417/6/#80; image online at <http://aalt.law.uh.edu/AALT7/E101/E101no417/E101no417no6/IMG_0194.htm>.

124 Maria Hayward *The Great Wardrobe Accounts of Henry VII and Henry VIII* (London: The Boydell Press, 2012) xii.

125 *English Court Music* edited Ashbee 7 25.

126 *English Court Music* edited Ashbee 7 29.

players of the same rank – the Marshall of the King's Trumpets merited half a yard of extra material – as well as that of the sackbut and shawm players.[127] But these recorded amounts of material represent issues of uniform, and do not represent wages. If John Blanke had wanted to obtain more costly clothes, these would not have been used for his work, or 'service' as he implies in his petition, because he was issued with everything necessary for that.

III

In short, although many a court musician may have resided at court where he would have enjoyed 'bouge of court' and free accommodation, several examples – as provided by Kisby – show that musicians sometimes lived in the City of London, when, for example, they were married.[128] This indicates a greater independence but also expenses additional to those allowed for by Kaufmann.[129] Furthermore, the emphasis on wages and their purchasing power alone to determine a musician's wealth would disregard the fact that being a court musician was a potentially lucrative business, allowing for supplementary means of acquiring wealth in terms of time available, opportunity, and connections; and being a court servant meant that additional privileges were to be had, such as profitable jobs and licences to conduct business. The *Records of Early English Drama* volumes and Andrew Ashbee's *Records of English Court Music* provide a wealth of examples of such opportunities.

Let us now return to Onyeka Nubia's warning that, 'By making John Blanke an exception, he is marginalised and his existence made strange'.[130] As I have attempted to show in this contribution, the record evidence on John Blanke is scarce, but that which is extant is generally consistent with that of other musicians and court servants at the Tudor court. From this it follows that not only was John Blanke not an 'exception' in terms of black presence in the society in which he performed his musical skills but also he was neither privileged nor disadvantaged within the context in which he worked. His starting on half wages of 20s equals John de Cecil's first

---

127 *English Court Music* edited Ashbee 7, at 25 and 29.
128 Kisby 'Royal Minstrels in the City' 208-12.
129 Kaufmann *Black Tudors* 22.
130 Onyeka Nubia 'The Author of *Blackamoores: Africans in Tudor England*' in *The John Blanke Project*, at <https://www.johnblanke.com/onyeka.html>.

entering the records on starting wages; Blanke's marriage gift of clothes sits in a trend of such gifts made to other servants; and, indeed, Blanke's petitioning for Dominic Justinian's position as a trumpet player with the accompanying wages of 16d a day appears to have been completely in line with other petitions made by royal musicians hoping to fill a 'room' that had become vacant. To return to Miranda Kaufmann's question: perhaps it is not so much that John Blanke 'needed' anything in particular that his current wages could not buy him. Rather, the reference to the 'other trumpets' in John Blanke's petition is strongly reminiscent of the petition by Antony Etfeld, which similarly asked for a position as trumpet player with wages of 16d a day 'as the other trumpeters receive'.[131] With this in mind, I suggest that we read John Blanke's petition to Henry VIII as a routine document within a context in which petitions were the means through which to apply for any change that needed the king's approval.

Delft University of Technology

Acknowledgements

This article would not be anywhere near its current form if it were not for the scholarly generosity of Meg Twycross, to whom I am very much indebted. This article has also benefited greatly from suggestions from Sarah Carpenter, Elisabeth Dutton, and John J. McGavin, and from the anonymous peer reviewers at *Medieval English Theatre*.

---

131 *English Court Music* edited Ashbee 7 408.

PERPETUALLY EDITING TOWNELEY
A Speculative Textual Note on Mrs Noah's 'Stafford Blue'

Pamela M. King

Many of us grew up with England and Pollard's edition of *The Towneley Plays*[1] and with Arthur Cawley's selection, *The Wakefield Pageants in the Towneley Cycle*.[2] We now work with the Early English Text Society edition by Stevens and Cawley,[3] which took so long to appear that aspects of its commentary were already out of date by the time it was published, and with Garrett Epp's TEAMS edition,[4] which moved faster. The Towneley manuscript, San Marino, CA: Huntington Library MS HM1, to give it its full designation, has attracted, and is still attracting, so much new scholarship, especially in the last fifty years, that all editors do their best to hit a moving target while fundamentals such as the provenance and date of the contents of the manuscript remain contentious.

In recent years we have lost Barbara Palmer and Olga Horner, both of whom made important contributions to those fundamental conundrums. The latter was working with Meg Twycross on research into the catalogues of the library of the Towneley family that exposed the anomaly that, although the manuscript has a Towneley shelf-mark, it is absent from any of their catalogues. Barbara Palmer is largely responsible for definitively undermining the commonplace understanding that the manuscript represented a 'cycle' from Wakefield, as her work on the West Riding revealed plays in many other locations that may have been drawn together in what is emerging as a compilation. Meg Twycross is still working on the Towneley family and the history of the manuscript and investigating the possible relationship between the manuscript and the great Catholic survivalist houses of the West Yorkshire/East Lancashire

---

1 *The Towneley Plays: Re-edited from the Unique MS* edited G. England and A.W. Pollard *EETS ES 71* (1897).

2 *The Wakefield Pageants in the Towneley Cycle* edited Arthur C. Cawley (Manchester UP, 1958).

3 *The Towneley Plays* edited Martin Stevens and A.C. Cawley, 2 vols *EETS SS 13* and 14 (1994).

4 *The Towneley Plays* edited Garret P.J. Epp (TEAMS Middle English Texts Series; Kalamazoo MI: Medieval Institute Publications, 2018).

border. Most recently, Alexandra Johnston has pursued another line of enquiry, prompted by correspondence with the late Malcolm Parkes, who identified the hand of the manuscript as that of a Chancery clerk writing during the reign of Mary Tudor – that is, 1553–8:

> He also believed that the manuscript is, in some ways, a legal document intended as an official copy for reference purposes by someone in authority, possibly a member of an ecclesiastical court.[5]

Johnston goes on to contextualise this suggestion within the history of the Reformation in the archdiocese of York.

Meanwhile, informed by historical and codicological investigation, fresh critical studies of its contents proceed. Notably Camille Marshall has written a significant PhD thesis parsing internal references to doctrinal matters in a different approach to dating, suggesting that the so-called 'Wakefield Master' demonstrates equivocations commensurate with the years during which Reformation theology had yet to solidify. Prior to that, Peter Happé wrote an important analysis of the borrowings from the York Cycle in the manuscript. Nor should it be forgotten that, in the early 1960s, the late Marshal Rose prepared an adaptation of the plays for the professional stage, the first professional production of English 'mystery plays' in the modern theatre.[6]

---

5   See Barbara D. Palmer '"Towneley Plays" or "Wakefield Cycle" Revisited' *Comparative Drama* 21: 4 (1987/8) 318–48, and 'Recycling "The Wakefield Cycle": The Records' *Research Opportunities in Renaissance Drama* 41 (2002) 88–130; Theresa Coletti and Gail McMurray Gibson 'The Tudor Origins of Mediaeval Drama' in *A Companion to Tudor Literature* edited Kent Cartwright (London: Wiley-Blackwell, 2010) 228–45. Gail Gibson continues to work on the after-history of the manuscript. Meg Twycross published her initial findings in 'They did not come out of an Abbey in Lancashire: Francis Douce and the manuscript of the Towneley Plays', in *The Best Pairt of Our Play: Essays Presented to John J. McGavin Part One*, edited Sarah Carpenter, Pamela M. King, Meg Twycross, and Greg Walker *Medieval English Theatre 37* (2015) 149–65. See also Alexandra F. Johnston 'The Towneley Plays' in *Early British Drama in Manuscript* edited Tamara Atkin and Laura Estill (Turnhout: Brepols, 2019) 55–70, at page 56.

6   Camille Marshall 'Playing, Seeing, and Doubting the Godhead in the Sixteenth-Century Towneley Collection of Biblical Plays' (unpublished thèse de doctorat, Faculté des Lettres de l'Université de Lausanne, 2019); Peter Happé *The Towneley Cycle: Unity and Diversity* (Cardiff: University of Wales Press, 2007). For Rose's

The present author's minor contribution to the ongoing endeavours is to draw attention to some idiomatic moments in the so-called 'Wakefield pageants', tying them to contemporary sources. I am generating what I hope will be new textual notes for future editors and for second editions, but the wider project is to help substantiate, complementing Camille Marshall's approach, a mid-sixteenth-century date for this clutch of excellent pageants. I have so far linked specifics in both Shepherds' Pageants with the politics of Tudor enclosures (not with fifteenth-century bastard feudalism, as has previously been assumed), and the Tutivillus elements in the *Judicium* with popular demonology from the same date.[7] The second, now published, part of this long episodic project links to the fifteenth-century burlesque Scots romance *Rauf Colyer*, circulating in the north of England in print in the mid-sixteenth century, in which there is a notable consonance between Rauf's request for entry to his humble cot and Mak's lines in *Secunda Pastorum*.[8]

Processus Noe cum Filiis Wakefield is the problematic heading on the Noah pageant in the manuscript, the subject of the present exploration. It is attributed to the single hand known traditionally as 'The Wakefield Master', not only because it mentions the word *Wakefield* but because it is written in the distinctive bob-and-wheel stanza and is of comparable quality. The present article focuses on one line, in fact two words, from Noah's Wife's opening salvo against her elderly husband before he has even revealed his momentous news about the need to build an ark:

> Bot thou were worthi be cled
> In Stafford blew,
> For thou art alway adred,
> Be it fals or trew.   289–92

As is the case in the other plays attributed to this hand, one of the markers of the shift into a demotic register is the inclusion of aphorisms and references to the playwright's contemporary culture. These have

---

adaptation see *The Wakefield Mystery Plays* edited Martial Rose (London: Norton, 1969).

[7] Pamela King 'The Wakefield Master Revisited' in *Performance, Ceremony and Display in Late Medieval England: Essays from the 2018 Harlaxton Symposium* edited Julia Boffey (Harlaxton Medieval Studies 30; Donington: Shaun Tyas, 2020) 110–28.

[8] Pamela King '*The Tale of Rauf Coilȝear* and *Secunda Pastorum*' Notes and Queries 68: 2 (2021) 168–9.

sometimes proved obscure to modern editors and commentators. Cawley and Stevens annotate as follows:

> *Stafford blew*: the name of a blue cloth. The *OED* quotations (s. Stafford) make it clear that a humorous pun on 'staff' is intended, and that 'to be clad in Stafford Blue' means 'to be beaten black and blue'.

Epp accepts the metaphorical interpretation, but also the understanding that Stafford blue refers to a type of cloth. According to *MED* there is only one other reference:[9]

> 2. When here herte from yow doth pas … let here passe and goo lyghtly, And clothe here well yn Stafford blewe.[10]

Our problem is that there is no surviving connection between Stafford and cloth of blue or any other colour. The persistent association with cloth must, therefore, derive from *clad* and cognates, but in late medieval and early modern idiomatic usage there are things other than cloth in which a body may be clad. We note, relating to our two citations from *MED*, that *clad* and *clothed* are essentially the same word, derived from the Old English *claðian*. *OED* observes that the verb 'to clad' in connection with clothing is now obsolete, but cites a cluster of examples from the sixteenth and seventeenth centuries, including metaphorical ones. As an adjective the range is greater and moves from applying to literal coverings for the body to metaphorical attributes and metonymic appurtenances.[11]

One of these has a much more secure connection with Stafford, or Staffordshire, and that is clay. Most medievalists will recall the dreamer in *Pearl* lamenting

---

9 See also 'Lexis of Cloth and Clothing' database at <http://lexissearch.arts.manchester.ac.uk/entry.aspx?id=4441>. I am grateful to Mark Chambers for pointing this out to me. Thanks also to Philip Butterworth who later drew my attention to the *MED* reference.

10 Cited from 'Who carpys', Trinity College Cambridge MS O.9.38 (Glastonbury Commonplace Book) fols 21r–22r, at fol 21v. Digitised at <https://mss-cat.trin.cam.ac.uk/Manuscript/O.9.38/UV#?c=0&m=0&s=0&cv=28&r=0&xywh=656%2C78%2C2595%2C1281>.

11 *OED* sv *clad* adj. See the *MED* sv *clothen* v. 4c for the overlap of *clad* and *clothe* in a wide range of uses beyond that of cloth.

> For soþe þer fleten to me fele
> To þenke hir color so clad in clot.
> O moul, þou marreȝ a myry iuele,
> My priuy perle wythouten spotte. 21–4

In discussing the lines in *Pearl*, Patricia Kean quotes a fifteenth-century lyric that gloomily promises, 'Clottes of clay þi cors schal cleth, | Þi careyne vn-to wormes cast'.[12] The alliteration of *clad* and its cognates with *clot* or *clay* is in fact a commonplace of late medieval mortality verse, such as the fifteenth-century lyric spin-off from the Dance of Death tradition that contains the lines, spoken by one of those summoned to death,

> I weende to ded, a kynge I-wisse;
> What helpis honor or werldis blysse?
> Dede is to mane the kynde wai —
> i wende to be clad in clay.[13]

Keen goes on to observe that the actual phrase 'clad in clay' in fact lived on into the seventeenth century and beyond, citing the shift from concrete examples to the figurative nature of Henry Vaughan's use, where, in the poem addressed to Christ, *Disorder and Frailty*, he 'threatens heaven' from his 'cell | of clay' – that is, his mortal body (lines 16–17).[14] The Peterborough gravedigger Old Scarlett, who died in 1594 in his ninety-eighth year, and is sometimes considered the original of the gravedigger in *Hamlet*, dug the graves of both Katherine of Aragon and Mary, Queen of Scots. He is commemorated in a verse on his own memorial which concludes,

> But at length his own time came;
> What hee for others did for him the same
> Was done: No doubt his soule doth live for aye
> In heaven: Tho here his body clad in clay.[15]

---

12 Patricia Kean *The Pearl: an Interpretation* (London: Routledge, 1967) 22–3.
13 *Religious Lyrics of the XVth Century* edited Carleton Brown (Oxford: Clarendon Press, 1939) 248–9.
14 Kean *Pearl* 22–3 note 36.
15 See George Searle Philipps *A Guide to Peterborough Cathedral* (Peterborough: J.S. Clarke, 1849) 85.

It seems, therefore, that the idea of being 'clad in clay' is a commonplace expression for being dead. If we were to accept that 'Stafford blue' might be clay, rather than fabric, the line may simply suggest that Noah's wife, like Gil in *Secunda Pastorum*, wishes her useless old husband dead: but that does not account for the other reference.

Before turning to that, we shall consider 'Stafford blew' as a term for clay, which can be accounted for. Burslem in Staffordshire, one of the five towns in what came to be known as 'the Potteries', is the home of the world-famous Wedgwood ceramic production works. Classic Wedgwood is glazed in the shade of blue to which it gives its name, but the factory did not begin production until the very end of the seventeenth century.[16] Before the rise of the Wedgwood brand, however, and going back to at least the thirteenth century, clay had been dug in the area of the five towns and, in the late fifteenth and sixteenth centuries, a number of factors conspired to bring a different and valued kind of 'blue' to prominence. The growth of the coal industry throughout the later fifteenth century made it possible for pots to be fired at higher temperatures than was previously the case, and a particular clay, sometimes called 'Midland Purple', actually Etruria marl, came into its own.

Etruria marl in its raw state is red, but 'when fired at a high temperature in a low-oxygen reducing atmosphere takes on a deep blue colour and attains a very hard, impervious surface with high crushing strength and low water absorption'.[17] In the nineteenth and twentieth centuries this clay was mined on an industrial scale and bricks and roof-tiles made from it were in great demand because of their low porosity and striking colour.[18]

The Staffordshire antiquarian Robert Plot, writing in 1686, illuminates further:

> Amongst the *underturf Earths*, the next that present themselves, are the *arable soiles*, which to mention more particularly than above, are either *Clay*, *marly*, *sandy*, *gravelly*, *light mould*, *black land*, *moorish* and *gouty land*; each of which they fit with their

---

16   Josiah Wedgwood *Staffordshire Pottery and its History* (London: Sampson Low and Marston, 1913) 13.
17   See <https://www.wikiwand.com/en/Staffordshire_blue_brick>.
18   See <http://www.thepotteries.org/six_towns/index.htm>; <http://www.thepotteries.org/focus/006.htm>.

> most agreeable *grains* and *manures* ... I shall consider only here the severall sorts of *Marles* ... Whereof I find in *Staffordshire* about four or five sorts. 1. a *red fat earthy* sort, having some *veins* of *blew* (which is the most common) found upon the *Trent* side about *Ingestre*, *Tixall*, *Heywood* &c, lyeing generally about 18 inches or two foot under the surface, though sometimes it lyes so *ebb* (as they call it) that they plow up the *head* of it, otherwise that which covers it, is a *hungry clay*, which yet makes them this recompence, that it holds the *Marle* so together above, that undermining it, they can have a *fall* of seven or eightscore loads at a time, which could not be, were this taken away, beside being commonly blended with 3 or 4 yards depth of good *marle* underneath, it is hardly seen, much less doth any hurt. 2 About *Swynnerton*, and the more *Northerly* parts of the *Country* they have a *stiff blewish* sort *Marle* with *red* veines; and 3 another sort mixt for the most part *blew* and *red*, that is not so *stiff*, much better for *corne*; both which (like the former) will fall with undermining, & are commonly dug for 4 shillings 6 pence the hundred load, each load containing 12 measures: And 4 the learned and inquisitive Sr. *Simon Degg* told me of another *blew Marle*, somewhere about *Kinston*, much like *Fullers earth*, which but that it differs in colour, I should otherwise have thought to have been the *Gischromargon* of *Pliny*.[19]

Here he is discussing the agricultural advantages of clay soil, but he continues:

> But beside the use of *Marle* in matters of *Husbandry*, they have another use of them here in order to *building* ... I met with a peculiar sort of *brick-earth*, which when burnt became all over *blew*, those bricks only which were placed furthest from the fire, having any *redness* in them ... [20]

After a discussion of white tobacco-pipe clays he reverts to blue-ware again:

---

19 Robert Plot *The natural history of Stafford-shire* (Oxford: Sheldonian Theatre, 1686) 119–20; transcription online at <https://quod.lib.umich.edu/e/eebo2/A55155.0001.001/1:9.3?rgn=div2;view=fulltext>.
20 Plot *Natural History of Stafford-shire* 120.

> I say the most preferrable *clay* of any, is that of *Amblecot*, of a *dark blewish* colour, whereof they make the best *pots* for the *Glass-houses* of any in *England*: Nay so very good is it for this purpose, that it is sold on the place for sevenpence the bushell, whereof Mr. *Gray* has sixpence, and the *Workman* one penny, and so very necessary to be had, that it is sent as far as *London*, sometimes by *Waggon*, and sometimes by *Land* to *Beaudley*, and so down the *Severn* to *Bristol*, and thence to *London*: the goodness of which *clay*, and cheapness of *coal* hereabout, no doubt has drawn the *glass-houses*, both for *Vessells* and *broad-glass*, into these parts; there being divers set up in different formes here at *Amblecot*, *old-Swynford, Holloways-end* and *Cobourn brook*.[21]

This blue clay is then contrasted with potters' clays 'for the more common wares'.

Robert Plot's antiquarian account is endorsed and clarified by a profusion of archaeological evidence that helps with modern translations of 'Stafford blew'. More recent archaeological papers concur that 'Midland Purple Ware' was made and used between 1450 and 1600. It was very hard, red to dark purplish-grey in colour, and usually with a dark purple to black glaze. It was used for a wide range of different vessels, such as jars, bowls, and jugs. It is often linked to 'Cistercian Ware', which was made between 1475 and 1700, and so-called because it was first found during the excavation of Cistercian monasteries, though not made by the monks. A number of different places are known to have been making this pottery, particularly in the north of England and the Midlands. The two related varieties describe pots that are very thin and hard, as they were made in the first coal-fired pottery kilns, which reached much higher temperatures than the wood-fired types of the medieval period. The clay fabric is usually brick red or purple, and the pots covered with a dark brown or purplish-black glaze, generally on both surfaces.[22] The main type of pot in Cistercian Ware was a small drinking cup with up to six handles, known as a 'tyg'. These pots were sometimes decorated with

---

21 Plot *Natural History of Stafford-shire* 121–2.
22 See, for example, Susan M. Wright and Derek Hurst (2011) *Midlands purple and Cistercian-type wares in the west Midlands in the 15th–16th centuries* [data-set] (York: Archaeology Data Service [distributor]) at <https://doi.org/10.5284/1010824>, and <https://www.archaeologs.com/w/cistercian-ware/en>.

painted dots and other designs in yellow clay, and were very popular, being found all over England. We should also bear in mind that in the immediate post-Reformation period pottery and tiles from dissolved Cistercian monasteries found a lively second-hand market.

Further evidence couples the diversification of working with the hard blue clays with the need to fire them at high temperatures. By the seventeenth century potters working around Burslem were using coal as the fuel of choice. Etruria marl requires firing at high temperatures that cannot be produced in timber-fired kilns, but it also occurs in areas where coal was abundant.

More evidence about the social context of rural potting has come to light from the archaeological exploration of medieval kiln sites in Chilvers Coton, near Nuneaton, another site of deposits of Etruria marl.[23] Here there is very early evidence of coal-fired kilns, but the manorial system constrained potting activity because of the shortage of grazing. It was only when crofts were combined by substantial yeoman farmers in the 1520s that the local clay could truly be exploited on a large scale, and presumably exported further afield. On the other hand, Joan Thirsk draws the distinction between those areas lately enclosed as grasslands that were formerly arable – such as the shepherds in both Towneley pageants complain about, and about which commentators, notably Thomas More, raged – and those that had always been 'woodland' – that is, uncultivated grazing with a scattered population. Staffordshire was one of the latter. No-one chose to plough areas of strong clay more than necessary, and modern agriculturalists know that highly nutritious clay soils perform well when minimally disturbed. These areas were seen as less civilised by travellers from the south, because there were not evidently acres of corn, settlements were small and scattered, and grand houses were concealed rather than prominently at the centre of villages. She concludes,

> Staffordshire holds many secrets which it has not yet yielded up to us on the way the partnership between agriculture and industry

---

23 Martin D. Wilson 'Medieval pottery production at Chilvers Coton, Warwickshire: Re-examination of the archaeological evidence and the historic landscape context' *Medieval Ceramics* 36 (2015) 61–79; online at <https://www.academia.edu/38542940/Medieval_pottery_production_at_Chilvers_Coton_Warwickshire_Re_examination_of_the_archaeological_evidence_and_the_historic_landscape_context>.

developed and shaped a distinctive economy and a distinctive form of family life.

Enterprises were small and family-based, but their products, made from timber, leather, iron, and clay, were in demand: 'in the north-west of the county the pottery industry was firmly established in the neighbourhood of Burslem, exploiting the many different types of clay in the locality'.[24] Over all these areas were small-scale craft industries, unlike the civic cloth industries of, for example, Coventry.

The family-based nature of these mixed agricultural and small-scale industrial activities has another dimension. Through the whole period of the shift from wood to coal-firing and the exploitation of and increasing demand for harder clays there is a notable absence of evidence in census reports from the Midlands of 'potter' as an occupation. It was commonly assumed that pottery production continued to be constrained by being a sideline for agricultural workers. However, Eileen Gooder proposed an alternative solution, which is that many of the potters were female, so concealed in census results as 'wife' or 'widow'. Gooder discovered an Amice Potkyn who worked for Nuneaton Priory in the 1320s, while Elena Pott and Agnes Butterton ran a tile house in Nuneaton in 1553.[25]

'Stafford blew' delivers the rhyme in Noah's Wife's outburst, but may also deliver one of those contemporary jokes that this playwright is so good at. The sole other reference to 'Stafford blue', while rather compromising the enticing suggestion that Noah's wife wishes her husband clad in clay, and therefore dead, I believe gives us secure access to the playwright's pithy contemporary reference.

The term is used in a poem headed simply 'A Ballad' in its published form, taken from Trinity College, Cambridge, MS O. 9. 38, where it is titled 'pluk of her belles & let here flee'.[26] Thought to have been written 'about

---

24 Joan Thirsk *The Rural Economy of England* (London: Hambledon, 1984) 173–4.

25 Eileen Gooder 'Clayworking in the Nuneaton Area, Part 1' in Philip Mayes and Keith Scott *Pottery Kilns at Chilvers Coton, Nuneaton* (Society for Medieval Archaeology Monograph Series 10; London: Society for Medieval Archaeology, 1984) 3–13.

26 *Reliquæ Antiquæ: Scraps from Ancient Manuscripts illustrating chiefly Early English Literature and the English Language* edited Thomas Wright and James Orchard Halliwell (London: John Russell Smith, 1865) 27–9; online at <https://archive.org/details/reliquaeantiqua01wriguoft/page/28/mode/2up>. With thanks to the *METh* editors.

the reign of Henry VI', the ballad is written in the voice of a male spurned lover. Its overarching conceit is the comparison of the treacherous lover with the sparrowhawk, which 'puttys to morte' small birds. When she refused to return to his, the falconer's, glove, he removed her bells and let her fly free. The refrain of each of the stanzas is some variant of 'plukk of here bellys, and let here fly'. The narrator tells how he provided his hawk with the finest of bells, jesses, and mews, but her eye was caught by another, male, hawk, and she pined after her freedom, so, despite all the attention he had lavished on her, he set her free. He goes on to argue that she is better moving from one shallow lover to another as she, like all women, is fickle in her affections, and advises other lovers to behave in the same manner, as such women will bleed them dry and never be satisfied. They will always effect an escape to indulge in infidelities. The poem has little to offer that is not predictable, and ends in its thirteenth stanza with the 'all men take example of me' trope. It is the tenth stanza, however, that is of interest to us:

> They be as fals as was Judas,
>   That with a cosse dyssevyd owre lorde Jhesu;
> For when here herte from yow doth pas,
>   Full sone sche thynkes to have a newe.
> But let here passe and goo lyghtly,
>   And clothe here well yn Stafford blewe;
> Kepe here not then to longe yn mewe,
> Then pluk of here bellys and let here fly.   29

Clothing in Stafford blue by this point in the poem is a kind of punishment. In the final stanza the narrator forcefully suggests, 'Y wolde suche damsellys yn fyre were brent' – that is, 'small damsellys and tender of age' who are responsible not only for men's heartache and impoverishment but for the break-up of marriages with their 'mysgovernawnce'.

Despite the bitterness of the final outburst, it is not within the logic of the syntax of the tenth stanza that slighted lovers should murder their paramours, so clothing in Stafford blue here rather undermines the possibility that Noah's wife is wishing her husband dead and buried. The sense that does work in both contexts is, however, that Noah, and the unfaithful paramour, should receive a sound beating until they are 'clad' all over in bruises. As we have seen, the fashionable blue pottery produced in the Staffordshire area from the mid-fifteenth century is more commonly referred to as Midland Purple, and examples, fired from clay that is originally red, run a range of hues from dark bluish red, in those fired furthest from the fire, through purple to bluish black.

So have we simply come full circle, to the conclusions of the published editions? Not quite: it seems there is no *prima facie* evidence whatever in these two sole instances of the use of the term, nor in literature or archival sources, that 'Stafford blue' is, or ever was, a type of cloth, nor does it need to be. It is much more likely that the term refers to bruising, as the result of a beating, to the colour of Staffordshire clay. *Clad* or *clothed*, as in the case of 'clad in clot' (meaning dead and buried) is, then, primarily metaphorical; it also works for beating because it is transitive, the cladding being done by an agent. This also preserves the understanding that the metaphor incorporates a pun on *staff* as the instrument of the beating, or *cladding*. Given the larger evidence that our playwright revels in rich contemporary allusions, he may well be suggesting that Noah should be beaten to the range of colours of fashionable Midland Purple clay products, and we at least may enjoy the further knowledge that their manufacture was also largely the product of female agency.

University of Glasgow

UNDERSTANDING THE BLANKET-TOSS IN MEDIEVAL DRAMA
The Case of *Een Cluijt van Lijsgen en Jan Lichthart*

Ben Parsons and Bas Jongenelen

This article, and the translation appended to it, will explore one of the most enduring riddles in medieval English drama: the significance of the canvas-tossing episode in the Towneley *Second Shepherds' Play*. As the play itself makes clear, the offences of the sheep-thief and black magician Mak, and of his wife and accomplice Gill, should by rights prompt their victims to 'do thaym to dede'; even Mak himself admits that the shepherds are entitled to 'gyrd of my heede'.[1] However, for some undisclosed reason, the group instead decide to 'cast hym in canvas'. Although the shepherds' change of heart clearly shows justice tempered with mercy, why they should moderate their punishment along these exact lines has proven difficult to determine.[2] Criticism has struggled to know precisely what to make of the canvas penalty, generating a range of suggestions but little consensus. It has been seen as a sign of 'contempt for an unworthy adversary', a method of inducing miscarriage, and a reference to sifting grain that in turn evokes the Apocalypse.[3] Even the most commonly cited interpretation, Chidamian's claim that it evokes a 'traditional way of hastening childbirth', has attracted as much scepticism as support.[4] The problem is exacerbated by the lack of analogues in the theatrical

---

1 *The Towneley Plays* edited Martin Stevens and A.C. Cawley, 2 vols *EETS SS 13* and *14* (1994) *1* 152 lines 901–6.

2 Edmund M. Taft 'Surprised By Love: The Dramatic Structure and Popular Appeal of the *Wakefield Second Shepherds' Pageant*' in *Popular Culture in the Middle Ages* edited Josie P. Campbell *Journal of Popular Culture 14: 1* (1980) 131–40; Josie P. Campbell 'Farce as Function in the Wakefield Shepherds' Plays' *Chaucer Review 14* (1980) 336–43.

3 John C. Hirsh 'Mak Tossed in a Blanket' *Notes and Queries 28* (1981) 117–18, at 118; Norma Kroll 'The Towneley and Chester Plays of the Shepherds: The Dynamic Interweaving of Power, Conflict, and Destiny' *Studies in Philology 100* (2003) 315–45; Ordelle G. Hill *The Manor, the Plowman, and the Shepherd: Agrarian Themes and Imagery in Late Medieval and Early Renaissance English Literature* (Cranbury, NJ: Associated University Presses, 1993) 123.

4 Claude Chidamian 'Mak and the Tossing in the Blanket' *Speculum 22* (1947) 186–90; Maynard Mack, Jr. 'The Second Shepherds' Play: A Reconsideration' *PMLA 93: 1* (1978) 78–85, at 85.

record. Although there are tantalising references to the practice in popular culture more widely, as we will discuss in due course, English drama contains no scene that replicates Mak's punishment and which might provide a clue to its larger meanings; indeed, it features on the English stage in only a few passing allusions from Greene, Shakespeare, Dekker, and Jonson.[5] To echo Jean Goodich, in the absence of any basis of comparison, the Towneley tossing is likely to remain a 'moment that always puzzles'.[6]

Yet, despite the absence of similar scenes in English theatre, instructive parallels can be found by looking to the continent. Especially relevant is the rich body of comic performance that emanated from the cities of the Low Countries. This *rederijker* (rhetorician) drama has a close kinship with medieval English performance: the two literatures overlap with one another at a number of points, to the extent that some commentators have been able to consider them aspects of a 'common tradition'; medieval Yorkshire, in fact, seems to have been a particularly important node in this interchange, owing to its longstanding trade links with the Low Countries.[7] More to the point, Dutch-language drama also makes occasional use of blanket tossing, or of similar types of slapstick abuse. A number of *kluchten* (interludes) and *esbattementen* (farces) see characters bounced on canvas or wrapped in animal hide and assaulted, either to advance trickery, to provide a punitive climax to their action, or to conclude a battle of wits. A recognisable variation can be seen, for instance, at the close of *Moorkens-vel vandequade wijuen* ('Dobbin's Hide, or the Angry Shrews', c.1525) and in Macropedius' closely related Neo-latin comedy *Andrisca* (1537), where unruly wives are 'sewn into

---

5   Susan E. Deskis 'Canvassed, or Tossed in a Blanket: Tracing a Motif from the Second Shepherds' Play through the Seventeenth Century' *Notes and Queries 54: 3* (2007) 325–8.

6   Jean A. Goodich '"So I Thought as I Stood, To Mirth Us Among": The Function of Laughter in *The Second Shepherds' Play*' in *Laughter in the Middle Ages and Early Modern Times: Epistemology of a Fundamental Human Behavior, its Meaning, and Consequences* edited Albrecht Classen (Berlin: De Gruyter, 2010) 531–45, at 543.

7   Claire Sponsler *Drama and Resistance: Bodies, Goods and Theatricality in Late Medieval England* (Minneapolis: University of Minnesota Press, 1997) 96; Leonard Forster 'Literary relations between the Low Countries, England and Germany' *Dutch Crossing 24* (1984) 16–31; Ben Parsons and Bas Jongenelen '"In Which Land Were You Born?" Cultural Transmission in the *Historie van Jan van Beverley*' *METh 34* (2012) 30–76.

the hide of a horse' (*insuta equino tergori*) and jostled until they 'now lie bloodied, salted as well' (*nunc lacera, salsa quoque iacet*); also comparable are *tCalf van wondere* ('The Miraculous Calf', 1559), *Vitulus* (1596), and *Lacchelijke cluchte van een boer die in een calfsvel benayt was* ('Amusing Farce of a Farmer who was Sewn into a Calfskin', 1619), which involve drunken farmers being cheated by innkeepers before undergoing similar treatment.[8] The idea is persistent as well as pervasive. A late variant from 1711 is found in Pieter Langendijk's *Don Quichot op de bruiloft van Kamacho* ('Don Quixote at the Wedding of Kamacho'), in which Sancho, following Cervantes' lead, is *in de deken gesold* ('entangled in a blanket') and thrown around until he pleads *Help! ik word vermoord!* ('Help me! I'm being murdered!').[9]

However, the most revealing example is the text we translate and discuss here, *Een cluijt van Lijsgen en van Jan Lichthart* ('A Farce of Lizzy and John Lightheart'). While it differs from the Towneley play in a number of ways, its treatment of the blanket toss is a particularly valuable one in both practical and theoretical terms. Not only does its toss mirror the events of the Towneley play, but the unusual level of detail in which it is described indicates how such actions might have been realised in performance, especially in the restricted playing-spaces where *rederijker* and Corpus Christi drama were habitually staged. On top of this, the framework in which it places this episode points to some of the wider meanings it might express, as the play sets up a deliberate counterpoint between the toss and other possible resolutions. As a consequence, it allows our appreciation of this problematic gesture to be illuminated, or at least deepens our sense of its potential implications. It is in this spirit of comparative interpretation that we offer our translation.

This is not to say that the climax of *Lijsgen en Jan Lichthart* is its sole point of interest. The play has value across a range of fronts, and it provides impressive testimony to the *rederijkers*' ability to make

---

8   *Veelderhande geneuchlijcke dichten, tafelspelen ende refereynen* (Utrecht: HES Publishers, 1977) 21–39; Frank Leys 'The "Andrisca" of G. Macropedius: A Critical Edition' *Humanistica Lovaniensia 31* (1982) 76–119, at 114; *Esbatementen van de Rode Lelije te Brouwershaven* edited Herman Meijling (Groningen: De Waal, 1946) 25–54; Cornelius Schonaeus Goudanus *Blijspelen* edited Hans van de Venne (Amersfoort: Florivallis, 2008) 8–55; *Het Nederlandse Kluchtspel van de 14e tot de 18e Eeuw* edited J. van Vloten (Haarlem: W.C. De Graaff, 1878) *1* 26–35.

9   Pieter Langendijk *Don Quichot op de bruiloft van Kamacho* edited G.A. van Es (Zutphen: W.J. Thieme and Cie, 1973) 157–8 line 1422.

slapstick raise serious moral and social questions. Although its structure is a typical one – Femke Kramer places it among the subgroup of *esbatementen* that open with a *noodsituatie* or crisis – even a casual reading reveals a sophisticated use of language and interwoven images.[10] It is also animated by a complex sense of gender politics, as it authorises a group of women to act as moral custodians to a profligate and drunken husband. Even the target of its ridicule, the wastrel Jan, is drawn with a startling level of sensitivity, albeit using a moral and economic rather than a psychological prism. He is not merely a comic sot but a pitiable figure trapped in a cycle of regret, self-disgust, desperation, and defensiveness: his speeches make clear that he is driven by compulsions he cannot control, and betray his ambivalence towards the alcohol that both demeans and attracts him. Equally striking is the playwright's careful management of audience sympathy. Lijsgen starts out as an object of mockery, much like Mak's wife Gill: her first speech paints her as a delusional figure convinced of the beauty of her 'hips and buttocks' (*heupen en billen*) and 'waist as slender as a carrier's cart' (*middel so smal als een vracht wagen*), claims rendered especially comic by the fact that these lines would have been delivered by a male actor. However, as soon as her intoxicated husband enters the stage she is quickly placed in a more sympathetic light, and is eventually shown to be the moral core of the text. The *klucht* is, in short, a bold and skilfully written piece, whose rough physical comedy belies the thoughtfulness and elegance of its warnings against intemperance and its social dangers.

Similarly interesting is the history of the play and its modern recovery. The play owes its survival to the Haarlem chamber of *De Pellicanisten*, more commonly known by its motto *Trou Moet Blijcken* ('Faith Must Be Shown'). The chamber itself was among the oldest foundations of its kind in Holland, and also one of the most enduring, still maintaining a small ceremonial role into the late nineteenth century.[11] It was certainly active by 1502, when it shows up in an invoice for a shipment of red wine, and may have been formed substantially earlier: a petition of 1600 to the *burgemeesteren* of Haarlem on behalf of the *camerbroeders* claims that the chamber had been *over de hondert jaren tot stadts eere ende dienste*

---

10   Femke Kramer 'Rederijkers-esbatementen: Om tot lachen te berueren' *Literatuur 16* (1999) 90–7, at 92.

11   K. ter Laan *Letterkundig woordenboek voor Noord en Zuid* (The Hague: G.B. van Goor Zonen's Uitgeversmaatschappij, 1952) 401.

toegelaten ende gheauctoriseert ('admitted and authorised to the honour and service of the city for more than a hundred years').[12] It participated widely in the civic and festive life of Haarlem and the Low Countries as a whole, most notably in 1504, when it entertained Philip I of Castile, and in 1609, when it hosted a lavish *retorijkfeest* (festival of rhetoric) that drew chambers from across the County of Holland.[13] Nevertheless, it still managed to fall foul of the ideological ructions that marked the period: in 1568 its official verse-maker or *factor* Heyns Adriaensz was hanged as part of a larger clampdown on unorthodoxy among the *rederijkers*.[14] As well as producing, hosting, and participating in dramatic spectacles, however, the chamber is also notable for conserving them. One of its key achievements is the exceptional *toneelcollectie* or library of dramatic texts its members compiled in the first decades of the seventeenth century; this stands as a vital monument to the vibrancy of *rederijker* culture, but also to the neglect into which it had fallen until comparatively recently. Originally fourteen volumes in length, of which eleven now survive, the collection comprises some 147 texts, or about 20 per cent of the total corpus of extant plays written in Dutch before 1620.[15] The collection came to light only in the late nineteenth century: in the intervening period the premises of *Trou Moet Blijcken*, the so-called *Huis met de trappen* ('House with the steps') in Haarlem's Grote Houtstraat, had become a gentleman's club, and the library itself unceremoniously deposited in a bookcase *tussen biljartkrijt en kaartspelen* ('between billiard-chalk and card-games').[16] Although Van Vloten published the first account of this *gansche schat* ('true treasure') in the 1870s, its full extent began to be recognised only in the 1920s; most of its contents remained unpublished until a full edition of the archive appeared in the

---

12 Th.C.J. van der Heijden and F.C. van Boheemen *Retoricaal memoriaal. Bronnen voor de geschiedenis van de Hollandse rederijkers vanaf de middeleeuwen tot het begin van de achttiende eeuw* (Delft: Eburon, 1999) 293.

13 Van der Heijden and Van Boheemen *Retoricaal memoriaal* 274; George W. Brandt and Wiebe Hogendoorn *German and Dutch theatre, 1600–1848* (Cambridge UP, 1993) 345–8.

14 J.A. Worp *Geschiedenis van het drama en van het tooneel in Nederland* 2 vols (Groningen: Wolters, 1903–7) *1* 191.

15 W.M.H. Hummelen *Repertorium van het rederijkersdrama 1500–ca. 1620* (Assen: Van Gorcum, 1968).

16 Herman Pleij *Het gevleugelde woord. Geschiedenis van de Nederlandse literatuur 1400–1560* (Amsterdam UP, 2007) 533.

1990s.¹⁷ Yet the plays are remarkable not merely for their quantity but for their panoramic range. Many are preceded by brief headnotes that make clear that they originate from across the Low Countries, recording their city, chamber, and on occasion the festival or *landjuweel* at which they were staged, especially those that won prizes in particular categories of performance.¹⁸

Lijsgen en Jan Lichthart itself occurs in book G of *Trou Moet Blijcken*'s library, and is the twelfth item in its volume. Its precise date and provenance are unclear, however, since it lacks a detailed headnote. The only comment it receives from the copyist is a list of its speaking *parsonages* and its length in *regelen* or rhymed lines.¹⁹ Nevertheless, it is still possible to infer its place and date of composition. It was probably a production of *Trou Moet Blijcken* itself. Geographic references, such as its allusions to Schoten and Velsen, both of which were historical townships (*gemeentes*) in the northern part of Holland, place it in the vicinity of Haarlem.²⁰ Its language likewise ties it to this region, showing an unusual preponderance of northern Dutch morphology and vocabulary.²¹ Although southern terms do intrude periodically, their inclusion simply shows Brabantine and Flemish forms serving as a literary standard (*schrijftaalvorm*) for the *rederijkers*, owing to the dominance of the chambers at Antwerp; this was especially true after 1585, when the city's capture by the Spanish in the Eighty Years War drove many Protestant refugees northwards.²² Even the lack of an explanatory note might indicate such an origin, since there was obviously little need for *Trou Moet*

17 Johannes van Vloten 'Onuitgegeven Rederijkersspelen' *De Levensbode 5* (1872) 461-74; C.G.N. Vooys 'Rederijkersspelen in het archief van "Trou moet blijcken"' *Tijdschrift voor Nederlandse taal- en letterkunde 45* (1926) 265-86, *46* (1927) 161-201, and *49* (1930) 1-25; *Trou moet blijcken. Bronnenuitgave van de boeken der Haarlemse rederijkerskamer 'de Pellicanisten'* edited W.N.M. Hüsken, B.A.M. Ramakers, and F.A.M. Schaars, 6 vols (Assen: Uitgeverij Quarto, 1997).

18 For examples, see *Comic Drama in the Low Countries c.1450-c.1560: A Critical Anthology* edited Ben Parsons and Bas Jongenelen (Cambridge: D.S. Brewer, 2012) 125, 206.

19 Hummelen *Repertorium* 91.

20 Vooys 'Rederijkersspelen in het archief' 277-8.

21 N. van der Laan *Uit het archief der Pellicanisten. Vier zestiende-eeuwse esbatementen* (Leiden: Brill, 1938) xiv-xv.

22 J.W. Muller 'Bijdragen tot de geschiedenis onzer Nieuwnederlandsche aanspreekvormen' *De Nieuwe Taalgids 20* (1926) 113-28, at 118.

Blijcken to keep track of its own recent productions. Further evidence is also provided by the reappearance of *Lijsgen*'s main plot points in *Jan onder de deecken* ('Jan under the Blanket'), written in 1690 by Laurens van Elstland; although based in the Dutch East Indies' colony of Batavia (modern-day Indonesia), Van Elstland was himself born and raised in Haarlem.[23] In terms of date, the manuscript is again silent on the issue, although there is some likelihood that it was first performed in 1593. At the end of February of that year, in order to mark the transition from *Vastenavond* (Shrovetide) to Lent, the authorities of Haarlem granted *Trou Moet Blijcken* a subsidy of twelve *pond* for a dual performance of *de cluyt van de Deeckenspringer* ('The Farce of the Blanket-leaper') and *het spel van den soberen tijt* ('The Play of the Temperate Period', i.e. Lent).[24] Given the central scene of the play, the farce of the *Deeckenspringer* is probably *Lijsgen en Jan Lichthart* under an alternative name; this date would also fit the play's references to *Vastenavond* in its prologue and opening lines, and its later allusion to the 'new archery butts' (*nieuwe doelen*), which had been constructed for Haarlem's citizen militia in 1592 to replace an earlier range destroyed by fire.[25]

Nevertheless, for all its merits and points of interest, it is the climax of *Lijsgen en Jan Lichthart* that remains its most arresting feature and the one most likely to stand out for readers familiar with English dramatic tradition. Indeed, if the farce can be identified with the *Deeckenspringer*, then it appears that the contemporary audience also regarded Jan's final humiliation as its main highlight, elevating it into a shorthand for the play as a whole. In its treatment of this device *Lijsgen en Jan Lichthart* gives a number of hints about how this motif was both accomplished and received. Perhaps most immediately significant are its implications for staging; while these are broad, they are also suggestive. In the first place, it is obvious that the action does not call for Jan to be wrapped in a cloth and thrown around, as in Macropedius' earlier take on the idea in *Andrisca*. Jan's lengthy outcry and the references to him being made *suijsebollen* ('giddy', literally 'hiss-headed') show that the tossing is a sustained set-piece. It obviously calls for the character to be hurled

---

23 Laurens van Elstland *Jan onder de deecken* edited K.J. Bostoen, Marja Geesink, and Mary Zijlstra (Leiden: KITLV Uitgeverij, 2005) 20.
24 Van der Heijden and Van Boheemen *Retoricaal memoriaal* 373.
25 See the discussion by Bostoen, Geesink, and Zijlstra in Van Elstland *Jan onder de deecken* 20–1.

into the air repeatedly over several minutes, and the blanket itself to be stretched into a trampoline-like surface. It is less clear whether the toss involves pitching around an actor or a prop dummy. The fact that Jan speaks throughout his ordeal, even if only to exclaim fragments and interjections such as 'Och Och Och', would certainly hint at the former possibility. However, the latter remains most likely. Projecting voices on to inanimate figures is relatively common in the theatre of the period, whether in popular marionette-plays (*dockenspelen* or *poppenspelen*) or in comic monologues, which sometimes incorporate exchanges between the main speaker and his *marot* or bauble.[26] The play also seems to be structured so that Jan might be substituted for a doll immediately before the toss. The play includes four breaks, marked *pausa* in the manuscript, of a kind that routinely appear in Dutch and French plays to mark musical interludes or similar points at which the action is suspended.[27] One of these interruptions occurs between the couple's second fight and the blanket toss, which would naturally allow the actor playing Jan to leave the stage while a prop replica takes his place. The play might even jokingly call attention to Jan's replacement when it has him lie motionless on the floor and declare 'my legs are sausages; I cannot follow you' (*mijn beenen sijn worsten | Ick can u niet nalopen*). The use of a dummy might also be inferred from the play's association with *Vastenavond*. Its treatment of Jan is remarkably similar to a local variant of the carnival procession (*Ommegang*) documented at Mechelen from the mid-seventeenth century. This custom features comparable mockery of masculine excess and focuses specifically on the ritual mistreatment of a doll. It sees the townswomen singing a traditional song while tossing a wooden effigy, called the *Sotscop* ('Drunken-head'), *vuilen bras* ('filthy drunk'), or *vuilen*

---

26 See G. Kalff 'Bijdragen tot de geschiedenis van ons Middeleeuwsch drama' *Tijdschrift voor Nederlandse Taal- en Letterkunde* 22 (1903) 304-20, at 317-20; Jeannette M. Hollaar and E.W.F. Van Den Elzen 'Het vroegste toneelleven in enkele Noordnederlandse plaatsen' *De Nieuwe Taalgids* 73 (1980) 302-24, at 318-19; Herman Brinkman 'Spelen om den brode. Het vroegste beroepstoneel in de Nederlanden' *Literatuur* 17 (2000) 98-106, at 101-2; Hinke van Kampen, Herman Pleij, Bob Stumpel, Annebel Venmans, and Paul Vriesema *Het zal koud zijn in 't water als 't vriest* (The Hague: Martinus Nijhoff, 1980) 58.

27 W.M.H. Hummelen 'Types and Methods of the Dutch Rhetoricians' Theatre' translated H.S. Lake in *The Third Globe: Symposium for the Reconstruction of the Globe Playhouse* edited C. Walter Hodges, S. Schoenbaum, and Leonard Leone (Detroit: Wayne State University, 1979) 164-89, at 169.

bruidegom ('filthy bridegroom') until 1775, when an accident caused it to be renamed *Opsinjoorke* (a pejorative name for a person from Antwerp, based on the Spanish title 'Señor') after it landed on a spectator and sparked a mass brawl.[28] An early, possibly original, doll made by the carver Valentyn Van Lantscroon (d. 1650) is held at Mechelen's Hof van Busleyden Museum, and the custom itself is commemorated by a bronze sculpture in the Grote Markt of the city.[29] While the exact relationship between this customary performance and the Haarlem play is obscure, at the very least it provides a further clue as to how the comedy might have been staged.

However, the play's links to *Vastenavond* open up interpretive possibilities beyond the practicalities of staging. They also shed light on the meanings the toss might have carried for its audience, and even allow a few tentative inferences to be drawn about the Towneley play by extension. In the first place, the fact that the toss appears in an entertainment intended for pre-Lenten performance, and is even called *een vastelavent spul* ('a Shrovetide game') in the course of the play, obviously connects it with the world of popular celebration and the misrule and relaxation of order that Shrovetide entailed. A few sources do in fact situate blanket tossing in carnival festivity quite directly. Almost inevitably, one of the key witnesses is Rabelais, whose *Gargantua* (1534) includes a cryptic allusion to the practice while running through the jumble of carnivalesque images that comprises its second chapter: at one stage, this sequence pictures heretics being 'tossed at the tanning mill' (*berné sus le moulin à tan*).[30] More explicit still is the work of the Protestant polemicist and theologian Thomas Naogeorgus in the 1550s. In a lengthy attack on popular and official observance, Naogeorgus addresses tossing in his wider critique of Quinquagesima: while denouncing the use of costumes and effigies in urban celebration, Naogeorgus states that the citizens of an undisclosed city 'by long

---

28 Jozef Cornelissen *Nederlandsche volkshumor op stad en dorp, land en volk* 6 vols (Antwerp: De Sikkel, 1929-37) *1* 214-15.

29 François Van der Jeught 'Valentijn van der Lantscroon, poirter deser stadt Mechelen ende beltsnijer van sijnen stiel, herbekeken' *Mededelingenblad Gidsenbond Mechelen 329* (2019) 3-22.

30 François Rabelais *Oeuvres completes* edited Jacques Boulenger and Lucien Scheler, 2 vols (Paris: Gallimard, 1955) *1* 10. On Rabelais' terminology, see Gerard J. Brault 'The Date of French *berner*' *Romance Philology 12: 3* (1959) 232-4.

Fig. 1. The *Vuilen Bruidegom* being tossed (though by men) in the Giants' section of the *Ommegang* of St Rumbold of 1775, the year in which his name was changed. His costume suggests he is the same dummy as *Opsinjoorke* in Fig. 2. Detail from image in *Prael-treyn verrykt door ry-benden, prael-wagens, zinnebeelden en andere oppronkingen toegeschikt aen het duyzend-jaerig jubilé van ... den heyligen Rumoldus* (Mechelen: Johannes-Franciscus van der Elst, 1775) plate opposite page 32. British Library 1482 d. 1(1), © British Library Board.

FIG. 2. Valentijn van der Lantscroon *Opsinjoorke* (1645). Wooden head, stuffed body. Museum Hof van Busleyden, Mechelen, reproduced with their permission. Photo credit: David Lainé/IPARC, Belgium.

tradition construct a great man, stuffed within with straw or cloth' (*formant hominem uel stramine magnum, | Vel panno fartum ueteri intus*), dress it in clothing, boots, and a waistcoat or breastplate (*vestes cum caligis habet et thorace*), and finally 'carry him wrapped in a blanket, and next, by pulling apart the four edges, throw him up on high to the stars' (*velatum lodice gerunt, mox quattuor imis | finibus attractis astra ad sublimia iactant*). Since Naogeorgus presents the custom as a grotesque parody of a funeral procession, adding that the dummy is made to appear 'as though recently dead, and deserving honours' (*quasi defunctum nuper, meritumque suprema*), he seems to have in mind one of the many rituals in which a personification of carnival is executed or buried to signify the closure of festivities and start of the Lenten fast.[31] His account provides eloquent testimony to the festive aspect of tossing and its capacity to support the general inversion or suspension of everyday conventions that is the hallmark of carnival.

Yet, despite these links to Shrovetide revelry, other sources paint a more complex picture. Most evidence shows the toss being used in popular culture in a broader, more irregular and intermittent manner, rather than being tied to any one occasion. Across the medieval and early modern sources, blanket tossing appears in a formidable range of contexts and proves highly variable in terms of its circumstances, objectives, and participants. Several European languages have a term to describe the practice – *berner* or *bernement* in French, *prellen* in German, *manteo*, *manteaban* or *pelele* in Spanish, *sollen* or *jonassen* in Dutch – but even witnesses from the same or neighbouring cultures show pronounced disagreement about when it might be performed, who might perform it, and even how severe its consequences could be. In other Dutch-language texts, for example, it appears at times as a relatively benign, if sexually charged, component of sixteenth- and seventeenth-century *bruiloftspret* (wedding celebrations), inflicted on a bridegroom to mark his entry into married life; however, it might also be used by young men to ridicule and harrass unmarried women in a

---

31 Thomas Naogeorg *Regnum Papisticum* edited Hans-Gert Roloff *Sämtliche Werke, Band 6:1* (Berlin: De Gruyter, 2015) 106. Translated by Barnabe Googe as *The popish kingdome, or reigne of Antichrist* (London: Henry Denham for Richarde Watkins, 1570) book 4 fol. 48v; text online at <https://quod.lib.umich.edu/cgi/t/text/text-idx?c=eebo;idno=A04873.0001.001>. The classic discussion of the Death of Carnival or *Fastnacht vergraben* is still J.G. Frazer *The Golden Bough* 12 vols (London: Macmillan, 3rd edition 1906–15) 4 220–33.

rural tradition called *in de zeef kriegen* ('to catch in the sieve'), a term that later expanded into a proverbial phrase meaning humiliation or trickery.[32] Early French texts after Rabelais present it as a relatively mild indignity, even an act of self-abasement. In his *Zélinde* (1664), Donneau de Visé makes his title character fantasise about Molière 'being cast in a blanket, and the blanket held by four Marquises' since they 'love him to excess' (*le faire berner, et faire tenir la couverture par quatre Marquis ... les Marquis l'aiment trop*), while a letter by Vincent Voiture, *maître de plaisir* to the marquise de Rambouillet, surrenders its author to the penalty 'this Friday after dinner' for his failure to 'make you laugh' (*je fus berné vendredy après disné, pource que je ne vous avois pas fait rire*).[33] Spanish references stretch the range of meanings even further. One of the key literary archetypes of tossing, Sancho Panza's manhandling at the inn in Cervantes' *Don Quixote* (1605), is a more aggressive degradation, which looks like a drunken act of vigilantism: although supposedly carried out in a 'mischievous and playful' (*maleante y juguetona*) spirit, it leaves Sancho 'bruised and broken' (*molido y quebrantado*) and is performed by a bunch of tavern-goers in response to the Don welshing on his bill.[34] In Fernando de Rojas' *Tragicomedia de Calisto y Melibea* (1499) it has a still graver cast. Here the bawd Celestina frets that exposure of her schemes will cause her to be put to death, tossed in a blanket, or mercilessly thrashed (*quisiessen, manteándome o açotándome cruelmente*), and apparently regards each alternative as equally severe.[35] Occasional

32 G.J. Boekenoogen 'Onze rijmen' *De Gids* 57 (1893) 1–34, at 22–3; F.A. Stoett *Nederlandsche spreekwoorden, spreekwijzen, uitdrukkingen en gezegden* 5 vols (Zutphen: W.J. Thieme, 1923–5) 4 525.

33 *Molière Mocked: Three Contemporary Hostile Comedies* edited Frederick Wright Vogler (North Carolina Studies in the Romance Languages and Literatures 129; Chapel Hill, NC: Longleaf Services for University of North Carolina, 2017) 44; Vincent Voiture *Les Lettres de Mr de Voiture* (Paris: Martin de Pinchesne, 1654) 17. On the letter, see Marika Takanishi Knowles *Realism and Role-Play: the Human Figure in French Art from Callot to the Brothers Le Nain* (Newark, DE: University of Delaware Press, 2020) 155.

34 Miguel de Cervantes Saavedra *El Ingenioso Hidalgo Don Quijote de la Mancha* edited Martín Alonso (Madrid: Biblioteca EDAF, revised edition 2005) 118. While Cervantes compares Sancho's ordeal to that of 'a dog at Shrovetide' (*como con perro por carnestolendas*), this episode makes equally clear that it could be staged as a more *ad hoc* event.

35 Fernando de Rojas *Comedia de Calisto y Melibea* edited Josep Lluís Canet Vallés (Universitat de València Press, 2011) 225. See further the English translation:

references in classical sources add still further variations. In his account of Otho's 'extravagant and dissolute youth' (*adulescentia prodigus ac procax*), for instance, Suetonius discusses a similar game as the means by which a privileged group would intimidate plebeians: he describes the future emperor and his wealthy friends patrolling the streets of Rome at night and forcing the 'crippled or drunk' (*invalidum ... vel potulentum*) 'to leap up high on a stretched-out cloak' for their amusement (*distento sago impositum in sublime iactare*).[36] A little earlier, Martial refers to his own book undergoing similar treatment in the *Epigrammata* (1.3), expecting that it will be 'sent to the stars in a cloak' (*missus in astra sago*) once its fickle readership have ceased to greet it 'with copious cheers' (*cum grande sophos*).[37] Again, while the toss remains a form of group play, it seems to lurch between sadistic victimisation and teasing mockery in its aims, and shows little consistency in its timing, targets, or actors.

Much the same can be said of England, where the toss is if anything even more loosely defined. Although the Towneley play is the lone depiction of blanket tossing in English, and there is no evidence to show its association with any particular point in the ritual calendar, a number of texts show some familiarity with the custom; indeed, its commonplace status is underscored by interlingual texts, such as Percival's Spanish dictionary or Palsgrave's French grammar, which show no difficulty in converting continental terms into English as 'canuassed in a blanket or sheete', 'kanuas a dogge or a mater', or 'this mater hath be canuassed'.[38] As Deskis demonstrates in her survey of sixteenth- and seventeenth-century witnesses, it occurs widely as an expression of 'contempt and violence (real or imagined) against an enemy': Shakespeare unmistakably uses it in this sense when he has Gloucester threaten the bishop of Winchester 'I'll canvass thee in thy broad cardinal's hat' or Falstaff say of Pistol 'I will

---

Fernando de Rojas *Celestina* translated Margaret Sayers Peden (New Haven CT: Yale UP, 2009) 57.

36   Suetonius *Lives of the Caesars* in *Suetonius* edited J.C. Rolfe, 2 vols (Loeb Classical Library 31 and 32; London: Heinemann, 1970) 2 228.

37   Martial *Epigrams* edited D.R. Shackleton-Bailey, 2 vols (Loeb Classical Library 94 and 95; London: Heinemann, 1991) 1 44.

38   Richard Perceval *A Dictionarie in Spanish and English* (London: Edmund Bollifant, 1599) 164 (STC 19620); John Palsgrave *Lesclarcissement de la langue francoyse* (London: John Haukyns, 1530) fol. 270v (STC 19166).

toss the rogue in a blanket'.[39] When depicted as a practice rather than a turn of phrase, however, it proves as free-floating in its associations as the continental examples. There is some indication that tossing was used in a household setting to discipline or make sport of junior servants: another early reference, possibly close in date to the Towneley play, mentions a kitchen-boy being 'kanwased' before the duke of Buckingham on 22 May 1508, perhaps as part of an entertainment, since the boy received 8d for his trouble; similarly, in the interlude *Iacke Iugeler* (c.1562), the servant Jenkin Careawaie says of his ill-treatment by his master and mistress 'I was neuer this canuased and tost'.[40] Elsewhere, however, John Foxe makes it an element of popular resistance akin to a lynching: while describing the persecution of Waldensians in the Alpine village of Rioclareto in 1560, Foxe claims that one of the papal enforcers held a grudge against the villagers after he was 'almost strangled' by them the previous year and his men 'so canuased, that they had no liste to come there agayne'.[41] An even more curious variation occurs towards the end of the seventeenth century, when the blanket toss features in a conflict between two rival political authorities: in 1688 one Captain Ousley apparently subjected Thomas Aislabie, mayor of Scarborough, to this indignity after Aislabie personally beat a minister who refused to endorse James II's declaration for liberty of conscience. Ousley was later called to defend his behaviour in the capital and brought 'with him a collection of Articles against the said Mayor'; the episode was sufficiently notorious to give rise to the satirical ballad 'Fumbumis; or the North-Country Mayor'.[42] Later sources see an even greater range of functions at work in tossing, variously

39 Deskis 'Canvassed, or Tossed in a Blanket' 326; *1 Henry VI 1*: 3, 36; *2 Henry IV 2*: 4, 222. Writing in 1621, Burton uses the phrase in a somewhat different sense, to emphasise aimless play and confusion rather than aggression; referring to the innovations of astronomers, he says 'the world is tossed in a blanket amongst them, they hoist the earth up and down like a ball': Robert Burton *Anatomy of Melancholy* edited Holbrook Jackson, 3 vols (London: Dent, 1961) *2* 57.
40 *Letters and Papers 3* 497 #1285, online at <https://www.british-history.ac.uk/letters-papers-hen8/vol3/pp485–516>; *Jacke Jugeler* edited W.H. Williams (Cambridge UP, 1914) 71.
41 John Foxe *Actes and Monuments* (London: John Day, 1583) 958 (STC 11225).
42 *Original Letters, Illustrative of English History* edited Henry Ellis, 4 vols (London: Harding and Lepard, 1827) *4* 125; Dale B.J. Randall and Jackson C. Boswell *Cervantes in Seventeenth-Century England: The Tapestry Turned* (Oxford UP, 2009) 486–7.

treating it as an impromptu punishment for petty theft, an Ascension Day ritual at Westminster school, and a reprimand for perceived gender transgressions 'inflicted by women, upon men who have been guilty of something peculiarly unmanly'.[43]

As these witnesses make clear, therefore, blanket tossing was a relatively fluid element in popular culture, capable of being deployed in multiple contexts to fulfil a number of ends; although it might be absorbed into formal celebration from time to time, it was obviously not bound to any one ritual framework, having instead a larger life and currency. Nevertheless, the sources do not only hint at the mutability of tossing. In spite of their obvious differences, it is still possible to identify a number of recurring meanings across them. With the exception of a few outliers, most of the texts treat the blanket toss as a raucous and disorderly game first and foremost (at least for its main actors), a feature that probably explains why it proved so conducive to festivity. Yet at the same time they do not see it as carnivalesque in the Bakhtinian sense.[44] While it could disrupt some patterns of authority – being used by women against men, for instance, or in mockery of prominent citizens – it does not seem to denote a temporary collapse of moral and political hierarchies of the kind Bakhtin imagines. In most cases it clearly carries a corrective dimension, and in several others is used to cement rather than relax existing power structures: it seems primarily intended to inflict symbolic disgrace or embarrassment on a social inferior or a violator of a behavioural code. In short, it seems to belong to the peculiarly punitive species of revelry that Tom Pettitt terms 'rough justice', sitting at the point where popular celebration and retribution intersect. Like Pettitt's examples of the noisy informal processions of charivari and skimmington rides, it also serves as a form of ritualised, extra-judicial shaming by which members of a community might penalise an offender against its values or norms, a process that is subversive in the sense that it operates 'outside the official institutions, and without official sanction, to demonstrate public

---

43 John Mathers *History of Elsmere and Rosa* 3 vols (London: Baldwin, Cradock and Joy, 1817) *2* 310; George Webbe Dasent *Half a Life* 3 vols (London: Chapman and Hall, 1874) *1* 222–3; John Good, Olinthus Gregory, and Newton Bosworth *Pantalogia: A New Cyclopedia* 12 vols (London: G. Kearsley and others, 1813) *2* sig. N8v.

44 Mikhail Bakhtin's theory of carnival is most fully developed in *Rabelais and his World* translated Hélène Iswolsky (Bloomington: Indiana University Press, 1984).

disapproval of and (to varying degrees) to punish other members of the community'.[45] Its overall function is a sort of comic victimisation, especially of a person who has breached the standards of a community in some way. In fact, blanket tossing could be said to dramatise this process as it enacts it, since the very form it takes is communal and cooperative. Since it demands the involvement of several people acting in concert, in order to stretch out the blanket or canvas and make it sufficiently taut, it performs social collaboration while defending it: as David Booth writes it in the nineteenth century, as an act of 'summary vengeance' it requires 'a number of men' to work the 'Blanket, which was held, at the corners and sides'.[46] It pits the group against an individual transgressor or inferior in physical as well as abstract terms.

These wider attitudes filter directly into *Lijsgen en Jan Lichthart*, where many of the functions detectible in the other sources work their way into its action. In the first place, the play also understands the blanket toss as an emphatically communal enterprise. It uses it to redress an offence against the community, one that has been inflicted on a collective by a member who has failed to respect its norms. Jan's habitual drunkenness is conceived from the first as an infraction against what the play calls *buerlijcke geselschap* ('neighbourly fellowship'). It is a large-scale disturbance that reverberates beyond the walls of his household and threatens the wider settlement Jan and Lijsgen inhabit. The first altercation between the two main characters attaches a whole sequence of ill-effects to Jan's drinking: the *leckerste bier* ('tastiest beer') Jan has sampled quickly sours, giving way to a sense of wastefulness and violence, and of Jan's failure as a husband, provider, and tradesman. Not only has he 'drunk up his wife's mantle and rings' (*verdrinckt twijffs huijck en ringen*), but there are heavy hints that his behaviour might eventually drive her to the darker crime of prostitution. The violence that quickly erupts between the couple likewise underscores that drinking is not merely a personal problem but an interpersonal one, comprising a disturbance of proper social relations.

Along the same lines, the blanket toss is also a solution that originates from and is implemented by the group whose cohesion Jan

---

45 Thomas Pettitt 'Protesting Inversions: Charivary as Folk Pageantry and Folk-Law' *METh 21* (1999) 21–51, at 43–4.

46 David Booth *An Analytical Dictionary of the English Language* (London: Simpkin, Marshall and Co, 1836) 181.

threatens. As well as taking a cooperative form, showing a number of individuals acting in concert against their chosen target, the play takes pains to emphasise the collaboration between its agents of justice. The ill-defined identities of the toss's performers make this point clear. The two women who aid Lijsgen in putting an end to Jan's caprices are entirely undifferentiated: the stage directions stipulate that they 'come out and speak together' (*beijde tsaemen uijt ende spreecken*), and this adequately summarises their activity throughout the play. They are denied names or any obvious characteristics that might set them apart from one another; the only designation they receive stresses their close proximity to Lijsgen and Jan and to each other, as they are referred to merely as *buerwijven* ('neighbouring wives') or *bueren* ('neighbours'). In their lack of individualisation they embody, it might be said, the wisdom of the crowd and the utility of common sense and knowledge; the fact that their remedy is a popular one, and stands in contrast with the elitist, pseudo-intellectualism parodied in the first half of the play, only adds to this impression. This sense of collective action reaches its highest pitch towards the play's conclusion, when the wives deliver a song that both cements their union and draws the audience into it, acting in harmony in a literal and unmistakable way.[47] In fact, the entire act of turning Jan into a comic spectacle could be said to carry out the same process, uniting characters and spectators in common mirth against him; tellingly, Jan is the only figure who remains outside this unification, oblivious to the fact he has not been assailed by the *geesten* ('ghosts') and *alven* ('elves') he imagines his neighbours to be.

Finally, one further remarkable feature of the play is the restorative character it assigns to the toss. By the end of the play Jan's experiences have given rise to reconciliation as much as retaliation: the toss not only expresses the opprobrium of Jan's community but manages to integrate him back into it. But what is especially noteworthy is that the play chooses to spell out these qualities explicitly, drawing a direct comparison between the quack doctor Meester Huijbert's bogus cure and the neighbours' intervention. Both are presented as competing remedies for the same deficiencies that differ only in their efficacy; moreover, the play often characterises Jan's fondness for drinking as a physiological

---

47 Dirk Coigneau 'Poetry Onstage: The *refrein* in Rederijker Drama' in *Controversial Poetry 1400–1625* edited Judith Keßler, Ursula Kundert, and Johan Oosterman (Radboud Studies in Humanities 11; Leiden: Brill, 2020) 183–212, at 195.

ailment, attributing it to heat in his body and referring repeatedly to him being *cranck van hooft* ('sick in the head') or *cranchooft* ('sick-headed'). By setting its two solutions side by side in this way, the play makes plain that it sees the blanket toss as a cure more than a penalty, comparable to formal medicine in its results. There is also some suggestion that this curative effect is meant to extend to the audience as well. The reference to *vreucht* ('joy', 'delight') in the prologue picks up on the common idea that laughter works as a purgative for melancholy: the term is used fairly frequently in *rederijker* drama to describe this effect and justify the utility of comic performance in general.[48] Once again, the toss is treated first and foremost as a tool in the service of community and community-building, and is framed as a positive gesture that heals rather than merely chastises.

As even this brief overview should make clear, therefore, there are some provocative overlaps between the events of *Lijsgen en Jan Lichthart* and the *Second Shepherds' Play*. Both share a rural setting that frames the blanket toss as a type of rough country justice, and both direct their aggression against a rogue element marked by his waywardness, disruption, and discordance. Both also set the toss against other possible measures, to stress either its remedial capacities or its relative mercy. Perhaps more interestingly, each incorporates a song in order to consolidate an onstage community (and, implicitly, an offstage one), and seem to implicate the blanket toss in this process. Of course, none of this is to say that *Lijsgen en Jan Lichthart* can be seen as the key to unlocking the events of the Towneley play. Despite the insistent cultural and economic links between Yorkshire and the Low Countries, we cannot simply map one piece straightforwardly on to the other. But this example of *rederijkersdrama* does show how a neighbouring and in some respects interrelated theatrical tradition made use of the same motif as the Wakefield playwright, and what meanings it attached to the same gesture. As such, it gives food for thought when considering its analogue over the North Sea.

---

48 See Wayne Franits 'René van Stipriaan's concept of the ludic in seventeenth-century Dutch farces and its application to contemporary Dutch painting' *De zeventiende eeuw* 15 (1999) 24–33. See further C.H.A. Kruyskamp *Dichten en spelen van Jan den Berghe* (The Hague: Martinus Nijhoff, 1950) 61–88.

Item: here begins A Farce of Lizzy and of John Lightheart.[1] The characters are these:

Lizzy
John Lightheart [John]
Master Hubert[2] [Hubert]
Two Neighbour-Women [N1 & N2]

  Prologue

ONE: Everything has its season, as wise men teach:[3]
   There is a time for sorrow, and a time for joy.[4]
TWO: And so, at Shrovetide, to help joy flourish,
   We will play a comical farce.
ONE: We hope that you all, men and women,   5
   Will listen to us with close attention.
TWO: And sit still long enough in silence here,
   Until you have fully understood our performance.
ONE: It is about a woman, whose thoughts and desire
   Were fixed on marriage; and she caught a man,   10

---

1 Our translation is based on the edition of *Lijsgen en Jan Lichthart* included by W.N.M. Hüsken, B.A.M. Ramakers, and F.A.M. Schaars in *Trou moet blijcken. Bronnenuitgave van de boeken der Haarlemse rederijkerskamer 'de Pellicanisten'* 6 vols (Assen: Uitgeverij Quarto, 1997) 7 335–62. Since this provides a purely diplomatic transcription of the manuscript, we have also consulted the edition of Van der Laan in *Uit het archief der Pellicanisten* 55–81, and incorporated Van der Laan's emendations where necessary.

2 The characters are listed as Lijsgen, Jan, Meester Huijbert; Lijsgen, like the modern-day Elsken, is a late medieval diminutive of Elisabeth.

3 The manuscript of the play is disordered at this point, opening with Lijsgen's speech and Jan's response to it, before breaking off after forty-one lines to deliver this preparatory dialogue. While Hüsken, Ramakers, and Schaars preserve this order, the error is clear from the introductory header to the prologue: the copyist sought to remedy his mistake by writing 'Item: here begins a spoken prologue for Light-hearted Jan, after which the farce follows' (*Item hier begint Een spreeckende prologe van Lichthertigen Jan waer af de Cluijt volcht*). For the sake of clarity, we follow Van der Laan's edition, and reorganise the lines into their intended order.

4 Compare Ecclesiastes 3: 1, 3: 4. The text uses the term *vreucht* here ('joy', 'delight'), a concept frequently evoked by the *rederijkerskamers* as the effect, purpose, and rationale of comic performance.

	Just as she wanted. But he made no mention	
	That he would drink till he was sozzled, all to her great sorrow.	
TWO:	For when this Lighthearted John was drunk,	
	He was nearly legless and out of his mind:[5]	
	Nevertheless, he found it too hard	15
	To stop drinking, and regularly drank himself stupid.	
ONE:	His wife searched for advice. She trusted a quack doctor[6]	
	Who advised her to pour away the beer;	
	But that did not help: he remained just as stubborn[7]	
	And indulged his habit, drinking even stronger stuff.	20
TWO:	Instead of beer, he spent his money on wine	
	Which made him even crazier than before,	
	And made his wife unhappier still.	
	But the neighbouring women gave her a word of advice.	
ONE:	They played a Shrovetide game with him,	25
	Tossing and hurling him in a blanket	
	So that he began to groan and tremble	
	For fear, until he could not hear, see, or speak.	
TWO:	Whoever saw in all his days such a trick,	
	Or heard such pleading and begging at the same time?	30
	They set before him all his failings	
	And let him know he was suffering because of them.	
ONE:	But this remedy must have pleased his wife greatly,	
	Since it made him turn away from drinking to excess.	
TWO:	And he forsook his evil life from this point	35

---

5   The Dutch emphasises a link between madness and drunkenness, characterising Jan as *cranck van hooft* ('sick in the head'). Variants of this phrase recur no fewer than five times in the course of the play, at lines 128, 243, 280, 293, and 372.

6   *Lapsalver*, literally 'poultice-smearer': the quack doctor, usually *quaksalver*, is a stock character in Dutch-language comic drama, much as he is in medieval English theatre. The most famous example is Rijckhart from Bredero's *De Hoochduytschen Quacksalver* (1619): see G.A. Bredero *Kluchten* edited Jo Daan (Culemborg: Tjeenk Willink-Noorduijn, 1971) 193–212. See further Jacques Tersteeg 'The Brouwershaven Chamber of Rhetoric De Roode Lelie and the *Esbatement van vijf personagien ghenaemt Jan Goemoete*' European Medieval Drama 4 (2001) 127–40, at 138.

7   *Verdooft*, literally 'deafened'. The play is probably drawing on a proverbial connection between deafness and wilful ignorance; this meaning is also found in the contemporary sayings *den dooverik spelen* ('to play the deaf man') and *den doove maken* ('to make deaf'): F.A. Stoett *Nederlandsche spreekwoorden* 1 181.

	Living with his wife in perfect companionship.	
ONE:	Oh, if only all you drunkards, notorious throughout Haarlem,	
	Might be converted as you'll see played before your eyes!	
TWO:	They would not burn[8] up their cash so often.	
	You have now heard all, just as I've told you:	40
	Look, listen, and keep quiet. Now we begin.	

Finis, this [poem] is 43 lines long[9]

LIZZY[10]	Good evening to all you good people. I must ask you something.	
	What do you think, all of you: aren't I slim and fine?	
	After all, my waist is as small as a carrier's cart.	
	My hips and buttocks are as thick-set	45
	As a Schooten[11] mare's – have a good look!	
	I am the finest, at least I think so.	
	I wonder whether anyone in Velsen[12] is my match,	

8   The original text has *gram* ('rage', or 'rave'). The phrase *gram op haer gelt* is probably proverbial: compare H.C. Landheer *Het dialect van Overflakkee* (Taalkundige bijdragen van noord en Zuid 1; Assen: Van Gorcum, 1955) 255. The merging of moral and economic concerns visible here is typical of the practical, commercial *burgermoraal* ('middle-class morality') often espoused in *rederijker* drama. See Herman Pleij *De Gilde van de Blauwe Schuit: Literatuur, volksfeest, en burgermoraal in de late Middeleeuwen* (Amsterdam: Meulenhoff, 1979) 209.

9   Although the rest of the play is composed in rhyming couplets, the prologue assumes a complex, highly repetitive scheme, following the pattern ABABBCBCCDCDDED, etc. This is probably intended to recall the intricate forms favoured by the *rederijkers*, especially the *refreinen* and *rondelen*. It is not unusual for plays of the period to present their opening and closing sequences as self-enclosed poems, and to call attention to the number of *regelen* over which a rhyme scheme has been sustained.

10 The direction stipulates that Lizzy enters and speaks alone, stating *Item Lijsgen Eerst* ('Lizzy first').

11 A village in the vicinity of Haarlem; also the toponymic surname of a prominent family in the city with branches at Amsterdam and Leiden: see Reindert Leonard Falkenburg *Kunst voor de markt, 1500–1700* (Zwolle: Waanders, 2000) 209–11. Their longstanding connection to Haarlem is detailed by Dirk Schrevel in his 1647 description of the city, where Schooten itself is described as *een vermaard Dorp* ('a renowned hamlet'): Theodorus Schrevelius *Harlemias, of eerste stichting der Stad Haarlem* (Haarlem: Joannes Marshoorn, 1754) 331.

12 At this point in its history, a small hamlet in the County of Holland, known especially for its cherry orchards, and situated directly to the north of Haarlem: see Siebe Rolle and Pieter van Hove *Velsen-IJmuiden. De doorsnee van Holland*

>Whether poor or rich, or whatever else she may be.
>I think not. But, more to the point, I'm relieved 50
>Of the great weight that lay upon my heart.
>I thank my old mother, who saw my anguish
>That made me pester her all day long –
>It was for a lover, to be exact. I longed to give myself
>In marriage; to marry was all I wanted. 55
>So I thought: will I still be alone this Shrovetide?
>What should I do, a poor wench like me?
>I made my mother's ears ring with my pleas
>Until at last she was convinced – listen to me –
>And she helped me get the lover I was pleading for, 60
>One with good prospects, which is why I should be glad.
>However, although I was desperate for a man,[13]
>Don't pity me and don't reproach me; I'm not alone in this.
>Look, you'll find lots like me in Velsen, some great, some small.
>I wish everyone would drop the subject 65
>And not pick on me – that is all I want
>From the ladies and gentlemen who are present here.
>Now it's time to leave here and go into my house
>Before John Lightheart returns, rolling home drunk.
>Since, if he finds me standing here in the street[14] 70
>He may box me on both ears with his fists.
>Hallo! I think I can hear him coming,
>And so I'm leaving here, right now!

John enters acting drunkenly

JOHN: Oh, I have drunk the most delicious beer
          That a man could ever drink at any time. 75

(Haarlem: De Vrieseborch, 2001). Rural settings are a recurring feature of *rederijker* comedy, no doubt to draw a humorous contrast between rustic manners and the supposedly greater sophistication of the urban audience and players.

13   The original has *mansieck*, 'sickening for a man'. Presumably Lijsgen means that her desperation made her resort to the first man she could get, or that her mother bundled her off to the first available suitor to shut her up.

14   Hüsken, Ramakers, and Schaars omit this line, although it appears to be a mere transcription error on their part.

>   But what will my wife say – Lizzy Cherrylips?[15]
>   I bet she will make me eat shit.[16]
>   Nonetheless, I shall clobber her if she grumbles,
>   As hard as though I had run at her full speed.
>   Hey, quick, open up!
> LIZZY: Well, drunken beast, you call this a day's work?   80
>   How can we earn a livelihood this way?
> JOHN: Lizzy, watch yourself, or I'll keep my money to myself,[17]
>   Or are you trying to catch flies with your big mouth?[18]

15 *Rodermont*, literally 'red mouth', is a Dutch variant of the 'cherry lips' or 'ruby lips' common in ekphrastic love poetry from at least the thirteenth century; here it refers to Lizzy's perpetually open mouth, and perhaps reprises the burlesque blazon of lines 45–8. For less ironic examples of the *rodermont* convention in late medieval Dutch literature, see *Een abel spel van Lanseloet van Denemerken* edited Robert J. Roemans (Klassieke galerij 123; Antwerp: De Nederlandsche Boekhandel, 1979) 118; 'Tmeiskin was jonck' in *De meerstemmige Nederlandse liederen van de vijftiende en zestiende eeuw* edited Jan Willem Bonda (Hilversum: Verloren, 1996) 292. See further Stoett *Nederlandsche spreekwoorden* 1 189.

16 The text has *sij een stront' wenscht in mij caecken* ('she will wish a turd in my cheeks'), punning on *caecken* ('cheeks', 'jaws') and *cacken* ('to shit'). Jan's meaning is not far removed from the analogous modern insult, and indeed from Nowadays' abuse of Mercy in the English *Mankynde* (c.1470), 'I have schetun yowr mowth full of turdys': *Mankind* edited Kathleen M. Ashley and Gerard NeCastro (Kalamazoo MI: Medieval Institute Publications, 2010) 17.

17 The Dutch reads *dat ghij de cas niet en verbost* ('so that you do not lose the cash'). Jan's threat is obviously a feeble one, given that his drinking impoverishes his household and occupies the time he should be spending at work.

18 In the original, *backhuijs* ('bake-house'), a popular metaphor for the mouth of a garrulous person. Compare, for instance, the morality *Van Nyeuvont, Loosheit ende Practike* (c.1500), in which the fool *Scoon tooch* (False Appearance) threatens another character with the statement *swijcht, oft ic clop u op uwen bach ouen* ('silence, or I will clobber you on your bake oven'); *Van Nyeuvont, Loosheit ende Practike: hoe sij Vrou Lortse verheffen* edited Elisabeth Neurdenburg (Utrecht: Oosthoek, 1910) 71. The analogy is clearly commonplace, as it occurs in a wide range of proverbs and popular imagery: an early French–Dutch dictionary contains the phrase *een zoo groote mond, als een oven gat* ('a mouth so great, like the opening of an oven'), and misericords on the theme are found across the Low Countries, including at the Oude Kerk of Amsterdam: see J. Robert Des Pepliers *Nieuwen en volmaakte koninglyke, Fransche en Hollandsche Spraakkunst* (Amsterdam: Steven van Esveldt, 1764) 237; Stoett *Nederlandse spreekwoorden* 1 124; Elaine C. Block *Corpus of Medieval Misericords, Belgium and the Netherlands* (Corpus of Medieval Misericords 3; Turnhout: Brepols, 2007) 19, 29, 53. Taking a still wider view, the same idea also occurs in English, most famously in Chaucer's

LIZZY:	No, John: I always hate to hear that song,	
	I'd sooner see you hang than see you beat me.	85
	I'm warning you: don't test me. You'd better listen,	
	For I will strike first, I won't hold back.	
	Take that, filthy drunkard!	
JOHN:	Yes, yes. Are you trying to beat me up?	
	I would sooner fast[19] than eat this cheese.	
	But I'll answer your fury tit for tat:	90
	Call me a fool all you want. Take that! This is just the start.	
LIZZY:	John, I used to think you one of the best:	
	Are you going to start beating me now?	
	I shall bite you back so ferociously	
	That you will shit yourself, you drunken pig.	95
	Do you think you can live with me like this,	
	Or in your crazy mind do you want to drive me away	
	With your horrible behaviour, so that everyone will know	
	Here and now, right here, what you are?	
	No: I shall make you look through new spectacles.	100
	You drunken windmill,[20] you never change.	
JOHN:	And I will trample you underfoot	
	To make you sorry that you taunted me like this.	
	Will you bring even more torments on my head	
	And addle my brains, you scum of all women?[21]	105

description of Robyn the Miller: see entry M.1262.11 in Robert William Dent *Proverbial Language in English Drama Exclusive of Shakespeare, 1495–1616: An Index* (University of California Press, 1984) 539.

19   Jan's reference to *vasten* ('fasting') is perhaps a veiled allusion to the probable occasion of the text (*Vastenavond*, literally 'Fasting Eve'), and a reminder of the Lenten fast that will follow its celebrations.

20   Lijsgen's term *droncken moolen* draws on a widespread association between milling technology and madness or inebriation. Although traceable across Europe (*Don Quixote* being the best-known example), the link is most abundantly expressed in the Low Countries, where mill-sails and waterwheels became a standard part of the iconography of foolery and merrymaking: see especially the proverb *hij is zoo dronken als een staartmolen* ('he is as drunk as a fantailed mill') recorded in Pieter Jacob Harrebomée *Spreekwoordenboek der nederlandsche taal: of Verzameling van Nederlandsche spreekwoorden* 3 vols (Utrecht: Kemink and Zoon, 1858–70) *2* 95.

21   Although the stage directions are silent at this point, the tone of Lijsgen's next speech suggests that Jan has assaulted her, and is probably making good on his

LIZZY: Oh no, John. Let me explain.
       You should let your mind settle down:
       I will study this lesson very thoroughly,
       And do everything that you want me to.
JOHN: What do you think, Lizzy? How does this camomile[22] smell? 110
       Will you keep following your silly ways?
       I have other headache pills[23] to give you,
       So I'm telling you for your own good to do what I say.
LIZZY: No, dear John, those pills do me no good;
       So I will always do what you say,   115
       And follow your command as best I can,
       And learn to be good and submissive in every way.
JOHN: Come, come with me, and put me to bed:
       I must sleep a while, so tuck me in,
       And when the clock strikes three, come quickly and wake me. 120

Pause[24]

LIZZY: Oh, marrying, marrying, what's the use of marrying?

   threat to kick her to the ground and stamp on her.
22 Van der Laan notes a popular belief that the camomile plant reached full potency only when trampled underfoot. Medical works also associate camomile with the treatment of foot complaints specifically, usually through the preparation of aromatic baths: see Johann Wilhelm Weinmann *Taalryk register der plaat- ofte figuur-beschryvingen der bloemdragende gewassen* 4 vols (Amsterdam: Zacharias Romberg, 1736–48) 2 164. A popular herbarium states that green camomile is in fact only good for bathing the feet (*grone Camillen hebben veel steelen ende dienen alleen om in voet water die voeten in te wassen*); likewise, an early work on maritime surgery recommends treating rheumatic swelling of the feet (*het Flerecijn der Voeten*) with 'man's urine infused with camomile' (*Menschen-pis met Camomillen opgesoden*), and promises that such a remedy is 'invariably good' (*uytnemende goet*): *Den clennen herbarius ofte Krundt-Boecxken* (Amsterdam: Henrick Barentsz, 1606) 74; *De nieuwe verbeterde chirurgyns scheeps-kist* (Amsterdam: Jan ten Hoorn, 1693) 65.
23 Jan's term *hooftpillen* contains an untranslatable pun on *pille* ('a medicinal tablet') and *pijl* (an arrow, dart, or other projectile weapon); Mak notes several further expressions in mock-prescriptions and the names of parodic saints that allude to blows to the head (*betekenis van klappen*): J.J. Mak *Rhetoricaal Glossarium* (Assen: Van Gorcum, 1959) viii–ix.
24 Following Hummelen's remarks on the function of the *pausa* in *rederijker* drama, a brief musical interlude would be fitting here to suggest the passage of time.

> Oh marrying was for me the start of my trouble,
> As I realised within a short time.
> Our John is good, but when drunk he is just deranged:
> Such is the bitter harvest I reap, and a great sorrow. 125
> Nevertheless, I can't really complain,
> Since he told me beforehand and swore to me
> That when he was drunk he would be bad-tempered.
> Did I take leave of my senses when I still married[25] him?
> Now I have this man and I must keep him; 130
> So I will stroke him with sweet reason[26]
> And see if I can win him with softness.
>
> HUBERT: Hey merchants, gather around, locals and strangers,[27]
> Burghers or citizens, according to your rank,
> Come and seek out the master while he may be found,[28] 135
> Don't be embarrassed to sample my expertise.
> Are you suffering from any shameful sicknesses,
> Such as pox or lesions, or anything that bothers you?[29]

---

25 Lijsgen's speech here might serve as a reminder that the *trou* ('truth', 'fidelity') celebrated in the motto of the *Pellicanisten* has a practical and matrimonial application, since it is echoed in her use of the term *trouwen* ('marry').

26 An alternate reading might be 'scratch him with gentle claws', since Lijsgen uses the verb *clouwen*.

27 Van der Laan notes that the formula *ven buijten en binnen* recurs throughout the plays of the *Pellicanisten*, referring to strangers and natives of Haarlem.

28 A parody of Isaiah 55: 6: 'seek ye the Lord, while he may be found: call upon him, while he is near'.

29 The 'pox' (*pocken*) and 'shameful sicknesses' (*sieckten van blamen*) to which Hubert refers are of course syphilis; its 'harm' extends to one's reputation as well as one's body. Many of the ailments he goes on to describe are popularly associated with the disease. In his treatise of 1690, Gervais Ucay, doctor at l'Hôtel-Dieu Saint-Jacques at Toulouse, not only calls the condition *schaamagtig* (shameful) and *eerloos* (infamous), but lists its symptoms as 'ringing ears, or inflammation in the glands of the joints, blisters, pustules, genital welts, warts, tumours, joint-swellings, glandular swellings, pains, rashes, bony growths, scurf, itching, purulent boils, necrosis and deterioration, especially of the bones, as though they are broken, shedding the hair, and other outbreaks besides' (*Klap-ooren, ofte geswellen in de klieren der las, Sweeringen, Puisten, vyg-werten, Wratten, Wild-vleis, Knoop-swellen, Klier-geswellen, Pynen, Vlekken, Kalk-builen, Schurft, Krawagie, Etter-builen, Verrottingen en doorknagingen, soo van de Beenen, als krakebeenen, uitvallen des haars, en meer andere toevallen*): Gervais Ucay *Nieuwe Verhandeling van de Venus-Ziekten* (Amsterdam: Nicolaus ten Hoorn,

Do you have warts, or corns that pinch your feet badly?
Do you have swollen glands, or any blood-blisters?   140
Come to me: I will cure you with my arts,
With tonics and herbs – all scientific –
With oil and ointments which fortify health,
Because I can cure a man of all illnesses,
Internal or external: don't be afraid to come forward,   145
Sample my art with its secrets
For believe me, it cannot be overpraised.
No-one is like me, I dare to boast.
Do you have ringing ears[30] or the clap?[31] Let me know.
Or secret troubles that none dare to name?   150
Or have you been bitten by a mad dog
So that you are half rabid yourself?[32] Then come to me.

1700) 6–7. On Ucay and his career, see Jean-Paul Martineaud *L'amour au temps de la vérole: histoire de la syphilis* (Paris: Glyphe, 2010) 48. See further Bruce Thomas Boehrer 'Early Modern Syphilis' *Journal of the History of Sexuality 1: 2* (1990) 197–214.

30 Disturbances in hearing (here *claporen*, literally 'chiming-ears') typically feature in lists of the symptoms of syphilis drawn up by early modern medical authorities: see François de la Calmette *Riverius reformatus, renovatus et auctus* 2 vols (Geneva: n.p., 1706) *2* 343, where *aurium tinnitus* leads the signs of *morbus venereis*.

31 *Druijpers* (literally 'the drip') remains slang for gonorrheal infection in contemporary Dutch. Gonorrhea and syphilis were often conflated in the early modern period; hence in the subtitle of his treatise on syphilis Blankaart can speak of 'the pox and its assaults, the clap, chancres, ringing ears' (*de pokken en deszelfs toevallen, van Druypers, chankers, klap-ooren*): Stephan Blankaart *Venus belegert en ontset* (Amsterdam: Timotheus ten Hoorn, 1684). It was not until 1837 and the work of Phillipe Ricord that the two were formally differentiated: see Allan M. Brandt 'Sexually Transmitted Diseases' in *Companion Encyclopedia of the History of Medicine* edited W. F. Bynum and Roy Porter, 2 vols (London: Routledge, 1993) 562–84, at 567–8.

32 These lines are probably a play on Hubert's name. His namesake St Hubertus, the eighth-century bishop of Maastricht and Liège, was traditionally evoked in cures for rabies, such as the *Hubertussleutel* ('Hubertus key'), a branding implement used to cauterise wounds inflicted by rabid dogs. In 1475, for instance, one Wynout Cornelisz of Leeuwenhorst in South Holland underwent a pilgrimage to the Abbey of Saint-Hubert in the Ardennes after being bitten by a mad dog: W.J.C. Rammelman Elsevier 'Geneeskunde in de Abdij van Leeuwenhorst' *Navorscher 13* (1863) 167–8.

	Women in trouble, come without hesitation:³³	
	Have you an outbreak of abscesses, or a secret problem?	
	I know how to help you, no word of a lie:	155
	Come in the dark of night, when no man can see,	
	If you do not dare to come by day.	
	I will assist you with help and advice:	
	If I fail, may I be eternally shamed.³⁴	
LIZZY:	Good day, master. Now, to business:³⁵	160
	I need to ask you for some good advice	
	About my husband's manic behaviour	
	Especially when he is drunk, if you get my drift.	
HUBERT:	What the devil, woman? That is really dreadful.	
	But what if beer itself might make him sorry?	165
	Would that not be a great help to you,	
	Or would you turn down such a scheme?	
LIZZY:	O master, if we could make that happen	
	I would give you a good load of gold in hand;	
	All other quack doctors I would then forsake	170
	And say that you are smarter than all the others.	
HUBERT:	I will prescribe you something, so that the fire	
	Within his body may be cooled a little.	
	And you must give him what I tell you to,	
	Or else he will feel no benefit from it.	175
LIZZY:	It would be no problem if he went to the New Ranges³⁶	

33 Almost certainly an innuendo, since the lechery of quack doctors was conventional: see, for instance, lyric 193 in the so-called *Antwerps Liedboek* ('Antwerp Songbook'), in which 'a skilful surgeon' (*een aerdich medecijn*) probes a lady's 'deep wound' (*diepen wonde*) with his 'instrument' (*tente*) until his jar of ointment is depleted: *Het Antwerps Liedboek* edited Dieuwke van der Poel, Dirk Geimaert, Hermine Joldersma, Johan Oosterman, and Louis Peter Grijp 2 vols (Tielt: Delta, 2004).

34 Perhaps another ironic echo of the *Pellicanisten*'s motto, since Hubert claims that he will *beschaempt blijven* ('stand ashamed').

35 In the original, *sout ghij niet kijven* ('do not dither').

36 Headquarters of the Haarlem *schutterij*, one of many citizen militias found throughout the cities of the Low Countries, and named after the bows and firearms with which its members were armed. The new *doelen* ('targets') had been built in 1592 on the site of the convent of St Michiel, after the original premises were destroyed in the great Haarlem fire of 1576. See Marijke Carasso-Kok and J. Levy-Van Helm *Schutters in Holland: kracht en zenuwen van*

	For a pint, two or three times a week.	
	I know he must sometimes rinse out his mouth.	
	But it happens every day. This is why I've come to you.	
HUBERT:	Woman, you should take a pint of vinegar,	180
	And mix it with this powder, both together.	
	In three days' time he will see good results	
	And the beer will be agony to him, I swear in truth.	
LIZZY:	Will this really do the trick, master?	
HUBERT:	Oh yes, the course is clear.	
	But although it will hit him hard, there should be no problem,	185
	Since it won't make his life too miserable.	
LIZZY:	Now, master, your art is greater than all others,	
	What shall I give you – just say the word –	
	For your expenses and herbs? I won't hold back,	
	But will pay you right away: tell me, what is your price?	190
HUBERT:	Woman, the herbs have been granted by our good Lord:	
	As for the art, just give me what you think is fair.	
	But if you don't think it turned out as you expected,	
	As will be revealed in due course,	
	Even if you gave me a hundred crowns,	195
	I will not give you a single one back.	
LIZZY:	Well, master, take this: I will not insult you.	
	I hand it over to you – spend it in good company.	
	But I beg you, master, not to expose me,	
	In case others find out about my affairs.	200
	Now adieu, master.[37]	
HUBERT:	Adieu, woman, do not worry about it.	
	Adieu, and go freely: you've already been cheated.	
	I can say this without a lie, as the gold is already in my purse.	
	I'm going, and shall feast this evening all the better.	

John, now awake, comes out yawning widely.

---

de stad (Zwolle: Waanders, 1988) 60–7; Paul Knevel *Burgers in het geweer: de schutterijen in Holland, 1550–1700* (Hollandse studiën 32; Hilversum: Verloren, 1994) 271–7.

37 There is no stage direction here, but Lijsgen is obviously meant to return to her house.

JOHN:	Although I am up now, I still feel very drowsy:	205
	I really would like a little more sleep.	
LIZZY:	Well, how goes it now, tell me, John Crookjaw?	
	Hey, you filthy dragon, must you yawn so much?	
JOHN:	Dear wife, I'll admit my guilt to masters and servants,	
	So knock off your scolding just for once.	210
LIZZY:	Damn it, John, I take no pleasure in chiding you,	
	Since our love will be thoroughly spoiled by it.	
JOHN:	Wife, I hope all that will be over, now and forever,	
	And will never happen again; if only I could shield myself	
	Against the taste of beer.	
LIZZY:	John, you must be on guard	215
	By day and by night, or else the game is lost.	
JOHN:	Yes indeed, wife, well said. But all men's powers	
	Come from good beer, even if women don't want to hear it.	
LIZZY:	But John, if I had taken medical advice, would you object	
	If beer itself could make you never drink again?	220
JOHN:	Heavens! then I would not get blind drunk	
	(Unless someone poured me some wine).	
	Nonetheless, wife, please do consider doing it:	
	I give you my consent, since it is for a good cause.	
LIZZY:	John, I will suggest something to you that will not hurt you,	225
	Not your goods or your blood, or any limb.	
	Here, drink this.[38]	
JOHN:	Well, wife, you should be pleased now:	
	It is all gone. Do you think it will do any good?	
LIZZY:	I hope so, yes.	
JOHN:	Well, then I'll take a little stroll,	
	And see how I feel this evening and in the morning.	230
	But I hope the wait will only be a small burden for you.	
	'Bye for now, wife.	
LIZZY:	'Bye, John: may God watch over you,	
	And keep you wise, as I expect you will be,	
	Goodbye. I'll leave too, and see what needs doing in the house.	

---

38 There is no direction here, but Jan is clearly intended to swallow Huijbert's preparation.

Pause[39]

Lizzy comes out again.

LIZZY:	My husband is still out; where could he be?	235
	I do long to see him, for I really love him.	
	He can drive away all my melancholy –	
	Especially when he does his husbandly duties.[40]	
	He used to write me so many letters,	
	When he first began to court me,	240
	And then he came sometimes, creeping like a thief,[41]	
	And I enjoyed everything he did to me in the dark.	
	But his drunken madness gives me no pleasure,[42]	
	As he has proved for quite some time:	
	But he has vowed to be better, and hopes to restrain himself,	245
	And when that is done, then all the past will be forgiven.	

The Neighbour-Women[43] *both come out at once and speak.*

N1 & N2:	Good day, neighbour.	
LIZZY:	May God reward you,	
	Dear neighbours, for coming to speak with me.	
N1:	Neighbour, you have not been living here long,	
	So we came to see whether you might need anything.	250
N2:	You shan't go without neighbourly friendship	
	Since we can give it, as women of honour.	

39 Again, there may well be a brief musical interlude here to show time moving on; at least there is some sort of break in the action, since all characters have vacated the stage.

40 The text has *hij mij doet het vrouwengerieff*, which might be more literally rendered as 'he gives me womanly pleasure'.

41 Probably an allusion to 1 Thessalonians 5: 2 ('for yourselves know perfectly, that the day of the Lord shall so come, as a thief in the night'), especially since St Paul goes on to urge his reader to 'be sober ... they that are drunk, are drunk in the night' (5: 6–7).

42 The original has *is mij een cleijn verblijen* ('is little joy to me').

43 The text uses the term *buerwijff* to describe these figures and in their dialogue; this untranslatable compound applies to a female neighbour specifically, and means something like 'neighbour-housewife'.

N1:	Our help and advice have never let anyone down
	Among all the neighbours who search us out.
N2:	Do you need us? Speak freely. Our advice will not fail you 255
	In the morning, in the evening, by day, or by night.
N1:	It sometimes happens that women are needed,
	Especially when younger women are in the family way.
LIZZY:	That is true, neighbour. That hadn't even occurred to me,
	But it is far from being the case with me. 260
N2:	Well, if God wills it, it must happen,
	And when it comes, you should embrace it gladly,
	Nor should you regret it, for you are young of days.
N1:	Neighbour, one thing, yes, one thing must I ask you,
	And you should answer me truthfully: 265
	Do you have any problems in your marriage?
	Tell me freely, don't hold back, in all frankness.
LIZZY:	Well, neighbour, I'm quite ready to do that.
	Listen to me closely, it shouldn't be hushed up:
	My heart was fixed on getting married 270
	And I have got hold of a man just as I wanted.
N1:	Yes, yes, is that how things are?
	Then you needn't complain, if I understand it,
	Because your marriage had a good beginning.
	But how do you find your husband now? Tell me all about it. 275
LIZZY:	My husband is truly good, and I love him for it –
	When he is sober and keeps his word.
	But when he is drunk, then you should pity me
	For ever getting married; who would have believed it?
	Because then he rages, as though he were insane, 280
	And has taken leave of his senses; I just hate it!
N2:	O neighbour, is that the case?
	Then you may well be heading to the Guild of Sorrow.[44]
LIZZY:	No, neighbour. I hope for better things, you see,

---

[44] Similar phrases are used in other plays of the period to denote enforced prostitution: compare Bredero's farce *Spaanschen Brabander* (1617), Hendrik Moor's tragicomedy *Hel en Hemel-vaert* (1630), or the shepherd masque (*Herders balet*) 'Rijst morgen-son van Célidon', which each refer to women going or having gone 'into the great guild to live' (*in't groote gilt te leven*): H. Moor *Hel en Hemel-vaert van Theodore en Constancy* (Amsterdam: Cornelis Blaeu-laecken, 1630) sig. B2v; G.A. Bredero *Spaanschen Brabander* edited C.F.P. Stutterheim (Culemborg:

	Since he has promised that it won't happen again.	285
N1:	The pledge will be fine if he sticks to it,	
	But I saw you doubting it will work out.	
N2:	Neighbour, I'll tell you how to avoid all quarrels,	
	So pay close attention to what I say:	
	If we could make your husband hate drinking	290
	To help you out, would you be happy with that?	
LIZZY:	Oh yes, if you can stop his crazy cravings, it would be a double trump,	
	And make him calm his cracked brain.	
N1:	That is true, but how should his loose screw	
	Be tightened up to help his wife?	295
N2:	I know what to do, so let me give it a go,	
	I am by no means ignorant of these things.	
LIZZY:	Will you hurt him at all?	
N2:	No ... not especially.	
	I shall just make him leap around on a blanket.	
	When he next comes home drunk	300
	Don't argue with him, but come and tell us.	
	If he falls down dead drunk, just let him lie there,	
	Until he is fast asleep – he'll look so stupid.	
	I bet we'll easily bring him to heel	
	And mend his manners for him,	305
	But I must have some help from the neighbours.[45]	
N1:	Happy to help; whatever you need.	
	We'll come back when you are ready.	
N2:	But first you must dress entirely in white –	
	It must be done like so, with our faces covered –	
	And when he lies stretched out on the blanket	310
	He will be woken up by our harsh gibbering.	
	He will think that we are elves or nightmares;	
	It will make his heart and the blood in his body ache.	
LIZZY:	Now, goodbye, and, dear neighbour, I hope that[46]	

Tjeenk Willink-Noorduijn, 1974) 211; Amsteldamse Vrolikheyt *Vervult met Veel'erhande gesangen, en Nieuwe Voysen* (Amsterdam: Josua Rex, 1647) 141.

45 The text uses another compound here, *buerhulp*, or 'neighbourly-help'. This line might plausibly be inviting audience participation in the eventual toss.

46 There appears to be verb missing from this line in the original. Van der Laan suggests *ick hoop* ('I hope'), an amendment we also follow.

	We can do this without harsh words:	315
	I'll give you all a huge pile of pancakes.	

All go in together. Pause.

Lizzy comes out again.

LIZZY:	Our John hasn't come back yet. What can the matter be?	
	I don't know where he might be hiding,	
	But I see that the sun is getting high;	
	It is about the time that we normally eat.	320
	But I'm afraid that he has forgotten me this time;	
	I can say it is so, for absolute certain.	
	Look, here he comes, and I think he's back on his old path;	
	He is full and drunk, as you can all see.	
JOHN:	Three cheers for the beer that they brew at St Bavo's![47]	325
	The rats there don't piss in the malt,[48] I reckon.	
LIZZY:	Well John, where, where the dickens[49] have you come from now?	
	I can't guess – I've no idea.	
	Are you soaked with booze?	
JOHN:	You are lying through your big mouth.[50]	
	I can't bear to listen to this.	330
	I do not care for beer, so don't hassle me;	
	I am not drunk, although my stomach is full.	

47 Bavo is a saint of some significance across the Low Countries. A Brabantine soldier who became a monk and died at Ghent in the mid-seventh century, he remains the patron of several cities in the Netherlands; this list includes Haarlem, where the Grote Kerk (or Sint-Bavokerk) is dedicated to him. Jan's reference probably relates to his feast day (*Bamis*, or *Baafmis*), which falls on 1 October, and traditionally coincides with harvest fairs to mark the onset of autumn (*Bamismarkt*), as well as the collection of taxes; the implication here, perhaps, is that Jan has frittered away money on beer that should have been more honestly spent. See J.R.S. Cauberghe *Vroomheid en volksgeloof in Vlaanderen. Folkloristisch calendarium* (Heideland: Hasselt, 1968) 119–20.

48 That is, as Van der Laan explains, because the malt is brewed and drunk too rapidly for vermin to contaminate it.

49 Mak defines *duycker* as a euphemistic name for the devil (*verzachtende vorm van duivel*), much like the early modern English 'dickens', 'ruffyn', 'Old One', or 'Old Harry': *Rhetoricaal Glossarium* 139.

50 Jan again refers to Lijsgen's *backhuijs*. Compare line 83.

LIZZY:	Well, what are you then?	
JOHN:	Well, I am half mad;	
	My head's in a whirl, I'm almost flying –	
	But it is not because of beer.	
LIZZY:	John, what is it from then? Don't lie to me.	335
	Tell me straight, how come you're standing there swaying?	
JOHN:	Well, I ladled out a little brandy,	
	And after that sipped some sweet malmsey wine.[51]	
LIZZY:	Is that why you are staggering as though you were crippled,	
	And stand there now so crooked in the head?[52]	340
	I'd rather see you hanging from a rope	
	Than see you filling your guts which such rotten stuff.[53]	
JOHN:	Liz, keep a civil tongue in your jaws,	
	Or you'll taste a knuckle sandwich.[54]	

She knocks him underfoot[55]

---

[51] The text has *bastart sop* ('bastard soup'). In his sixteenth-century vocabulary, Kiliaan defines *bastaerd wijn* as 'raisin wine, wine sweet and noble, pressed from the grape dried in the sun' (*vinum passum, vinum dulce & generosum ex vuis passis & sole siccatis expressum*): C. Kiliaan *Etymologicum Teutonicae Linguae* edited F. Claes (The Hague: Mouton, 1972) 28.

[52] Another common saying for madness or folly, found in various forms throughout the period: it occurs in a farce of 1552, where a character reports 'my senses run in discord, wholly crooked' (*mijn sinnen de rinnen in discoorde | geheel verdraijt*), and a lyric from the famous Gruuthuse manuscript (c.1400), which depicts unruly peasants with 'their caps fixed all crooked' (*tcaproen staet al verdraijt*): '*Wie voirmaels waeren de victorlöste*' edited P.J. Meertens *Jaarboek De Fonteine* 17 (1967) 82–105, at 84; '*Wi willen van den kerels zinghen*' *Het Gruuthuse-handschrift: Hs. Den Haag, Koninklijke bibliotheek, 79 K 10* edited Herman Brinkman and Ike de Loos, 2 vols (Middeleeuwse verzamelhandschriften uit de Nederlanden 13; Hilversum: Verloren, 2015) 1 443–4.

[53] *Aes*: literally 'carrion, rotten flesh'.

[54] In the original text, Jan threatens Lisjen with *kaes van mijn vuijst* ('cheese from my fist'), punning on the fact that *vuijst* means both 'fist' and a small portion of meat, bread, or cheese that can be held in the hand: see the relevant entry in Matthias Kraemer *Das Königliche Nider-Hoch-Teutsch, und Hoch-Nider-Teutsch Dictionarium* 2 vols (Nuremburg: Matthias Kraemer, 1719) 2 77.

[55] Although Van der Laan places this direction after Lijsgen's next speech, it is clear from both the manuscript and context that she retaliates against Jan at this point.

LIZZY:	Lie there, you drunken beast. May God make you sorry.	345
	I'll walk away right now so you can't get at me.	
JOHN:	Damn it, Lizzy, I'll give you	
	Such a blow on your jaw that you'll regret it tomorrow.	

He remains lying down.

Now, be off. My legs are sausages: I can't follow you.
And it's no use straining myself further by shouting, 350
So I'll sleep a little, while I lie here by myself.

Pause

LIZZY: I'd better come and find out whether the pig is sleeping.
I think so, yes, so I'll call my neighbours:
Come, neighbours! Come, all together!
The pig is asleep: come, you have to see him! 355
N1: We'll come to you right away
We must 'Show Our Good Faith'[56] at every hour.
LIZZY: I'd better come and find out whether the pig is sleeping:
I think so, yes, so I'll call you, dear neighbours.[57]

You know what to do now, work a strange cure – 360
I ask you as a friend, will you start the process?
N2: Where is he lying?
LIZZY: On the dung heap.
N2: He won't stay there for long:
We will gladly drag him off.
N1: What are we going to do? Please spell it out,
We are good friends, so don't mislead us. 365
N2: First cover your face, and then we'll roll him
Up on this blanket, so that his head will spin.
Even if he screeches like an angry cat
Make sure you echo everything I sing.[58]

---

56 *Trou moet blijcken* is, of course, the motto of the Pellicaen.
57 Lines 352–9 form a *rondeel*, one of the intricate, repetitive rhyme schemes favoured by the *rederijkers*, and derived from the French *roundel*.
58 A veiled instruction to the audience, indicating that they too should follow the *gebueren*'s lead and repeat their song line-by-line.

The song

  Harken you women, good of heart,   370
  Here have we a great drunkard:
  He refuses to restrain his bad temper:
  And so he must leap upon the blanket.

Second verse[59]

  Think about this drunken fool:
  He cares not for butter nor for cheese,   375
  For bread, for fish, for meat, nor for bacon:
  So his children live in great need.

JOHN: Oh, Oh, Oh, I am a poor fool:
  Are you human beings or ghosts? Oh, I was never so scared!
  Are you elves or women? Leave me alone!   380
  Oh *benedicite, magnificat!*[60] I must be dying!
N2: Oh yes: they will teach you not to beat up your wife;
  Even if you rot, you must truly repent.

Third stanza

  He does many strange things
  In full view of all the neighbours,   385
  He drinks up his wife's mantle and rings:
  And so he must leap upon the blanket.

Fourth stanza

  Whoever saw such a drunken fool?
  When he opens a chest or a cupboard
  He can't line the key up to the lock,[61]   390
  He just jabs everything to splinters.

---

59 The sections of the song are differentiated in the manuscript by means of the headers *2 vers, 3 vers*, etc.

60 Two garbled snippets of liturgical Latin: *benedicite* ('bless me') is taken from the opening petition of the Canticle of the Three Young Men and based on Daniel 3: 57; *magnificat* ('it magnifies', or 'my soul doth magnify the lord' in full) is the incipit of the widely known Song of Mary, based on Luke 1: 46, and a key part of the Liturgy of the Hours.

61 An obvious reference to the proverbial impotence of drunkards.

JOHN:	Oh, *venite exultemus*.[62] I don't dare speak:	
	Must I suffer this because of you, oh, dear wife?	
	I love you as much as the heart in my body:	
	Help me out of this, oh, please hear my prayers!	395
N2:	No, no: you still have more suffering to come,	
	So drop down into the folds like a good boy.	

Fifth stanza

	When he is drunk he is so very brave	
	That he shits his pants quite nobly.[63]	
	In all his actions he is disgusting:	400
	And so he must leap upon the blanket.	

N2:	All men should be taught to sing like this	
	If they maltreat their wives for no reason.	
N1:	I bet he will behave better from now on,	
	And stop terrorising his wife with his drunken habits.	405
N2:	Now he's fainted,[64] so let us lay him back	
	On the dung heap, and then we can all go home.	
	We will hear how long he stays there.	

John, coming to his senses, looks about painfully:

JOHN:	Oh, oh, where am I? Never did a man have worse luck!	
	Where have I been? It makes my heart tremble.	410

---

62 Another piece of liturgy, meaning 'come, let us praise', this time taken from the invitatory preceding matins, and based on Psalm 94 (or 95 in some later versions).

63 The incontinence of drunks is a frequent source of comedy in *rederijker* drama, ramped up to particular extremes in the parodic homily *Spotsermoen over Sint Niemand* ('Mock Sermon on Saint Nobody'); the obvious point here is that Jan's bravery is no bravery at all, as it simultaneously emboldens him and inflicts on him the most humiliating sign of cowardice. On the *Spotsermoen*, see *Comic Drama in the Low Countries c.1450–c.1560: A Critical Anthology* edited Ben Parsons and Bas Jongenelen (Cambridge: D.S. Brewer, 2012) 63–81.

64 *Swijm* ('swoon, dead faint') is perhaps intended to recall *swijn* ('pig') and *wijn* ('wine'), echoing both the cause and result of Jan's denigration.

> Were they elves or water-spirits?⁶⁵ It's a great wonder
> That I am still alive, I've been so tortured.
> But am I alive, or am I dead? What's my condition?
> Can someone tell me? Someone who's here?
> I think I am alive, so I will go and find my wife   415
> Before I am hurt again by those elvish scum.
> Hey, wife! Hey, open up!

*Lizzy, to her husband John:*⁶⁶

LIZZY: Well, who is making this ruckus?
                   It almost drives me mad. Is that you, John Runny-arse?⁶⁷

---

65   Jan refers to *nickertgen* (variant of *nikker*), a type of malevolent or mischievous water spirit given to abducting children, and equivalent to the German *Nixe* or Scandinavian *näck*. According to the Amsterdam controversialist Walich Sywaertsz, these creatures played a prominent role in medieval church processions, accompanying the other demons (*Duyveltgens*) who harassed Christ as he stormed *Helle gaet*, and provoking 'terror from any youngsters … threatening that afterwards somewhere a Nikker waits to stab them with a barb, in order to seize them in their claws when they sleep' (*verbaestheyt van eenighe jonghers … vreesende ofter noch erghens een Nickertgen in een hoeck was blijven steecken, om haer te betrappen ende met sijn clauwen wech te sleepen*): W.S. *Roomsche Mysteriën: ondeckt in een cleyn tractaetgen* (Amsterdam: Ambrosius Janszoon, 1604) sig. B4v. They are associated with drunkenness in Joost van den Vondel's beast fable of 1627, which refers to 'the nikkers and devils | the privileged or drunk' (*Daer Nickertgen en Haintgen / De wellekoemst of drinckt*): Joost van den Vondel '*Een Niew Lietgen van Reyntgen de Vos*' *De werken van Vondel* edited J.F.M. Sterck and others, 7 vols (Amsterdam: De Maatschappij voor goede en goedkoope lectuur, 1927–34) *3* 111–14.

66   The fact that this direction was deemed necessary suggests that Lijsgen is addressing Jan from within the structure of their 'house', or from its upper gallery or 'window'.

67   *Jan after lam* (literally, 'John Lame-Behind'), a popular term for a drunk more commonly spelled *Jan Achterlam*, and again alluding to the incontinence of drinkers. Compare a sixteenth-century *refrein* that lists various insulting surnames, such as John Dripnose (*Jan druypnuese*) and John the Hen-Toucher (*Jan den hinnentaster*), and which contains the line 'John Comfort, John Soft-Arse, John Seldom-Satisfied' (*Jan troost, Jan achterlam, Jan selden sadt*): '*Als een man gehout is, soo is hy gesint*' *Refereinen en andere gedichten uit de XVIe eeuw, verzameld en afgeschreven door Jan de Bruyne* edited C. Ruelens, 3 vols (Antwerp: P. Kockx, 1879–81) *1* 93–5. Compare also the *Farce of the Two Soldiers* (1612), the tragicomedy *Daraide* (1618), and other sources for further occurrences of the term: *Een cluchte*

[JOHN:][68]	O, dear wife, do not be angry	
	Because I barged in here so hastily:	420
	I pray you, by God's will, don't be upset	
	And don't blame me if I ever mistreated you.	
LIZZY:	Well, John, why exactly did you want to hit me this afternoon?	
	Do you have other plans now? That is a great improvement.	
JOHN:	I pray you, don't scold me for it now,	425
	But let me have your forgiveness:	
	We shall live peacefully together in harmony	
	Forever, believe me.	
LIZZY:	You say that whenever you are sober.	
JOHN:	No, no: I will no longer drink too much,	
	Even if they give me beer and wine for nothing,	430
	Because it has made me suffer dreadfully.	
	You can see it clearly: just look[69] in my eyes.	
LIZZY:	John, your eyes look as though they are racing:[70]	
	It's true; how come you look so exhausted?	
JOHN:	Oh, wife, I don't know myself what troubles me,	435
	I am so disturbed by a strange vision:	
	I think that elves dragged me away. I can't understand it;	
	I suspect it must have been 'white nightmares'.[71]	

van d'een ende d'ander twee soldaten in *Vier excellente cluchten* edited J.J. Mak (Antwerp: De Nederlandsche Boekhandel, 1950), 64-94, at 93; J. Starter *Daraide* (Rotterdam: Abraham Mexing, 1630) sig. D3; Jacob Westerbaen 'Boerenvrijage op de Haagse kermis' *Gedichten* edited Johan Koppenol (Amsterdam: Polak and Van Gennep, 2001) 23-4.

68   The manuscript omits a direction here, but it is clear from the reference to his *lieve wijffgen* that Jan is speaking.

69   The exact meaning of the original (*teijl van mijn oogen*) is uncertain, since *teijl* or *teyl* appears only rarely in early modern Dutch. Mak connects the term with *telen* ('to cultivate, to plough'), plausibly suggesting that it is intended to mean 'eyeline' or 'gaze' (*blik*): *Rhetoricaal Glossarium* 416.

70   The text describes Jan's eyes as *vlogen*, literally 'flying' or 'soaring'.

71   Jan seems to conflate two types of folkloric apparition here, the *witte wieven* ('white women') and *nachtmaren* or *nachtmerries* ('nightmares'): the former describes a group of ghosts said to inhabit bogs and swamps, while the latter is a species of shapeshifting witch who uses sleeping animals or humans as nocturnal steeds. For an accessible account, see Abe J. van der Veen *Witte wieven, Weerwolven en Waternekkers: een beschrijving van alle geesten, elfen en andere wonderlijke wezens uit Nederland* (Rotterdam: Mijnbestseller, 2017).

LIZZY:	John, I am half-terrified by what you say;	
	Spare no details, and tell me more.	440
JOHN:	O wife, I think I have been before Hell's gate –	
	Listen to my story, I must tell you –	
	I thought they laid me upon a blanket	
	And over hedges and bridges they threw me high	
	Into the air. I almost thought that I flew.	445
	It has left me with a black eye.	
LIZZY:	John, my heart almost starts to tremble	
	From hearing your story. But is it really true,	
	Or was it a dream?	
JOHN:	Wife, I don't know myself; that's why I'm upset,	
	And feeling so sorry for myself: I can't hide it.	450
LIZZY:	John, I'm starting to feel such terror	
	The hair is almost standing upright on my head.	
JOHN:	Yes, wife, I completely believe you:	
	But I have tasted it, and been right in the soup,[72]	
	Because all my failures were charged against me,	455
	And all my secrets, all I've ever done or thought.	
LIZZY:	John, I think in truth that our good Lord has visited you	
	And has brought these sorrows down on you	
	To make you hold off getting drunk,	
	And to teach you how to control your foolish mind.	460
JOHN:	Yes, wife, from now on I will start	
	To redeem my soul, and also to please you.	
	I will never drink again for the rest of my life,	
	So you won't have to complain about my evil ways.	
	And so I ask you, dear wife: please forgive me	465
	For all that I did wrong, or however I mistreated you.	
LIZZY:	Well, John, there is no problem with that:	
	All will be well if you do as you say.	
JOHN:	Wife, I will force myself to do it:	

---

[72] *Inde peeckel geseten* (literally 'to sit in the brine') is a proverb roughly equivalent to the English 'in a pickle', or 'in the soup'. Stoett lists numerous variants, including 'he sits in the rats' (*hij zit in de rats*), 'to sit in the shit' (*zitten de schijt*, or *kak krijgen*), 'in the soup' (*in de soep*), 'in the plums' (*in de pluimen*), and 'to sit in the shitty whirlpool' (*in de poepsche karn zitten*): Stoett *Nederlandse spreekwoorden 1* 148, 202.

	So give me a kiss of peace and let's make up.[73]	470
LIZZY:	With pleasure, John, but always remember the blanket:	
	Your crack-brained tricks will surely end then.	
JOHN:	Good burghers, all of you that are present here	
	Having come here to see us play,	
LIZZY:	We pray you, do not disgrace	475
	The good name of the brothers whose Faith must be shown.[74]	
JOHN:	If anything fell short – please listen, poor and rich –	
	Because of our carelessness, do not mock us,	
	But overlook our faults out of joyful friendship.	

Finis. This play is 458 verses long[75]
By Trou moet blijcken

University of Leicester
Fontys Lerarenopleiding, Tilburg

---

73   The kiss (*soen*) for peace (*pejis*) is curiously reminiscent of Chaucer's *Prologue of the Wife of Bath* and its ballad reworking 'Att the Townys ende', which both conclude with a comparable gesture, as a means of ending a pitched battle between spouses: see *Songs, Carols, and other Miscellaneous Poems* edited Roman Dyboski *EETS ES 101* (1907) 110–11.

74   *Trou moet blijcken*, a further reiteration of the Pellicaen's motto.

75   That is, excluding the song that accompanies the tossing, perhaps because it is written in a shorter line than the customary decasyllabic or dodecasyllabic *regel* of *rederijker* verse.

ALIMENTARY ADDRESS
and the Management of Appetite
and Hunger in *Jacob and Esau*

Ernst Gerhardt

The anonymous mid-Tudor biblical interlude *The History of Jacob and Esau* presents a set of uncertainties for its commentators.[1] While the interlude's composition has been dated broadly to the period between 1547 and 1558, narrowing that range decisively has proven difficult. The interlude's commitment to a Calvinist-influenced doctrine of election and reprobation might suggest a composition date in Edward VI's reign, but opinion remains divided.[2] As it was first entered in the Stationers' Register between June 1557 and June 1558 by Henry Sutton, it must have been composed by that date. Unfortunately, only a single fragment of the 1557/8 printing remains extant.[3] However, the complete text

---

1   'The Historie of Iacob and Esau' in *Reformation Biblical Drama in England: An Old-Spelling Critical Edition* edited Paul Whitfield White (New York & London: Garland, 1992). All citations of the play text will be made from this edition; hereinafter '*Iacob and Esau* edited White'.

2   For a composition date under King Edward VI, see C.C. Stopes *William Hunnis and the Revels of the Chapel Royal: A Study of His Period and the Influences Which Affected Shakespeare* (Louvain: Uystpruyst, 1910; reprinted Nendeln/Liechtenstein: Kraus Reprint, 1969) 269; David Bevington *Tudor Drama and Politics: A Critical Approach to Topical Meaning* (Cambridge MA: Harvard UP, 1968) 109; and John N. King *English Reformation Literature: The Tudor Origins of the Protestant Tradition* (Princeton UP, 1982) 301–5. For Queen Mary, see Lily B. Campbell *Divine Poetry and Drama in Sixteenth-Century England* (Cambridge UP, 1959) 215; Naomi Schwartz Pasachoff 'Playwrights, Preachers, and Politicians: A Study of Four Tudor Old Testament Dramas' (PhD thesis, Massachusetts: Brandeis University, 1974) 17–29 online at <http://www.proquest.com/docview/288280800/citation/68CE41E923A49F6PQ/1>; Helen Thomas '*Jacob and Esau* – "rigidly Calvinistic"?' *Studies in English Literature, 1500–1900* 9: 2 (1969) 199–213, at 211–13; and Paul Whitfield White *Theatre and Reformation: Protestantism, Patronage, and Playing in Tudor England* (Cambridge UP, 1993) 118–19. The prayer for the queen that concludes the printed version suggests performance in the reign of Mary or Elizabeth.

3   Paul Morgan 'Fragments of Three Lost Plays from the Stationers Register' *Bodleian Library Record* 7 (1962–7) 299–307, at 301; White 'Introduction' in *Reformation Biblical Drama* xxxiv–xxxv.

survives in seven copies of a 1568 edition 'newely imprinted' by Henry Bynneman.⁴ In addition, given that no direct evidence of the interlude's performance is known, ascertaining its provenance has been challenging. Its sophisticated Terentian comic structure along with its requirement for several singing parts have led to the now widely accepted view that the interlude was written for performance by children of the Chapel. Commentators have identified two main candidates for *Jacob and Esau*'s author: Nicholas Udall and William Hunnis, both of whom had Protestant leanings, worked with child performers, and wrote and produced plays at court in the relevant period.⁵

Taking these probabilities and uncertainties of time, place, and context into account, this essay explores the implications of the interlude's striking interest in food and its preparation and consumption. The serving of meals is central to the biblical story on which it is based, but the playwright develops the treatment of food into a complex mode of social interaction. Food becomes an 'alimentary address': a means by which one character addresses another, referring to or using food as a means of persuasion. Its provision and withholding are used to manage appetite and shape social hierarchies and relations.

The action of *Jacob and Esau*'s first two acts is based on the account, found at the end of Genesis 25, of Esau's selling of his birthright to Jacob in exchange for pottage; the action of the final three acts is based on Genesis 27's account of Rebecca and Jacob's deception of the blind Isaac in order to win for Jacob the paternal blessing Isaac intended for his first-born son, Esau. The interlude elaborates on these events, inventing several characters, mostly servants, not found in its biblical sources. *Jacob and Esau* also presents several scenes not grounded in its biblical sources, such as a scene in which neighbours complain of Esau's early-morning hunting, a Prologue, a concluding commentary by 'the Poet', and several songs.

---

4   Darryll Grantley *English Dramatic Interludes, 1300–1580: A Reference Guide* (Cambridge UP, 2004) 157.

5   See White 'Introduction' xxxvi–xxxvii; C.C. Stopes 'The Interlude, or, Comedie of Jacob and Esau' *Athenaeum 3783* (1900) 538–40; Robert Hornback 'The *Jacob and Esau* Paradigm: Nicholas Udall's Predestinarian Problem Comedy' in *Stages of Engagement: Drama and Religion in Post-Reformation England* edited James D. Mardock and Kathryn R. McPherson (Pittsburgh: Duquesne UP, 2014) 63–80, at 65.

The Prologue and concluding commentary frame the interlude's action with paraphrases of Pauline commentary drawn from Romans 8, 9, and 11, which address the Jacob-Esau story's exemplification of God's election of Jacob over Esau.[6] The Prologue and Poet's use of 'election' and 'reprobate' in these passages suggest the Calvinist influence underwriting the interlude. The Jacob and Esau story had become a key text in Protestant discussion of predestination, focusing on Paul's text: 'As it is wrytten: Iacob haue I loued, but Esau haue I hated', a divine decision made 'yer the chyldren were borne, when they had nether done good nether bad (that the purpose of God by eleccion, myghte stande)'.[7] The playwright cites Paul's words explicitly and comments on them in both the Prologue and Epilogue. But the doctrine, as illustrated in this biblical story, continued to provoke difficulty in spite of extensive discussion among commentators. This was partly because of its clear unfairness in terms of human morality. This affected not only the moral judgement of the two brothers but also the manipulative behaviour of Rebecca in deceiving her husband and favouring her younger son.[8] Both she and Jacob were often criticised for their actions, even while the expositors accepted that the outcome was ordained by God.[9] Calvin observed that, 'all this sprang from no other thing, then from [Rebecca's] fayth ... [but] ... her fayth was ioyned with a rash and undiscreete zeale'.[10] The Protestant Geneva Bible (1560) glosses Rebecca's deception 'This subtiltie is blameworthie because she shulde haue taried til God had performed his promes', and points out that 'Although Iaakob was assured of this blessing

---

6   See Thomas *'Jacob and Esau'*; Paul Whitfield White 'Predestinarian Theology in the Mid-Tudor Play *Jacob and Esau*' *Renaissance and Reformation/Renaissance et Réforme* 12: 4 (1988) 291–302.

7   Epistle of Paul to the Romans 9: 11–13, in the Great Bible: *The Byble in Englyshe that is to saye the content of all the holy scrypture, both of ye olde and newe testament* (London: Rychard Grafton [and] Edward Whitchurch, 1539) New Testament fol. lxiii verso.

8   See John Curran *'Jacob and Esau* and the Iconoclasm of Merit' *Studies in English Literature 1500-1900* 49: 2 (2009) 285–309; Arnold Ledgerwood Williams *The Common Expositor: an Account of the Commentaries on Genesis, 1527–1633* (Chapel Hill: University of North Carolina Press, 1948) 169–73.

9   Ledgerwood Williams *Common Expositor* 169–70.

10 Jean Calvin *A commentarie of Iohn Caluine, vpon the first booke of Moses called Genesis* translated by Thomas Tymme (London: [Henry Middleton] for John Harison and George Bishop, 1578) 570.

by faith yet he did euil to seke it by lies'.[11] While the playwright openly acknowledges the influence of the Calvinist doctrine, he does not address these criticisms directly, concentrating on positive dramatisation of the characters' actions in the light of God's election.[12] Like other mid-Tudor biblical interludes, *Jacob and Esau*, with the significant focus of its action on Rebecca's and Jacob's deception of Isaac, self-reflexively thematises play-acting or, in its own terms, 'counterfeiting'.[13] Yet, while it criticises some forms of counterfeiting, the interlude offers a defence of the counterfeiting its characters undertake, foregrounding playing's ability to reveal, if not fulfil, Jacob's election and Esau's reprobation.

Jacob and Esau's elaboration of these doctrinal, political, and self-reflexive theatrical themes converges in the interlude's treatment of food production, service, and consumption. Two meals are central to the interlude's plot, and both are depicted as coercive acts of theatrical hospitality. In the first of these, Jacob sells a mess of pottage to a hungry Esau, exchanging this 'grosse and homely' (line 594) meal for Esau's birthright. However, rather than Jacob's refusal to relieve his brother's hunger without compensation, it is Esau's ravenous consumption of the pottage that becomes the subject of later parodic and mocking counterfeitings by other characters. In the second meal episode, Rebecca advises Jacob to play the part of Esau – with a costume designed by herself – and serve a goat stew to his father, Isaac, who had requested venison from Esau. The interlude thus sets on display the power relations inherent in, and the tactics, including theatrical ones, for the management of, household members' hunger, appetites, and tastes.

---

11   The Geneva Bible: *The Bible and Holy Scriptures conteyned in the Olde and Newe Testament* (Geneva: Rouland Hall, 1560) Genesis 27 glosses to verses 9, 19.

12   *Jacob and Esau* has by some critics been understood as advancing a Protestant politics of the justified usurpation of traditional authority. The interlude's largely positive depiction of Rebecca and Jacob's seizure of Esau's birthright and blessing has been interpreted as a justification of 'revolutionary usurpation in the name of God' (Pasachoff 'Playwrights, Preachers, and Politicians' 29) with its 'chief ideological purpose ... to justify seizure of power' (Bevington *Tudor Drama and Politics* 112).

13   Some critics have understood the interlude's theatrical self-reflexivity to be either an iconoclastic attack on Catholic practices or a cautionary challenging of Calvinist doctrine. See Curran '*Jacob and Esau*' 286–7; Nadia T. van Pelt '"Counterfeiting his maister": Shared Folly in The History of Jacob and Esau' in 'Théâtre Tudor' *Theta 13* (2016) 131–48, especially 135–6.

Most obviously, it is Jacob and Rebecca who manage the household's food in order to manipulate Esau's hunger and Isaac's taste. But other characters also see the management of food as a mechanism of power. Esau understands his servant Ragau's hunger as a means to control him and so withholds food from him; Ragau responds in kind, concealing stolen food from Esau as a petty act of vengeful self-preservation and class transgression. Both Esau and Isaac consume their meals privately offstage, without allowing others a share. In response, the household's servants favour Jacob over Esau because Jacob promises them a part in the feast to come.

Characters' treatment of food addresses other characters' senses, particularly those of taste and smell, as well as embodied sensations such as hunger and satiety. Such alimentary addresses complement the verbal addresses in which they are couched, and it is often difficult to untangle them. However, untangling offers a way to think about the interlude's use of food beyond its symbolic or literary functions and to grasp food's deployment as a suasory device addressed to individuals' sensations. A statement by Rebecca articulates this notion of alimentary address: Rebecca intends to 'make such meate ... | As shall say come eate me, and make olde Isaac | Licke his lippes therat, so toothsom shall it smacke' (lines 1023–5). Prepared for Isaac, Rebecca's meal addresses his senses of smell and taste, compelling him to lick his lips and, implicitly, to consume the meal. Rebecca here describes the meal's alimentary address of Isaac in synaesthetic terms, personifying the meal so that it speaks to her blind husband in the imperative mood. While proverbial in nature, the meal's command ('Come eat me') exemplifies the persuasive effect the meal will have on Isaac.[14] Rebecca's alimentary address of Isaac helps win his blessing of Jacob, a blessing Rebecca could not win through either argument or petition. The interlude presents Rebecca's alimentary address of Isaac as a powerful technique of persuasion.

Though focused primarily on the food itself, the interlude's alimentary addresses are often highly theatrical in nature, involving counterfeiting, or moments of self-reflexive play-acting. The most salient of such counterfeiting is the multisensory entertainment – an interlude-within-the-interlude – that Rebecca devises for Isaac. In addition, Jacob's alimentary address of Esau's hunger occasions counterfeiting, notably in providing subject matter for the servants'

14   *Iacob and Esau* edited White 167 notes 1023–4.

mocking imitation of a hungry Esau's gluttonous gorging of Jacob's rice pottage. Characters re-enact the latter episode more than once in the interlude, each time subjecting Esau's unmannerly consumption to ridicule. Finally, alimentary addresses overlap with several direct addresses to the interlude's spectators, suggesting that the interlude's use and treatment of food complements the implication of the spectators in its action. Although there is no definitive evidence, critical opinion has tended to locate *Jacob and Esau* as a court interlude, and many internal details and references seem to point to a hall or household venue for performance.[15] This would certainly give resonance not only to the interlude's focus on the preparation and serving of food but to the potentially self-reflexive context it would provide for the staging of entertainments. In what follows I will discuss first the interlude's two meals, beginning with the counterfeit meal Rebecca prepares for Isaac before discussing the rice pottage Jacob serves to Esau. This will be followed by a consideration of the text's evocation of a household space, and its implications for the audience.

Jacob's tooth

Rebecca's alimentary address of Isaac takes the form of a multi-sensory mimetic and theatrical entertainment. The central component of this entertainment, which Jacob calls a 'deuise' (1028) and Esau a 'subtill fetche' (1499), is a meal in which kid-goat counterfeits venison. The entertainment requires mimetic performance as well as food; Rebecca asks Jacob to 'playe thy parte well' (1006), namely that of Esau, and she explicitly directs his speech, actions, and costuming to imitate his brother. Jacob, playing Esau, serves his blind father the counterfeit meal, which, satisfying Isaac's taste for venison, convinces the patriarch of the verisimilitude of the performance. Once convinced, Isaac blesses Jacob-as-Esau, effectively delivering the older son's legacy to the younger. Rebecca's entertainment addresses Isaac not simply in conventionally theatrical terms of spectacle (sight) and dialogue (hearing); since he

---

15   See White 'Introduction' xxxvii–xxxix. Suzanne R. Westfall *Patrons and Performance: Early Tudor Household Revels* (Oxford: Clarendon Press, 1990) includes *Jacob and Esau* in a table of plays (59) supporting her fuller discussion of chapel plays designed for household performance (58–62). Van Pelt '"Counterfeiting his maister"' and Grantley *English Dramatic Interludes* 157 both identify the play as a court or great hall interlude.

is blind, her device also addresses Isaac's senses of touch, smell, and, importantly, taste.

It is worth noting that Rebecca's alimentary address of Isaac is instigated by the logic of Isaac's own taste. Isaac's preferential love for Esau as his eldest son, which organises the hierarchy and legacy of the household, seems closely associated with an appetitive response similar to the one Rebecca plans to elicit with the meal that says 'Come eat me'. Against Rebecca's charge that his 'loue is bestowed on him [Esau] in vayne', Isaac defends his preference for Esau on two grounds: 'Fyrst actiue he is ... And many a good morsell he bringeth home to me. | Then he is myne eldest and first begotten sonne' (394–7). It is notable that Esau's provision of food for his father seems to precede, in Isaac's affection, his status as first-born son. Later, wishing to bless him, Isaac requests that Esau first 'Bring me of thy venison that is good ... And to make for mine owne tooth such meate as I loue. | Thus doo mine owne dere sonne, and then I shal thee kisse ... and thee for euer blisse' (961–6). Following its biblical source, Genesis 25: 28, which also states that 'Isaac loued Esau because he dyd eate of his venyson', the interlude here explicitly connects a patriarchal taste for venison with the blessing of a firstborn son.[16]

The satisfaction of Isaac's appetite is intertwined with his maintenance of primogeniture, which he declares to be 'Natures lawe' (445). As both taste and law justify his preference for Esau, Isaac's taste for venison – and Esau's ability to satisfy that taste – acquires the force of that law, and, conversely, the law acquires the taste for Esau's venison: the hierarchy of Isaac's household is organised by affect, by Isaac's taste for venison, and by his love of Esau for satisfying that taste.

The satisfaction of taste and appetite resonates with Isaac's image of God as a food-provider. Isaac explains to Rebecca that God is one that 'feedeth and gouerneth all that he hath sent: | Protecting his faithfull in euery degree, | And them to relieue in all their necessity' (313–15). Isaac's description ironically foreshadows the interlude's action – Esau will be fed pottage, Isaac himself a counterfeit stew – but both feedings will realise God's election of Jacob, contrary to Isaac's desire. Nevertheless, Isaac's taste – his declaration of what food he prefers – operates not simply as a symbol but as an organising principle of household hierarchy and legacy, because it is also a declaration of which son is preferred.

---

16 The Great Bible fol. x recto.

Rebecca's alimentary address of Isaac thus aims at both Isaac's maintenance of primogeniture and his taste for venison; they are two sides of the same coin.

Rebecca's address subverts both Isaac's authority over his household and its organisation, a subversion exemplified in part by her marshalling of the household's personnel and resources to produce the counterfeit meal that will win Isaac's blessing of Jacob. The preparation of her entertainment occupies several of the interlude's scenes.

Rebecca focuses sustained attention not on the visual but on the tactile and olfactory nature of Jacob's costume. To counterfeit Esau's hirsute body, Rebecca creates a costume made of kids' hides. She tells Jacob, 'because that Esau is so rough with heare: | I haue brought sleues of kid next to thy skin to weare. | They be made glouelike, and for eche finger a stall' (1241–3). As well, she has prepared 'a coller of roughe kiddes heare, | Fast vnto the skinne around about thy necke to weare' (1245–6). Both the smell of Esau's clothing, which Rebecca also provides for Jacob, and the feel of the kids' hair helps convince Isaac that Jacob is Esau, even despite the sound of Jacob's voice: 'Let me feele thy hande, right Esau by the heare, | And yet the voice of Iacob sowneth in mine eare' (1301–2). Together, the tactile and olfactory properties of Jacob's costume overcome the doubts occasioned by the sound of Jacob's voice.

Rebecca designs Jacob's costume so that it addresses the blind Isaac's primary modes of perception, feeling and smell. Just as she directs that kid-goats perform as venison, she directs Jacob to perform as Esau, instructing him 'To play thy parte well, and sticke vnto it throughout' (1006). Gloved and sleeved with kid hide, draped with a collar of kid hide, adorned with Esau's clothing – Jacob's costume is an obvious counterfeit, appearing absurd to other characters, and perhaps also to the interlude's spectators. Complaining that the 'raiment liketh not me' (1261), Jacob notes that 'my chekes will blushe red, | To be sene among our folke thus apparailed' (1277–8). Visually, Jacob's costume fails to work in conventional theatrical terms. Deborra draws attention to its visual absurdity, commenting snidely on Jacob's appearance:

> Mary sir now is maister Iacob trimme in deede,
> That is all triksie and gallaunt so God me speede,
> Now I see apparell setteth out a man.
> Doth it become Esau so? Nay shrewe me then.   1255–8

Rebecca sends Deborra away, apparently annoyed by her nurse's sarcastic comment on the costume's visual failure. Yet Deborra's comment makes explicit the counterfeit quality of Jacob's costume, calling attention to Jacob's performance as performance and, by extension, to the preparations for the deception as the production of a theatrical entertainment.

Alongside the costuming of Jacob, the interlude foregrounds the multisensory nature of the meal and its preparation. Rebecca orders Jacob to fetch two kids for the meal and instructs her servant Abra to make a broth in which to stew the kid-meat. Advising Abra to prepare the aromatic broth, Rebecca itemises its ingredients: 'cloaues, mace, and sinamom | Peper and saffron, then set hearbes for the pot' (1080–1). Abra later displays the herbs she has collected from the garden, and, addressing the spectators directly, itemises those she will use to make broth and farcing (*stuffing*):

> Here is time and percelie, spinache, and rosemary.
> Endiue, suckorie, lacteux, violette, clary,
> Liuerworte, marigolde, sorell, hartes tong, and sage:
> Peniryal, purselane, buglosse and borage,
> With many very good herbes mo than I do name.   1156–60

Like Rebecca, she too boasts of the meal's deliciousness, claiming of her broth that 'God almighty selfe may wet his finger therein' (1155). The kids, too, are set on display, with Jacob and Mido bringing them to Rebecca, which contrasts with Ragau's later lugging of venison into the kitchen for preparation (1382 sd).

Aside from setting the meal's ingredients on visual display, the preparations also cause smells to permeate and noises to echo through Isaac's household. Fearing that the simmering broth's aroma will reveal her plan to her husband, Rebecca sets herself at ease by noting that Isaac will assume he smells advance preparations for Esau's venison: 'in case he smell what we haue thus farre begonne, | He may thinke it all for Esau to be done' (1095–6). Similarly, Jacob worries that the bleating kids will make Isaac suspicious, a fear that is confirmed when Mido later informs Jacob that his father's suspicions were indeed aroused when he heard the bleating (1216–25).

When Isaac consumes it, Rebecca's meal satisfies his taste, convincing him to deliver his blessing to the meal's server, who is Jacob disguised as Esau. Despite eating a dish prepared with kids rather than venison,

Isaac declares that the meal truly satisfied his tastes: 'I haue eate meate euen to my minde. | It hath refreshed my soule wonderfully well. | Nor neuer dranke I better wine that I can tell' (1327–9). Immediately prior to blessing Jacob (whom he believes to be Esau), Isaac reiterates the pleasure he took in consuming the counterfeit meal: 'It was the best meat and wine that euer I had' (1331). The satisfaction of Isaac's taste occasions his blessing, thus ironically undermining his maintenance of primogeniture even as he thinks he upholds it.

In order to emphasise the importance of taste to Rebecca's device, the interlude slightly revises the biblical source. While in both accounts the feel of Jacob's costume and the taste of the meal convince Isaac of Esau's identity, the biblical account identifies the costume's odour as the final factor that convinces Isaac that Jacob is Esau. However, while in *Jacob and Esau* Isaac comments favourably on Jacob's costume's smell, he does so only after his declaration that he will bless Jacob (1333–7). The interlude emphasises the counterfeit meal's satisfaction of Isaac's taste as the deciding factor in Jacob's usurpation of the blessing intended for Esau.

While the nature of the meal that Rebecca devises for Isaac advances the interlude's thematic treatment of counterfeiting, it also participates in a culinary tradition of counterfeit dishes. Such dishes were common enough that several medieval recipes offer instructions on how to prepare them. The *Noble boke off cookry*, for example, offers at least two counterfeit dishes, one 'To counterfet a kidde' with ground figs, pork, ginger, and cinnamon, and the other 'braun counterfet for lesshe'.[17] Other possible counterfeits include a brawn royale, made with fish rather than meat and so appropriate for fish days or Lent.[18] Later collections of recipes also included such counterfeit dishes, demonstrating the longevity of such culinary practices. A seventeenth-century manuscript containing recipes attributable to Henry VIII's reign includes instructions

---

17 *A Noble boke off cookry ffor a prynce houssolde or eny other estately houssholde: reprinted verbatim from a rare ms. in the Holkham collection edited by Mrs. Alexander Napier* (London: E. Stock, 1882) transcribed in *The Corpus of Middle English Prose and Verse* (electronic resource, University of Michigan: 2018); online at <http://name.umdl.umich.edu/CME00005> 37 and 4.

18 Constance B. Hieatt *An Ordinance of Pottage: An Edition of the Fifteenth Century Culinary Recipes in Yale University's Ms Beinecke 163* (London: Prospect Books, 1988) 67–8.

for making 'a counterfeit red Deare pye' with beef.[19] Another seventeenth-century manuscript includes recipes for several counterfeit meat dishes, including one for 'counterfeit venison'.[20]

Terence Scully calls such dishes 'games of pretend-foods', which required the cook to manage ingredients so that the resultant dish masquerades as another, more desirable dish.[21] The point of counterfeit dishes appears to have been two-fold. First, the counterfeit dishes were aimed at the satisfaction of the diner's taste for a particular dish when the usual ingredients were not available or permitted for consumption. Secondly, the counterfeit dishes demonstrated the craft – or subtlety – of the cook, whose skill was on display in the quality of the masquerading dish. As Karen Raber notes of the period's attitude to feasting,

> Food was used to create almost anything, from small objects to entire environments ... The feast was a 'game of deceit', with edible trenchers, cups and so on – but also featuring meats layered or fused within, around and on top of other meats, meats disguised as other creatures or as their own living selves.[22]

The 'braun counterfet for lesshe' from the coronation feast of Henry V, for example, was used 'withe the ribe ther in a gret swan for suttellte sitting upon a grene stok displaid with a skriptur in his bille'.[23] While the meals

---

19   Robert Wilson 'Cookery and Medicinal Recipes' LUNA: Folger Manuscript Transcriptions Collection MS V.a. 562, Recipe 330: <https://luna.folger.edu/luna/servlet/detail/FOLGER~3~3~15101~271257:Cookery-and-medicinal-recipes--manu>. This manuscript, dating to 1660–80, contains recipes attributed to the reign of Henry VIII.

20   Sara Mueller 'Early Modern Banquet Receipts and Women's Theatre' *Medieval and Renaissance Drama in England 24* (2011) 106–30, at 127 note 30.

21   Terence Scully *The Art of Cookery in the Late Middle Ages* (Woodbridge: Boydell Press, 1995) 104; see 103–5 for a discussion of the development of *subtleties* and *entremets* from counterfeit dishes. By the mid-fifteenth century these had become spectacular in nature (105). See also Christina Normore *A Feast for the Eyes: Art, Performance, and the Late Medieval Banquet* (University of Chicago Press, 2015) 21–43.

22   Karen Raber 'Animals at the Table: Performing Meat in Early Modern England and Europe' in *Performing Animals: History, Agency, Theater* edited by Karen Raber and Monica Mattfeld (University Park, PA: Penn State UP, 2017) 21.

23   *A Noble Boke off Cookry* 4.

in *Jacob and Esau* do not aspire to the elaborateness that Raber discusses, they are nevertheless examples of food-disguisings.

The words used for such food confections, in particular the common term *subteltie/soteltie*, have a further resonance in the interlude. Esau's reference to Rebecca's plan as a 'subtill fetche' (1499) echoes the marginal gloss in the Geneva Bible that criticises Rebecca's plan to deceive Isaac with goat meat: 'This subtiltie is blameworthie because she shulde haue taried til God had performed his promes'.[24] The term 'subtiltie' works ambiguously here. It refers broadly to Rebecca's scheme to deceive Isaac in order that Jacob can receive his father's blessing in place of Esau, working as a synonym for Jacob's characterisation of Rebecca's plan in the interlude as a 'device' (1028). Yet the gloss specifically comments on Genesis 27: 9, which describes Rebecca's substitution of kid-goat for venison in the meal she will make for her husband: 'Get thee now to the flocke, & bring me thence two good kyds of the goates, that I maie make pleasant meat of them for thy father, such as he loueth'. This suggests a tacit implication that her 'subtiltie' lies also in her culinary ability. The skill required to concoct 'subtyll dyshes' was warned against by John Hales in his 1543 translation of Plutarch's *De tuenda sanitate praecepta*. Advising readers to consume simple foods, Hales contrasts 'commen fare' with:

> the cunning of those that bee deuysers and dressers of dyuersytee of meates, their subtyll dyshes, their swete sauces always dooe sette forwarde, and encreases the lymytes of appetyte and corrupte the vertue and holsomnesse of the meate.[25]

George Cavendish notes of one banquet laid before Henry VIII that it was comprised of 'wonderouse costly meates & devycys subtilly devysed'.[26] Of a feast Cardinal Wolsey held for French diplomats, Cavendish notes that

---

24 The Geneva Bible, Genesis 27: 9 gloss.

25 Plutarch *The Precepts of the Excellent Clerke [and] Graue Philosopher Plutarche for the Preseruation of Good Healthe* translated by John Hales (London: Richard Grafton, 1543) B5v.

26 George Cavendish *The Life and Death of Cardinal Wolsey* edited Richard S. Sylvester *EETS OS 243* (1959) 28.

> There ware, beastes, byrdes, fowles of dyuers kyndes And personages most lyvely made & counterfet in dysshes ... Among all oon I noted/ there was a Chesse bord subtilly made of spiced plate/ w*ith* men to the same.[27]

As Cavendish's comment indicates, *subtlety* connotes yet another sense of 'subtiltie', the edible figures or scenes that served as allegorical images at feasts. While Rebecca's proposed meal is not made from sugar, as sotelties often were, it nevertheless works figuratively, as sotelties did.[28] Whereas sotelties represented figures or scenes from sugar or other edible materials, Rebecca counterfeits venison with goat-kids, a form of soteltie that unduly hastens the fulfillment of God's promise. Rebecca's counterfeit dish elicits Isaac's blessing of Jacob, transforming a private meal to a political event, as Isaac declares Jacob's inheritance of his father's household.

Device, counterfeit, subtilte, soteltie: these terms indicate the deceptive yet productive quality of Rebecca's entertainment. Her 'subtletie' is troublesome, at once an act of theatrical deception and a bringer-about of God's will, at once counterfeit and a revelation of the truth of Jacob's divine election. The interlude stages both the duplicitousness of theatrical playing and its revelatory capacity. The counterfeit meal – an alimentary address – achieves its political aim (Jacob's inheritance) by eliciting Isaac's aesthetic response to the meal he consumes. By satisfying Isaac's 'tooth', thereby managing his appetite, Rebecca and Jacob win Isaac's blessing of Jacob, fulfilling God's promise. The category of counterfeiting is thus extended to cover both Jacob's playing of his brother and the preparation, service, and consumption of the meal: it includes both mimetic and edible performances.

Beastly hunger

The interlude grounds Jacob's election in his satisfaction, albeit through counterfeit means, of Isaac's taste for venison. In the same vein, it

---

27 Cavendish *Wolsey* 70–1.
28 See Robert Epstein 'Eating Their Words: Food and Text in the Coronation Banquet of Henry VI' *Journal of Medieval and Early Modern Studies 36: 2* (2006) 355–77; Claire Sponsler 'Edible Theater' in *The Queen's Dumbshows: John Lydgate and the Making of Early Theater* (Philadelphia: University of Pennsylvania Press, 2014) 147–66.

grounds Esau's reprobation in his unmannerly consumption of pottage, a consumption that satisfies the elder son's ravenous hunger. Whereas Rebecca devises an entertainment that addresses Isaac's taste, Jacob prepares a mess of pottage that addresses Esau's hunger. And while the interlude depicts Rebecca's device as the staging of a multi-sensory household entertainment, it also characterises Jacob's selling of the pottage meal as theatrical, staging it as an action subject to improvised re-enactment, with Esau's unmannerly consumption of the pottage counterfeited several times by other characters. This mimicry becomes a form of licensed household entertainment that subjects Esau to ridicule and undermines his authority in the household; in doing so, it takes Jacob's part in his usurpation of Esau's birthright.

In the second Act, having hunted unsuccessfully, Esau and Ragau return home hungry. Esau's hunger causes him to be excessively weary; the stage direction indicates that he *Commeth in so faint that he can scarce go* (495 sd). His hunger also makes his appetite both indiscriminate and grotesque. He complains that he will eat anything, including a raw cat or even the shoulder of one of his hunting dogs (501–4, 506). He claims to be so hungry that 'my teeth I can scarcely charme, | From gnawyng away the braune of my very arme' (508–9), and he later threatens to eat his servant, Ragau (521).

Jacob's pottage addresses Esau's intense hunger, and Esau purchases that pottage with his birthright. Within the interlude, his inability to restrain himself against his own hunger marks him as reprobate. Remarking that Esau's exchange of his birthright for 'a mease of pottage' is 'bothe unthriftinesse and dotage' (633–4), Ragau explains that the exchange was predetermined according to God's knowledge of Jacob's goodness: 'God this thyng hath wrought, | For Iacob is as good as Esau is nought' (637–8). Rebecca too sees the exchange as a sign of both Jacob's election and Esau's reprobation:

> Now dout not Iacob, but God hath appointed thee
> As the eldest sonne vnto Isaac to bee:
> And now haue no dout, but thou art sure elected,
> And that unthrift Esau of God reiected.   889–92

Esau's unrestrained hunger also marks him as an object of ridicule by Mido and Ragau, both of whom also wish to eat but are forestalled by Esau's ravenous consumption of all the pottage. Mido mocks Esau by likening his rude eating to animals' consumption. He laughingly informs Ragau that Esau has eaten all the pottage:

> Since I was borne, I neuer see any man
> So greedily eate rice out of a potte or pan.
> He woulde not haue a dishe, but take the pot and sup,
> Ye neuer saw hungry dogge so slabbe[29] potage vp.   644–7

In their improvised re-enactment of his unmannerly eating, Ragau and Mido mock Esau as a daw (657), with Mido explicitly likening Esau's ravenous consumption to the corvid: 'styll cogeld in lik Jacke daw that cries ka kob' (670). In his second re-enactment, Mido later returns to his mimicry, complaining that Esau ate both Mido's and his cat's share:

> Thus he licked, and thus he licked, and this way.
> I thought to haue lickt the potte my selfe once to day.
> But Esau beguilde me, I shrewe him for that,
> And left not so muche as a licke for pusse our catte.   857–60

In his mockery, Mido points out that Esau's ravenousness deprives even the lowliest members of the household of food.[30]

Jacob responds to Esau's hunger with alimentary addresses. Just as he directly addresses Isaac's 'tooth' with Rebecca's counterfeit stew, he directly addresses Esau's hunger with pottage. Jacob's satisfaction of Esau's hunger both wins his brother's birthright for himself and also reveals Esau's reprobation alongside Jacob's election. Both of Jacob's alimentary addresses might be seen as tests of individual will: of Esau's restraint of his hunger and of Isaac's discernment. That both fail these tests confirms Jacob's election.

While Jacob's alimentary addresses aim at Esau and Isaac, they also address others. Mido assists in the preparations for Rebecca's counterfeit stew, but is himself addressed by them: he hopes he will have 'some parte' of the feast (1058). Similarly, Jacob's rice pottage addresses not only the hungry Esau but the equally hungry Ragau. Ragau's hunger, however, is a

---

29 *Iacob and Esau* edited White has *stabbe*, but the original 1568 text reads *slabbe*. See *OED* sv *slab* v.2a 'transitive with *up*: To eat or drink in a hasty or untidy manner'.

30 Goodblatt, discussing animal imagery in the interlude, notes that in Genesis 25 'Esau's use of the term *hal' iteni* possesses the connotation of stuffing cattle with food': Chanita Goodblatt *Jewish and Christian Voices in English Reformation Biblical Drama: Enacting Family and Monarch* (London: Routledge, 2017) 109–14, at 110.

product of Esau's management of his servant's provisions. Esau absolves himself of his duty to feed him, insisting that Ragau's hunger results from his own moral defectiveness. Contrary to the interlude's action but in keeping with conventional complaints against hungry servants, Esau claims that Ragau 'doth none other good but eate and drink and slepe … And that maketh thee so slouthfull and so lyther' (763–5). Wondering whether he must 'prouide meate for euery glutton knave' (772), Esau chides Ragau that he must 'deserue thy dinner before thou do it craue' (774), later complaining, 'Haue I nothing to do but provide meate for you?' (783). When Ragau notes that Esau 'might haue geuen me som part [*of the pottage*] when ye had ynough' (784), Esau, noting the pottage's restorative effect on himself, scornfully asks, 'Is that meate for you? nay it would make you to ranke. | Nay soft brother mine, I must kepe you more lanke' (787–8). For Esau, food provision – or its lack – serves as a mechanism that maintains a hierarchical distinction between himself and his servant, in this case marked by a hierarchy of physical strength.

Keeping Ragau hungry keeps him 'lank' and thus manageable. The interlude characterises his hunger, like Esau's, as animal-like. Yet, whereas the beastliness of Esau's hunger derives from his unmannerly consumption, Ragau's derives from the low-quality food, usually consumed by animals, that his hunger has made him eat. For instance, on setting out on the hunt, Ragau complains that Esau 'hath no care' to provide him with food, leaving him to forage 'Acornes or Bearies from the Tree' (60). On returning from the hunt, Ragau exclaims:

> I haue hearde it ofte, but nowe I feele a wonder,
> In what grieuous paine they die, that die for hunger.
> Oh my greedie stomacke howe it doth bite and gnawe?
> If I were at a racke, I could eate hey or strawe. 472–5

Ragau's hunger makes him crave animal fodder, and he notes later, 'Woulde God I had a piece of some horsebread here' (477).[31] Ragau's willingness to consume vegetation and animal fodder likens him to a domesticated animal.

In this vein, Esau's management of Ragau's hunger parallels that of his hunting dogs. As they prepare to hunt, Esau accuses Ragau of having fed his dogs too much: 'I shrewe your cheekes, they haue had too much meat'

---

31 For *horsebread*, see William Rubel 'English Horse-Bread, 1590–1800' *Gastronomica* 6: 3 (2006) 40–51.

(101). Whereas Esau understands his dogs' hunger as productive (they will hunt all the better when hungry), Ragau replies that he does not blame the dogs for eating what they could get; for his part, he provides them a 'small releuauit of that that ye giue me', which was not enough to satisfy the dogs' hunger as he himself 'had not a good meales meat this weeke' (104–6). By keeping them hungry, Esau manages both Ragau and his hunting dogs in the same way.

The hunting-dog scene establishes a motif for the interlude's treatment of Esau's relationship to hunger, which is to treat it as a mechanism enforcing distinction and obedience. Notably, the dog whose behaviour occasions Esau's rebuke of Ragau is named Takepart. While addressing Takepart, Esau decides that the dogs' response to his calls are not satisfactory: 'come Takepart, here, how say you child | Wilt not thou do thy part? yes, else I am beguilde. | But I shrewe your cheekes, they haue had too much meat' (99–101). In this moment, the interlude foregrounds the multivalent term *part*, a term central to its treatment of hunger management. In this particular case, several of *part*'s valences come into focus. Esau demands that the dog live up to its name – Takepart – and perform its role – do its part – in the coming hunt. As well, Takepart and his fellow dogs have eaten too much, Ragau usually sharing a part (*releuauit*) of his food with them. Later, the interlude echoes these motifs in Ragau's concern that he receive 'som part' of the pottage; in Isaac's description of God as provider, taking 'all thing in good parte at Gods hande' (317); in Ragau's denial of Esau having 'any parte' of the stolen vitailes (988); in Mido's hope that he will have 'some parte' in the feast (1058); in Esau's belated offering to Isaac of 'part of my hunting' (1428), and his invitation to Isaac to 'Come eate your part' (1449). Importantly, *part* also connects the theme of hunger-management with counterfeiting – Rebecca instructs that Jacob 'play thy parte' in her entertainment. Importantly, Rebecca's and Jacob's more generous management of others' hunger wins over the household: Mido claims 'all good folkes are glad Iacobs parte to take. | And now by Esau no man wyll sette a pinne' (1408–9). Takepart returns here in a different guise: adequately fed with a part of the feast, the household favours Jacob over Esau.

Lenten taste

Jacob's desire to acquire Esau's birthright leads to another alimentary address as he offers his brother a 'mease of pottage' in a seriously unequal exchange. This too, addresses a primary audience (Esau), with its address widening to include the hungry Ragau. But Jacob's pottage also has strikingly local reference to the English audience of the interlude.

The Hebrew scriptures indicate that Jacob's meal was a red lentil pottage or stew.[32] Yet all sixteenth-century English biblical translations, save for the 1560 Geneva Bible, state that Jacob serves Esau a red rice pottage. The 1535 Coverdale translation describes the meal as both a 'meace of meate' and a 'meace of ryse' while the 1539 translation printed by Richard Taverner describes the meal as a 'potage of red ryse'.[33] Moreover, the same Hebrew word for lentils appears in three other passages: 2 Samuel 17: 28 and 23: 11 as well as Ezekiel 4: 9.[34] The early sixteenth-century translations – Coverdale's (1535), Matthew's Bible (1537), and the Great Bible (1539) – also render these occurrences as *ryse* (although the Coverdale has 'small corne' in 2 Samuel 23: 11).

The rendering of Jacob's lentil pottage as a rice pottage is unique to English translations. The Vulgate translates the meal as *lentis edulio* and early sixteenth-century continental translations of the Bible indicate that Jacob made a lentil pottage: a 1535 French translation of the passage gives *le potage de lentille*[35] and Luther's translation has *linsen gericht*.[36] In his lectures on Genesis, Luther even speculates on the pottage's preparation, indicating his familiarity with lentil consumption: 'But lentils are not red; they are yellow. Therefore I think that they were prepared with saffron or another condiment in order to stimulate the appetite'.[37] The translation of *lentil* to *rice* appears to have been a particularly English solution to a

---

32 James Strong *The New Strong's Expanded Exhaustive Concordance of the Bible* (Nashville: Thomas Nelson, 2010) 506 sv *lentiles* and 1316 note 5742; online at <http://archive.org/details/newstrongsexpand0000stro_v2a3>.

33 Genesis 25: 34. The Coverdale Bible: *Biblia the Byble, That Is, the Holy Scrypture of the Olde and New Testament, Faithfully Translated in to Englyshe* (London: J. Nycolson, 1535) fol. xi recto; the Great Bible fol. x recto.

34 Strong *Concordance* 205, 506.

35 *La Bible Qui est toute la Saincte escripture. En laquelle sont contenus, le Vieil Testament et le Nouveau ...* (Neufchastel: Pierre de Wingle, 1535) fol. 7v.

36 *William Tyndale's Five Books of Moses, Called the Pentateuch: Being a Verbatim Reprint of the Edition of M.CCCCC.XXX. : Compared with Tyndale's Genesis of 1534, and the Pentateuch in the Vulgate, Luther, and Matthew's Bible: With Various Collations and Prolegomena* edited by Jacob Isidor Mombert (New York: Randolph, 1884) 77 note 34.

37 Martin Luther *Luther's Works Vol. 4, Lectures on Genesis Chapters 21–25* edited by Jaroslav Pelikan and Walter A. Hansen (St. Louis: Concordia, 1964) 408.

particularly English problem, namely English unfamiliarity with lentils as a food for human consumption.

The early sixteenth-century biblical translation of Jacob's lentil pottage as 'rice pottage' suggests not only English unfamiliarity with the regular consumption of lentils but a familiarity with the consumption of rice pottage, with the English translators probably sacrificing accuracy for comprehension. English unfamiliarity with lentils and preference for rice is reflected in the several sixteenth-century printings of John of Garland's *Equivoca*, which may have influenced the early sixteenth-century biblical translators. Sometimes described as a book of homonyms, Garland's *Equivoca* also includes fifteenth-century English glosses made by Galfridus Grammaticus.[38] Noting the homonymic relationship between *lens* and *lentis*, the *Equivoca* explains that *lens: est quoddam legumen maxime in tempore quadragesimali vsitatum* (*anglice* ryce potage) ('is a kind of pulse especially used in the time of Lent, in English "ryce potage"').[39] The *Equivoca* thus identifies lentils as a food consumed most often during Lent, and the accompanying gloss indicates the English equivalent to be 'ryce potage'. It is just possible that the gloss *ryce* refers not to the grain *oryza sativa* but to the stalks of bean and pea plants.[40] However, Thomas Elyot confirms an English association of rice pottage with Lent, noting that the 'grayne callyd Ryce ... is moste commonly eaten in Lent, with almond mylke'.[41] In addition to associating rice pottage with Lent, an association discussed in further detail below, the *Equivoca*'s gloss indicates an English culinary tradition that commonly uses rice to replace lentils in Lenten pottage.

Lentils appear to have been uncommon if not unfamiliar English fare through the first half of the sixteenth century. Translators seem uncertain how to refer to them. In his 1543 translation of Plutarch's *De tuenda sanitate praecepta*, John Hales translates references to lentils as

---

38   R. Hugh Schram Jr. 'John of Garland and Erasmus on the Principle of Synonymy' *The University of Texas Studies in English 30* (1951) 24–39, at 25, 28; David J. Shaw 'An Unrecorded STC Item: Johannes de Garlandia's *Multorum Vocabulorum Equivocorum Interpretatio* Paris, 1502' *The Library 5* #4 (2004) 359–69, at 365.
39   John of Garland *Multorum vocabulorum equiuocorum interpretatio* (London, Wynand de Worde, 1517) sig. FF1r sv *Lens*.
40   *OED Online* sv *Rice* n.1.
41   Thomas Elyot *Bibliotheca Eliotæ Eliotis librarie* (London: Thomas Berthelet, 1542) sig. Aa3r sv *Oriza*.

'litle meate' and 'common fare'.[42] Thomas Elyot also seems uncertain as to how to translate *lens* into English. In 1538 he identified *lens* as a vetch, defining lentils as 'a kynde of poulse called fatches'.[43] Four years later, he revised his definition of *lens* to 'a kynde of pulse callyd lyntelles'.[44]

While they gradually became more familiar later in the century, lentils were thought of primarily as weeds or as animal fodder, understood, as Elyot noted, as a kind of vetch or tare. Tares, a form of vetch – or, in Elyot's term, *fatche* – were known to John Fitzherbert as the 'worst wede' that could nevertheless be harvested and dried for fodder.[45] In his 1548 *Names of herbes*, William Turner claims that 'Lentilles are sowen in corne fieldes and growe as Tares do' (sig. D8v); however, neither John Fitzherbert nor Thomas Tusser mention lentils at all in their guides to husbandry.[46] *Lentil* appears several times throughout Barnabe Googe's 1577 *Four bookes of Husbandry*, a translation of Konrad Heresbach's 1570 *Rei rusticae quator libri*. However, in a section that gives Latin, Greek, Italian, Spanish, French, and Dutch terms for *lens*, no English term is offered.[47] Nevertheless, along with others, the text likens lentils to the tare, describing them as

> a Pulse very thicke and busshy, with leaues lyke the Tare, with three or foure very small Graynes in euery Codde, of all Pulses the least, they are soft and flatte ... It is sowen with vs in Germanie in March and in April ... it flowreth in Iuly.　　　(sig. E2v)

By the late sixteenth century English writers increasingly differentiated lentils from other pulses, and, as they did, lentils were

---

42　Plutarch *The Precepts* translated Hales sig. B5r.
43　Thomas Elyot *The Dictionary of Syr Thomas Eliot Knyght* (London: Thomas Berthelet, 1538) sig. M2r sv *lens*.
44　Elyot *Bibliotheca Eliotæ* sig. V1r sv *lens*.
45　John Fitzherbert *Here Begynneth a Newe Tracte or Treatyse Moost Profytable for All Husbandmen and Very Frutefull for All Other Persons to Rede* (London: Richard Pynson, 1523) sig. C2r.
46　William Turner *The Names of Herbes in Greke, Latin, Englishe, Duche [and] Frenche with the Commune Names That Herbaries and Apotecaries vse* (London: John Day and Wyllyam Seres: 1548) sig. D8v.
47　Barnabe Googe *Foure Bookes of Husbandry, Collected by M. Conradus Heresbachius* translated and expanded by Barnabe Googe (London: Richard Watkins, 1577) sig. E2v.

identified primarily as animal fodder. William Harrison called such food 'horssecorne', which included 'beanes, peason, otes, tares, and lintels'.[48] Harrison noted that, when corn prices were high, 'the artificer and the poore laboring man' were driven to eat horse corn, proving the proverb that 'hunger setteth his first foot into the horsse manger' (153). Hugh Plat also saw lentils as a remedy to famine. In his 1596 *Sundrie New and Artificial Remedies against Famine*, Plat advised that bread could be made from 'All maner of pulse, as Lentils, vetches, beanes, & such like, if they be first rubbed ouer in Lee, & then hulled and after ground, they will yeelde both fayrer meale, and better bread'.[49] He noted, too, that 'drink may also bee made of Lentils' (sig. D3r). By 1578, Thomas Tymme's translation of Calvin's commentary on Genesis describes the meal as a 'pottage of Lentils', as does John Fielde's 1579 translation of Calvin's sermons on Jacob and Esau.[50] In Henry Lok's 'Sonnet 97' (printed in 1593), the speaker addresses God, repenting that he 'sell the patrimony to ensue ... And change for lentil pottage birthright due'.[51]

The 1560 Geneva Bible perhaps reflects this increasing English familiarity with lentils as it translates Jacob's meal as a 'pottage of lentiles'; it also uses *lentil* in the three other passages in which the Hebrew term for *lentil* appears in the source. However, the 1568 Bishop's Bible reverts to 'pottage of ryse' for its description of Jacob's meal even as it uses *lentil* in the three other relevant passages. The Bishop's Bible's return to rice pottage may indicate the translators' attempt to retain the pottage story's pertinence for an English audience. Even later, the 1609 Douai Rheims translation describes the meal as 'rice broth'.

Curiously, then, throughout much of the sixteenth century in England Esau ate a different sort of pottage than he did on the Continent: rice pottage in England, lentil pottage elsewhere. The history of Jacob's

48 William Harrison *Harrison's Description of England in Shakspere's Youth: Being the Second and Third Books of His Description of Britaine and England* edited by Frederick J. Furnivall (London: Trubner for New Shakspere Society, 1877) 153. For further discussion see Rubel 'English Horse-Bread'.
49 Hugh Plat *Sundrie Nevv and Artificiall Remedies against Famine* (London: Peter Short, 1596) sig. D1v.
50 Jean Calvin *Thirteene sermons of Maister Iohn Caluine, entreating of the free election of God in Iacob, and of reprobation in Esau* translated by John Fielde (London: [Thomas Dawson] for Thomas Man and Tobie Cooke, 1579) sig. H4v.
51 Henry Lok *Sundry Christian Passions Contained in Two Hundred Sonnets Diuided into Two Equall Parts* (London: Richard Field, 1593) sig. D1v.

pottage in the sixteenth-century English translations of the Bible and consequently in *Jacob and Esau* indicate that rice pottage addressed English audiences' familiarity with, if not taste for, the dish. In contrast with lentils, rice seems to have been a familiar comestible in England, despite it being an expensive import. Several fifteenth-century recipes for rice pottage attest to its consumption. The pottage usually required that almond milk be used, although at least one recipe indicates that cow's milk could serve as a substitute; another recipe indicates that sandalwood could be added to make the pottage red.[52] While sixteenth-century recipes for rice pottage are rare, this may be due to the simplicity and familiarity of its cooking.[53]

Rice was regularly imported to England throughout most of the fifteenth century and into the sixteenth.[54] Through the late sixteenth and seventeenth centuries, rice was purchased frequently, though not regularly, until the mid-seventeenth century.[55] However, purchases of rice appear less frequently through the first half of the sixteenth century and decrease in frequency from the records Rogers consulted from the mid-1550s to the 1570s.[56]

Rice pottage appears to have been consumed as a seasonal dish, perhaps associated, as Rogers suggests, with Christmas or, as Galfridus and Elyot indicate more clearly, with Lent. Categorised as a spice, rice was 'purchased as spices are for occasional feasts'.[57] Indeed, rice was frequently imported along with other more expensive comestibles and spices, such as almonds, cinnamon, or cumin. Although it was not

---

52 *Two Fifteenth-Century Cookery-Books* edited by Thomas Austin *EETS OS 91* (1888) 22, 114, 33.

53 However, see Thomas Paynell's instructions for cooking 'ryce or peasen' pottage in Joannes de Mediolano *Regimen sanitatis Salerni* translated Thomas Paynell (London: Thomas Berthelet, 1528) sigs P2r–v.

54 James Edwin Thorold Rogers *A History of Agriculture and Prices in England* 7 vols (Oxford: Clarendon Press, 1866–1902) *3* (1882) 523-33, *4* (1882) 673; *The Oxford Encyclopedia of Economic History* edited Joel Mokyr, 5 vols (Oxford UP, 2003) *5* 385; Aldo Ferrero and Francesca Vidotto 'History of Rice in Europe' in *Rice: Origin, Antiquity and History* ed. S.D. Sharma (Boca Raton: CRC Press, 2010) 341–72, at 343.

55 Rogers *History of Agriculture and Prices* 5 (1887) 460-1.

56 Rogers *History of Agriculture and Prices* 3 533-43.

57 Rogers *History of Agriculture and Prices* 5 460; see also *The regulations and establishment of the household of Henry Algernon Percy, the fifth Earl of Northumberland* edited Thomas Percy and others (London: Brown, 1905) 19, 343.

cheap, rice was perhaps the least expensive of the spice goods imported to England.

Noting that rice was typically purchased at Christmas, Rogers speculates that it 'may therefore have been used for some special dish, regularly supplied at that season [i.e. Christmas], as a custom or fashion'.[58] The seasonality of rice purchase may also be discerned in the accounts of Andrew Halyburton, a Scottish trader working in Antwerp. Although he occasionally made some rice purchases in May, July, October, and November, Halyburton usually purchased and shipped rice in December.[59]

The Lenten consumption of rice pottage is complemented by the traditional English Use's liturgical association of the Jacob and Esau story with Lent. The Hereford, York, and Sarum Uses all set Genesis 27, covering Rebecca and Jacob's deception of Isaac, as the lesson on the second Sunday of Lent. The Sarum Breviary stipulated that Genesis 27: 1–19 was to be read on that day, and the remainder of the chapter read the two following days.[60] The Sarum and York Missals indicate that Genesis 27: 6–39 was to be read on the Saturday before the Third Sunday of Lent; the Gospel to be read alongside is Luke 15: 11–32, the parable of

---

58   See Rogers *History of Agriculture and Prices 5* 461, who also notes, 'Generally, rice was purchased at Christmas only ... The fact that the price was ordinarily uniform suggests that the dealer knew and anticipated an occasional demand for it'.

59   Andrew Halyburton *Ledger of Andrew Halyburton, conservator of the privileges of the Scotch nation in the Netherlands, 1492–1503* edited Cosmo Innes (Edinburgh: Her Majesty's General Register, 1867) *passim*: see Index entry sv *Rice*. However, in 1505/6, rice imports were made in late spring and early summer: see *London Customs Accounts. 21 Henry VII (1505/06)* edited Stuart Jenks *Quellen und Darstellungen zur hansischen Geschichte* Neue Folge, Bd. 74, Part 4, Nr. 6 (Köln etc.: Hansischer Geschichtsverein, 2018) 94, 101, 105, 109, 110, 125.

60   *Dominica ij. quadragesime. Ebdomada ij. quadragesime* edited William Renwick in *The Sarum Rite: Breviarium Sarisburiense cum nota* (Hamilton ONT: Gregorian Institute of Canada, 2009) Tome *B* Fasciculus *24* 923–64; online at <https://hmcwordpress.humanities.mcmaster.ca/renwick/breviary/latin-breviary/temporale/> 929–32, 951–4; Sharon Frances Parrott 'Liturgical Sources of Old English and Middle English Epic Poems on Genesis and Exodus' (MA dissertation, University of Iowa, 1921) 79, online at <https://doi.org/10.17077/etd.rtnvgxvn>; also see John Mirk *Mirk's Festial: A Collection of Homilies* edited Theodor Erbe *EETS ES 96* (1905) 92–6, who indicates that Jacob's story 'ys red and songen of yn holy chyrche all þys weke' (93).

the Prodigal Son.⁶¹ Although Jacob's selling of pottage to Esau, recounted in Genesis 25: 26–34, was not part of the Sarum lectionary, the *Legenda Aurea* includes the narrative as a preface to its recounting of Genesis 27, 'the legende as it is redd in the chirche'.⁶² For its part, the Hereford Breviary, printed in 1505 at Rouen, indicates that the beginning of Genesis 25 is to be read on the second Sunday of Lent and completed in the following week, along with Genesis 26; Genesis 27 is to be read Friday to Sunday, the third Sunday of Lent.⁶³

This association of the Genesis 25 and 27 stories with Lent was disrupted by the liturgical changes occasioned by the 1549 and 1552 Books of Common Prayer. Although the 1559 Book of Common Prayer restored Genesis 27 as a Proper Lesson for matins on the second Sunday of Lent, the two earlier Books of Common Prayer omitted Lent from their lists of Proper Lessons for required readings and lessons. Moreover, the 1549 and 1552 Books of Common Prayer required the public reading of Genesis alongside the Gospel of Matthew and Romans throughout much of January. Of particular note, Genesis 25 and 27 were to be read aloud at evening prayer on 14 and 15 January respectively. Effectively, the Books of Common Prayer gave the two chapters of Genesis on which *Jacob and Esau* is based new temporal significance, shifting the story's association with Lent to mid-January.

Although weakening the story's relationship with Lent, the 1549 and 1552 Books of Common Prayer juxtaposed the story with Romans, the entirety of which was also read aloud at Evening Prayer through the first two-thirds of January. Significantly, Romans 11 was to be read at evensong on 13 January, the evening before Genesis 25. Romans 11: 33, which focuses on the unsearchability of God's judgements and was often cited to dispel anxieties about the Jacob and Esau story, is paraphrased in the interlude several times.⁶⁴ In addition, Romans 8 and 9, parts of which including the verses on predestination 'Iacob haue I loued, but

---

61 Pamela M. King *The York Mystery Cycle and the Worship of the City* (Cambridge: D.S. Brewer, 2006) 86.

62 Jacobus de Voragine *Legenda aurea sanctorum* translated William Caxton (London: William Caxton, 1483) fol. xliv verso.

63 *The Hereford Breviary* edited Walter Howard Frere and Langton E.G. Brown, 3 vols (London: Henry Bradshaw Society, 1904–15) *1* 268–73; online at <http://archive.org/details/herefordbreviar00diogoog>.

64 Thomas 'Jacob and Esau' 205.

Esau haue I hated' are paraphrased in the Prologue and Epilogue, were to be read on 10 and 11 January, shortly before the reading of Genesis 25 and 27 on 14 and 15 January.

Given that *Jacob and Esau* was probably written between 1547 and 1557, and that most commentators assign the composition date to Edward VI's reign, the 1549 and 1552 Books of Common Prayer provide valuable context for the interlude. At the very least, from 1549 onward, English audiences would have become familiar with Jacob's rice pottage, hearing the Great Bible's translation of Genesis 25 read aloud at Evensong.

Rice pottage marks the interlude's address of a particularly English audience, and the food works as an index to the sort of pottage English audiences commonly ate at this time of year. In this respect, the interlude (like the English Bibles) addresses itself to its contemporary audience in a manner similar to the Towneley *First Shepherds' Play*'s reference to 'the good ayll of Hely' or the provenance of the Chester Shepherds' food.[65] While those examples more overtly revel in their anachronistic and geographic counterfeitings of biblical food, *Jacob and Esau*'s rice pottage reflects a quieter anachronism, one silently imported from English culinary tradition, early sixteenth-century English biblical translations, and the 1549 and 1552 Books of Common Prayer's innovative liturgical requirement that the interlude's biblical sources be read aloud in mid-January Evensong services.

While the biblical source indicates that Rebecca's counterfeit stew is made from kids, kid-meat also gestures to a Christmas–Lent setting. Noting that 'Kyd is euer good', the 1545 *A Propre new booke of cokery* specified that 'Lambe and young kidde is best betwene Christmas and Lent, and good from Easter to whitsontide'.[66] While the kids used in Rebecca's counterfeit kid stew would have been thought to be 'euer good' throughout the year, the interlude's kids, along with its rice pottage, address an English audience's sense of seasonality, setting the interlude's action, if not its performance, in the season between Christmas and Lent.

---

65 'The First Shepherds' Play' in *The Towneley Plays* edited Martin Stevens and A.C. Cawley, 2 vols *EETS SS 13–14* (1994) line 352; 'The Paynters Playe' in *The Chester Mystery Cycle* edited R.M. Lumiansky and D. Mills 2 vols *EETS SS 3* and *9* (1974–86) lines 113–20.

66 *A Propre new booke of cokery declaryng what maner of meates bee best in ceason for all tymes of ye yere* (London: Richard Lant and Richarde Bankes, 1545) A2r; online at <http://www.proquest.com/eebo/docview/2240940956/citation/B46E59D6B1C4854PQ/14>.

Robert Hornback has pointed to the increased activity during the 1551–2 Christmas–Shrovetide season at Edward's court; yet he speculates that the interlude 'likely appear[ed] ... in the fall of 1552 in response' to a controversy over predestination involving Bartholomew Traheron and John Hooper.[67] Yet given its plot's association with Christmas and Lent, *Jacob and Esau* may well have been appropriate entertainment at Edward VI's court during the Christmas to Shrovetide season, following the introduction of the Book of Common Prayer at Whitsun in 1549.

Spectators' appetites, tastes, and hunger

Throughout this essay, I have focused on the alimentary addresses that appear in *Jacob and Esau*: that is, those addresses made by one character to another and that refer to or use food as a means of persuasion. The interlude's alimentary addresses include those that display food's preparation, service, and consumption; those that describe food's taste, odour, and appearance; and those that describe food's satisfaction of characters' hunger or appetite; as well as the inverse – the withholding of food in order to produce a hunger that provokes obedience. I have argued that these addresses draw on and perform techniques for the management of household alimentary resources and, more significantly, for the maintenance of the household authority. Isaac's household hierarchy is grounded in the patriarch's taste for venison, an appetitive desire that justifies both his love for Esau as well as his defence of the law of primogeniture.

Extending beyond Isaac's household, some of *Jacob and Esau*'s alimentary addresses take the form of direct address to the interlude's implied spectators. For instance, Abra's display and itemisation of herbs for the broth directly addresses the interlude's implied audience, as do Ragau's complaints of hunger and, later, his display of the bag of *vitailes* he has stolen, the contents of which he plans to withhold from Esau. Albeit less directly, Jacob's service of rice pottage also addresses an implied audience, one that is familiar with the seasonality of early sixteenth-century English rice pottage consumption.

The interlude presents Rebecca organising, directing, and producing a multi-sensory entertainment for Isaac as she stages the preparation of a counterfeit stew, an extended action that includes sounds of

---

67 Hornback 'The *Jacob and Esau* Paradigm' 69.

kids' bleating and reference to the aroma of broth simmering. Her preparations for this performance, which include the organisation of Jacob's costume as well as the provision of stage food, parallel what we know of the preparations for interludes as well as for parish *ludi* and for civic biblical drama.[68] In staging Rebecca's interlude-within-an-interlude, *Jacob and Esau* also addresses its implied spectators, offering a reflection not only on the requirements of its own counterfeiting but also on the interlude's alimentary address to – and management of – its implied spectators' varied tastes, appetites, and hunger.

Given the lack of evidence for *Jacob and Esau*'s performance, let alone contemporary descriptions of the features of that performance, it is impossible to confirm the extent to which a mid-sixteenth-century production of *Jacob and Esau* might have supplemented its alimentary addresses with consumable food or even with the aroma of simmering broth. However, the interlude is generally thought likely to have been performed within a household space such as a Great Hall – associated primarily with the sort of tasks, including both meal provision and the staging of entertainments, that Rebecca manages.[69] *Jacob and Esau*'s staging of Isaac's household and the activities performed in it would then

68 See Michelle Ephraim 'Jewish matriarchs and the staging of Elizabeth I in *The History of Jacob and Esau*' *Studies in English Literature 1500–1900* 43 (2003) 301–21, at 306; in 1538 Lady Lisle was involved in acquiring players' garments as well as the text for an interlude called 'Rex Diabole': see Muriel St. Clare Byrne *The Lisle Letters* (University of Chicago Press, 1981) 237–8; Suzanne Westfall '"A Commonty a Christmas Gambold or a Tumbling Trick": Household Theater' in *A New History of Early English Drama* edited John D. Cox and David Scott Kastan (New York: Columbia UP, 1997) 39–58 notes that 'Many women acted as producers, as patrons to drama' (50); James Stokes 'Women and Performance in Medieval and Early Modern Suffolk' *Early Theatre* 15: 1 (2012) 27–44. For leather garments, see W.A. Mepham 'Municipal Drama at Maldon in the Sixteenth Century' *Essex Review* 55 (1946) 169–75, and 56 (1947) 34–41, which notes payments 'for a peire of glovis dressynge and for iij skynnes and dyinge of Crist's cote', 'for ij calvesynnes for hym that pleid John Baptyste', and 'for dressyng of the same skynnes' (38); the play at Chelmsford required two pairs of leather sleeves as well as other garments for costumes (172–3).

69 See Note 15. See also Denise E. Cole 'Edible Performance: Feasting and Festivity in Early Tudor Entertainment' in *The Senses in Performance* edited Sally Banes and André Lepecki (New York: Routledge, 2007) 92–104; John J. McGavin and Greg Walker *Imagining Spectatorship: From the Mysteries to the Shakespearean Stage* (Oxford UP, 2016) 43–64.

have mirrored those of the household space in which the interlude was being performed.

The interlude itself suggests such household performance. Performers of household drama could draw on resources that touring players could not, and household performances often required the collaboration of an array of household members, including animal members.[70] *Jacob and Esau*'s action opens with the entrance of the servant Ragau, who leads *iij. greyhounds or one as may be gotten* (22 sd).[71] Like other stage directions in the text, this one seems clearly aimed at the producers or actors of the interlude, rather than later readers. While the stage direction's comment 'or one as may be gotten' indicates a flexibility for the interlude's performance, the requirement for greyhounds to be present indicates some degree of collaboration with a dog keeper. Later in the interlude, Rebecca requests that two kids be brought to her so that she may prepare them as counterfeit venison. The kids are central to Rebecca's household play, performing as venison as well as appearing as parts of Jacob's costume. Rebecca fears that their bleating will alert Isaac to the spectacle's preparations and, although there is no stage direction, the dialogue in the scene in which Jacob and Mido bring the kids to her suggests that they are both heard and seen on stage (1174–88). The possibility that actual kids were carried into the playing area depends, like the explicit stage direction regarding the dogs, on the goats' availability, the likelihood of which would be increased by household performance.

Another stage direction may suggest *Jacob and Esau*'s interface with a household space. This indicates that Ragau is to enter *with his hunting staffe and other things and a bag of vitailes* (982 sd). The bag is a significant prop for, in the short speech that follows, Ragau talks about it and its contents. Apparently gesturing to the bag of food, he notes that he has 'no time to tell what delicates here be, | But (thinke this to be true) for better men than me' (986–7). He plans to hide the

---

70 Suzanne Westfall '"A Commonty"' 54.
71 For a discussion of dogs in mid-Tudor interludes, see Andy Kesson 'Exit Pursuing a Human: Performing Animals on the Early Modern Stage' in *Reading Literary Animals: Medieval to Modern* edited Karen L. Edwards, Derek Ryan, and Jane Spencer (Perspectives on the Non-Human in Literature and Culture; New York: Routledge, 2020) 88–103, 89–90. For this interlude, Stopes *William Hunnis* 228, 232.

bag from Esau, and 'till the bag be clere, he shal it neuer see. | I shall, and if he faint, feede him as he fedde me' (990–1). By withholding the bag's contents from Esau, Ragau manages Esau's hunger to achieve revenge for his master's earlier treatment of him. Yet, more pertinently, the stage direction's stipulation that the bag contain 'vitailes' might imply that Ragau would be able to display and consume the bag's contents, perhaps while noting he has 'no time to tell what delicates here be'. Were no 'vitailes' required, the stage direction might have simply called for a bag. The direction assumes that a 'bag of vitailes' might easily be sourced and used in performance, and household performance would indeed make the procurement of the prop easier.

Of course, for all the props noted above – the greyhounds, the kids, and the bag of vitailes – counterfeit objects could have been, and may be, used in performance, just as Rebecca uses goat to counterfeit venison; the props' use may have been mimed, too. Yet, given what we know about the social technology of Tudor household interlude performance, such objects would have been, if not readily at hand, then readily made available. While textual references to such objects cannot be taken as evidence of a specific performance, they do suggest ways that the spaces in which the interludes were performed afforded certain performance possibilities. In a household setting, not everything must be constructed by the interlude; space and objects may have been afforded to the players by the performance environment. *Jacob and Esau*'s alimentary addresses, where the audience's attention is called to the sight and smell of food, the service of meals, and the provision of entertainment, might also be considered as traces of the interface with that historical performance environment. If we accept the likelihood of household, possibly court, performance, this entails the probability that the interlude's performance was associated with an occasion and a venue of feasting and hospitality. In that case, the production of the interlude itself, along with the service of a meal, both contribute to the nature of the hospitable event the audience experiences, and the array of tasks required within the performance echo those that would have contributed to the event. What appears in the interlude's text as a *depiction* of a household, may have been, from the perspective of interlude-performance practices, an *interface* with the household space that shaped, and was shaped by, the performance.

Despite the many alimentary addresses made in the interlude, its characters consume their meals privately, offstage and unseen; these consumptions are then re-enacted by other characters or reported in dialogue. *Jacob and Esau*'s stage geography creates a paradox: the interlude is fixated by food, but food is largely absent from the stage. Throughout *Jacob and Esau*, as in the scene of Mido's mockery of Esau, food both is and is not present, usually located *there*, off-stage, rather than *here*, in the playing space. When Mido and Ragau mimic Esau's rude devouring of pottage, Mido's mimicry derives from his off-stage witnessing of Esau's consumption, whereas Ragau's mockery is an improvised response to Mido's. Food's absence heightens the mimicry's comedic effect – both characters consume nothing, and the interlude emphasises the pottage's absence from the playing area, locating it and its consumption offstage. 'Here is good meate Iacob', says Mido, mocking Esau as he imitates him (654). The stage direction in the 1568 text instructs 'Here he counterfaiteth supping out the potte'.[72] Mido counterfeits Esau, as does Ragau, as, later, does Jacob. Significantly in this scene of mockery, *here* plays *there*, *now* plays *then*, and nothing plays the pot of rice pottage.

Similarly, characters display ingredients they have collected – herbs, kids, venison – before taking them away to cook or prepare as a broth, the aroma of which apparently wafts from offstage *there* to onstage *here*. Isaac eats goat stew – a counterfeit for venison stew – offstage, afterwards declaring it onstage to be the best he has ever eaten. Esau, too, consumes pottage offstage. Food's production, service, and consumption shape the spatial geography of the interlude's settings even as food does not appear onstage.

Jacob and Esau configures its offstage space as the imaginary place of alimentary consumption, a space where Isaac's taste and Esau's hunger are satisfied. Conversely, onstage space becomes the space of unfulfilled appetitive desire, heightened by the mimed performance of consumption. Mido's *here* ironises this relation: *here* becomes the space of imagination – of dramatic performance – of consumption's *there*. Dramatic mockery fleetingly folds the two spaces together; Mido's *here* is simultaneously a counterfeit space, and *here*'s lack of food is an index of that counterfeiting. Yet, even as he mocks, Mido does so hungrily, his hunger shaped by Esau's politics of hunger management.

In such moments, *Jacob and Esau* also manages its spectators' hunger, real or implied. Alexander Barclay satirises such household strategies in

---

72   For some reason, White replaces this with *Mido mimics Esau eating the pottage*.

his *Eclogues*. He ironically characterises dining halls as sites of hunger, competition, and antagonism, where hierarchy becomes apparent not through shared consumption but through its managed deferral. Barclay's speaker, Cornix, depicts courtiers waiting to be served while dishes pass by on the way to the lord's table:

> But whan these courters syt on the benches ydyll
> Smellynge those dysshes they byte on the brydyll
> And than is theyr payne and anger fell as gall
> Whan all passyth by / & they haue nought at all.[73]

Cornix adds that 'To se suche dysshes / & smell the swete odour | And nothynge to tast / is vtter dyspleasour'.

In turn, the courtiers' consumption tempts those serving the meal. Whereas the lord's food tempts the courtiers, the servants likewise are tempted by the courtiers' food. The 'seruynge rable', as Cornix calls them, so hungrily anticipate eating the diners' leftovers that they mime the courtiers' consumption of the meal:

> The hungry seruers / whiche at the table stande
> At euery morsell / hath iye vnto thy hande
> So moche on thy morsell dystract is theyr mynde
> They gape whan thou gapyst / oft bytynge ye wynde
> By cause that thy leuyngys / is only theyr part
> If thou fede the well / sore greued is theyr hart.   sig. K4r

Here, Cornix describes two consumptions, one actual and the other a mimicry of the first, predicated on a sort of sympathy: when the courtiers eat, the servants mimic that consumption, biting nothing but air; biting nothing but air, the servants hope to receive a part of the meal.

Like Mido and Ragau – and perhaps *Jacob and Esau*'s spectators – Barclay's courtiers and servants are tantalised by the sight and odour of food. Most obviously, the order in which food is consumed replicates the social hierarchy. But implicit in that ordered consumption is the management of appetites: the aesthetic, embodied elicitation of hunger from servants who hope to have a part in what remains. Such management of hunger is a central feature of the dining hall that both *Jacob and Esau* and Barclay describe.

---

73   Alexander Barclay *Eclogues* [or *De curialium miseria*] (London: P. Treveris, 1530) sig. K2v; online at <http://www.proquest.com/eebo/docview/2240900420/Sec0007?accountid=12005>.

Attending to *Jacob and Esau*'s address of and interface with household space sharpens our focus on the performance's status as itself a household task situated in relation to other household tasks. Rebecca's staging of an interlude-within-an-interlude is part of a staging of a household-within-a-household, her acts of alimentary service components of the Christmas–Shrovetide event of which the interlude apparently forms a part. When framed in this way, the interlude's alimentary addresses can be considered an aesthetic feature of its potential performance: even as Rebecca addresses Isaac's appetite, the interlude's performance addresses, or alludes to, the appetites of its spectators. The interlude's meal preparations not only foreshadow the meal for Isaac but also, possibly, represent a nod to the preparations for the audience's meal, even perhaps to the aromas in the hall signalling the food that was served before, during, or after the interlude.[74] The spectators, as Jacob promises Mido, 'may haue some parte' of the possible feast (1058–9). The interlude's alimentary addresses engage with, or even manage – as Rebecca does with Isaac's, and Jacob with Esau's – its spectators' appetites. And, just as Rebecca's and Jacob's addresses have secondary audiences – Mido and Ragau, for example – the interlude addresses its spectatorship multiply: some by taste and some by hunger.

I have attempted to demonstrate how *Jacob and Esau*'s characters manage the tastes, appetites, and hunger of other characters through scenes of counterfeit hospitality. These moments of theatrical hospitality aim to achieve political gains in Isaac's household: Jacob and Rebecca usurp Esau's birthright; Esau starves his servant Ragau to keep him obedient; and Ragau and Mido undermine Esau's authority by comically counterfeiting his unmannerly consumption of pottage, making Esau an object of ridicule. The achievement of these political goals relies on food's suasory power, particularly the power it derives from its address of characters' senses of smell and taste as well as of their embodied sensations of craving and hunger. The interlude identifies the subversion

74 See Greg Walker *Plays of Persuasion: Drama and politics at the Court of Henry VIII* (Cambridge UP, 1991) 11, who notes that the management of spectators' consumption functioned as a form of coercion, keeping spectators in their seats and thus subject to the arguments advanced by interludes, which had the advantage 'of being able to expound upon a theme at some length to guests who were perforce kept relatively silent and attentive ... Short of pointedly leaving the hall before the conclusion of the meal, the spectators could do little other than absorb the ideas presented'.

of the law of primogeniture with the unrestrained satisfaction of taste and hunger. While Isaac's gustatory satisfaction with Rebecca's counterfeit meal compels him to give Esau's blessing to Jacob, Esau's intense hunger compels him to sell his birthright for rice pottage.

Even as these moments of alimentary management lead to the subversion of primogeniture, they also confirm Esau's reprobation and Jacob's election. This confirmation validates the theatricality that elicited the confirmation in the first place. In this light, *Jacob and Esau* presents Rebecca's interlude-within-the-interlude as a defence of Protestant playing as a revelation of truth, despite its counterfeit nature. Insofar as Rebecca's 'devise' confirms the divine truth of Jacob's election, *Jacob and Esau* itself confirms the doctrinal and political truth of predestined usurpation.

Not only does *Jacob and Esau* elicit these revelations through its characters' embodied responses to alimentary addresses, but the interlude also addresses its implied spectators' tastes, appetites, and hunger. Rebecca's marshalling of household resources and household space perhaps interfaces with the household space in which the interlude was likely to have been performed. The interlude's stage geography, as does its staging of rice, rather than lentil, pottage, addresses its audience's alimentary practices and tastes; in doing so, *Jacob and Esau* manages its audience's hunger and tastes, aligning these varied embodied responses with a Christmas–Shrovetide performance as well as with the doctrinal and political usurpations staged by the interlude.

Laurentian University, Canada

LAST SUPPER, FIRST COMMUNION
Some Staging Challenges in N. Town and the Huy Nuns' Play based on Deguileville's *Pèlerinage de la vie humaine*

Elisabeth Dutton and Olivia Robinson

In March 2020 the COVID pandemic closed shops and pubs and restaurants, libraries, cinemas, gyms and theatres, and churches across Europe. As everyone learnt to shop online and technologically baffled academics tried to teach via Zoom, many churches also started to broadcast their services, in variously adapted forms, so that people could listen along at home, but, though the prayers and sermons continued, the singing stopped and, crucially for many believers, the sharing of the Eucharist became impossible. For Catholics in particular it became imperative to find creative ways in which the faithful could receive the consecrated Host, the Body of Christ. In Chalons-en-Champagne, France, the 'drive through Mass' became the unlikely solution at the height of lockdown. Priests, having performed the Elevation and Consecration of the Host in a newly choreographed ceremony in a large car park, protected by masks and with their hands sanitised, delivered wafers through the car windows of attendees.[1]

In England, the churches cautiously reopened as summer began, but government guidelines allowed only a single cantor – no choirs or congregational singing – and clergy had to find ways to administer the Eucharist that observed social distancing and appropriate hygienic practices. Communion was administered in one kind – wafers only – and, as the communicant inevitably had to remove his/her mask to receive the wafer, the priest had to be masked and silent. No 'The Body of Christ' whispered to each participant. Priests and worshippers sanitised their hands before Communion, and members of the congregation followed one-way systems around churches to avoid close contact with others in narrow aisles. It was all a rather sad inversion of what the Eucharist is meant to be: rather than bringing the community together into one body – 'Though we are many, we are one body, because we all share in one bread' – the participants in a COVID Communion were reminded that they must keep their bodies separate from the bodies of others, that it

---

1   *The Daily Telegraph*, 17 May 2020. Report by Johannes Lowe.

might bring them disease if they share one bread. For the devout who believe in the Real Presence, it was perhaps particularly distressing to see hand sanitising before receiving the Host, not out of reverence for the Body of Christ, but because it was a material health hazard.

COVID Communion highlighted, in surprising ways, two topics that we would like to consider in relation to medieval theatre's staging of the Eucharist: the complicated choreography of the participants and the multivalent materiality of the props involved. Theatre as a medium can allow performers and audiences to experience in time and space the relationships between Old Testament Passover and New Testament Last Supper, and between both of these and contemporary practice around the consumption of the Host. Clothing, movement, activity, or gesture, and performance locations and their implications or connotations, can all be mobilised to create a blend of these different occasions and activities, in which times and places are superimposed on one another. We would like to explore these issues in two very different plays: the first, better-known, example is N. Town Play 27, which stages the Last Supper in such a way as to draw attention to its roots in the Old Testament Passover as well as its future in the mass; the second, probably less familiar, example is the convent drama *Le jeu de pèlerinage humaine*, a verse morality play based on part of the first recension of Guillaume de Deguileville's c.1330 *Pèlerinage de Vie Humaine* (usually translated as *The Pilgrimage of the Life of Man*, though more literally meaning *The Pilgrimage of Human Life*) that was written and performed by Carmelite nuns in Huy (in modern-day Belgium) in the late fifteenth century. This play survives in the convent's manuscript playbook, which contains five complete plays: two of these dramatise Biblical material, and three are allegorical; of these three the *jeu de pèlerinage humaine* ('the play of the human pilgrimage') adapts closely an allegorical verse narrative for performance purposes.[2] The convent compositors adapt Deguileville's text carefully, removing

---

2   Olivia Robinson 'Chantilly, Musée Condé MS 617: Mystères as Convent Drama' *Essays on Les Mystères: Studies in Genre, Text and Theatricality* edited Peter Happé and Wim Hüsken (Leiden: Brill-Rodopi, 2012) 93–108, and Aurélie Blanc and Olivia Robinson 'The *Huy Nativity* from the Seventeenth to the Twenty-First Century: Translation, Play-Back and Pray-Back' *Medieval English Theatre 40* (2019) 66–97 offer further discussion of the Huy convent, its playbook, and some of its theatre. The two remaining allegorical plays in the manuscript are entitled *le Jeu des sept pechiés et des sept vertus*, and *l'Alliance de foy et de loyauté* ('the play of the seven sins and the seven virtues'; 'the alliance of faith and loyalty').

passages of description to leave dialogue among various personifications, thus drawing attention to the performative potential of Deguileville's multi-voiced allegory, but also leaving open the questions of whether, or how much, performers may have incorporated the non-dialogic aspects and descriptions of Deguileville's work into their performance(s). The section of the *Pèlerinage* that has been chosen for adaptation in the *jeu* covers discussion and debate among a range of allegorical characters concerning the nature and workings of the Eucharist: it therefore forms an intriguing counterpart to N. Town's treatment of the Last Supper and its significations.

Blocking the Last Supper in N. Town

N. Town, a collection of plays from various sources drawn together in a manuscript of the late fifteenth or early sixteenth century, possibly in imitation of the civic cycles, has the most developed and, in Rosemary Woolf's opinion at least, the most successful presentation of the Last Supper in medieval English theatre.[3] The play conflates two events entirely separate in the Gospels: the Passover supper and the meal, two days before Passover, at the house of Simon the Leper in Bethany, at which a woman anoints Christ with oil.[4] Although this conflation seems to be unique in the English dramatic tradition, it is perhaps justified by Gregory the Great's explicit connection between the foot-washing of the Last Supper and the scene in Bethany, typologically linked to Christ's death;[5] a few plays in the French and German traditions have Simon as the host of the Last Supper,[6] and the two dinners are presented as symbolically parallel in a German play of the Last Supper copied in the

3   Rosemary Woolf *The English Mystery Plays* (London: Routledge and Kegan Paul, 1972) 234-7. N. Town is here cited from *The N-Town Play Cotton MS Vespasian D.8* edited Stephen Spector, 2 vols *EETS SS 11* and *12* (1991). Play 27, the Last Supper, occupies pages 264-85 of volume 1, and is cited here by line number. Spector calls N. Town Play 27 'the most elaborately detailed and reconstituted portrayal of the Last Supper in the Middle English drama' (2: 495).

4   See Mark 14: 1.

5   See Gregorius Magnus *Opera Omnia: PL 78* (1849) cols 725-850, cols 766-7.

6   See Yumi Dohi *Das Abendmahl im spätmittelalterlichen Drama. Eine Unterschung dar Darstellungsprinzipien der Abendmahlslehre in den englischen Mystery Cycle und ihren Vorlagen mit den französischen und den deutschsprachigen biblischen Spielen* (Europäische Hochschulschriften series 18 volume 95; Frankfurt: Peter Lang, 2000) 327-9.

late fourteenth century in Silesian dialect.⁷ The N. Town play also has Christ drive seven demons out of the woman, here identified as Mary Magdalen, at this dinner, though in the gospels this is again a separate incident (and indeed it occurs on interpolated leaves in the N. Town manuscript).⁸ Simon *comyth ... owt of his hous to welcome Cryst* (68 sd) and Christ, having assured Simon that he will receive the bliss of heaven, enters that house and eats the Paschal lamb that is the Passover meal. Peter and John discuss the meal as Jesus' *sopere* (40) and his *Pasch* (44), which would indicate a Passover meal, but they also refer to the event, anachronistically, as *Maundé* (17), as does Jesus (366): *Maundy* is a contraction of the Latin *mandatum novum*, citing Christ's words that he is giving the disciples a 'new commandment', and it is the name given to the day before Good Friday on which the feet of the poor were washed in imitation of Christ's washing his disciples' feet and charitable coins were distributed. Given N. Town's relative lack of interest in the foot-washing,⁹ the word here seems primarily to signal the liturgical day, Maundy Thursday, as the day on which the Last Supper is commemorated.

---

7   See Cora Dietl '"Let Me Have the First Drink": Two Meals and One Table in the *Prague Ludus de Cena Domini*' *European Medieval Drama 12* (2017) 1–20. Dietl hypothesises (16) that this play was written for the parish of St Mary Magdalene in the city of Wroclaw, to celebrate the feasts of the Conversion of Mary Magdalene and Maundy Thursday coinciding in either 1390 or 1401.

8   All four Gospels tell of the woman who anoints Jesus while he dines at Simon's house, but only John identifies the woman as Mary Magdalen (see Mark 14: 3–9, Matthew 26: 6–10, Luke 7: 35–50, John 12: 1–8). Luke 8: 2 and Mark 16: 9 identify Mary Magdalen as the woman from whom seven demons had been driven out, though neither presents this as happening during the dinner at Simon's house. In the Prague *Ludus* Mary states that she has been delivered from seven demons but it is not clear whether this action happens during the scene: see J.H. Kuné '"In the Beginning was the Word ..." *Das Prager Abendmahlspiel*: The Words Rendered into Action and Images' *Neophilologus 87: 1* (2003) 79–96, at 86. Spector demonstrates (*N-Town Play* 495) that the Mary Magdalen episodes are interpolations, part of the 'O' quire added into the N. Town MS, but the choice to set the Last Supper at Simon the Leper's house is part of the play's original plan.

9   The foot-washing is presented at the end of N. Town's *Last Supper* play, but fairly briefly: Jesus declares that he will show 'another exawmpyl' of how to 'leve in charyté' (512–13); the foot-washing and discussion of it are completed within the next thirty lines (although of course the action itself would have occupied some time, particularly if Jesus did indeed wash each Disciple's feet). This contrasts with the number of lines, in excess of a hundred, devoted to the bread and wine.

The stage direction calls for simultaneous staging with separate mansions or scaffolds:

> *Here Cryst enteryth into þe hous with his disciplis and ete þe paschal lomb; and in þe menetyme þe cownsel hous befornseyd xal sodeynly onclose schewyng þe bushopys, prestys and jewgys syytyyng in here astat lych as it were a convocacyon*   76 sd

From this it seems that Christ and his disciples are visible on a separate stage, eating the lamb, during the action of the Conspiracy among Annas, Caiphas, Gamalyel, Rewfyn, and Leyon that occupies lines 77–140. Attention then returns to Simon's house as Mary Magdalen approaches Christ and anoints his feet with oil, and he casts 'vij develys' (174) out of her – after which he is apparently tired and hungry: *Here Cryst restyth and etyth a lytyl ... syttyng ...* (204 sd). It is not specified what he eats here, however. Jesus then predicts his betrayal, and Judas travels through *þe place* (268 sd) to meet the Conspirators.[10] On his returning *sotylly whereas he cam fro* the Conspirators *partyn in þe place* and, in an apparently rather dramatic reveal, we return to Christ and his Disciples at dinner:

> *And than xal þe place þer Cryst is in sodeynly vnclose rownd abowtyn shewyng Cryst syttyng at þe table and hese dyscypulis ech in ere degré*   348 sd

The sudden 'unclosing' implies that the stage has been hidden from view, perhaps with curtains,[11] during Judas's encounter with the Conspirators, whereas during the earlier Conspiracy episode it was apparently open. There is no stage direction to indicate at what point the curtains are closed, and there is no immediately obvious practical reason for this – the scene is still a dinner, on the same stage and presumably using the

---

10 Hans-Jürgen Diller says 'the interpolation allows ... the betrayed and the betrayers to be seen simultaneously, but the interpolated scene itself shows the "itinerant" on his way, allowing him to draw the audience into his confidence while crossing the *platea*'; *The Middle English Mystery Play: A Study in Dramatic Speech and Form* (Cambridge UP, 1992) 106. Diller's idea is attractive but raises the question of at what point the place of the 'betrayed' is concealed in order to be 'unclosed' at 348 sd.

11 Philip Butterworth assumes that curtains were used: see his *Functions of Medieval English Stage Directions: Analysis and Catalogue* (Abingdon: Routledge, 2022) 144.

same table¹² – but there is perhaps a dramatic reason: when the stage is 'suddenly' opened again the audience are presented with an iconic 'Last Supper' image. A seating plan has been imposed, and the disciples have taken their seats (perhaps for the first time, as discussed below). Christ and his Disciples eating the lamb is now reformulated as Christ sitting at a table with his Disciples disposed around him according to a strict hierarchy: in comparing the staging of the meal at Bethany and the Last Supper in the Prague *Ludus* Cora Dietl notes, 'the visual setting of all apostles and Christ taking a seat clearly plays on the association of the Last Supper'.¹³ The stage had been 'closed' in order to facilitate the reveal of this image which the audience must experience as a striking tableau,¹⁴ dining as spectacle, before Christ proceeds to discourse on 'þis lambe that was set us beforn | þat we alle haue etyn in þis nyth' (349–50).

Jesus declares that the Passover lamb was commanded of Moses and Aaron when they fled Egypt, it is eaten with unleavened bread ('swete bredys' 353) and bitter herbs ('byttyr sokelyng' 354), the head and the feet together (355), and that those present have their loins girded and their shoes on; they carry staves and eat in haste (357–60). Clearly, the meal has been celebrated in accordance with the Passover laws of Exodus 12: 8–11. But this means that the disciples have been *standing* during the eating of the paschal lamb ('And as we stodyn so ded þei stond', 357). The Gospels do not indicate that the disciples ate the Last Supper standing, but the idea appears in the pseudo-Bonaventuran *Meditationes Vitae Christi*, which Spector notes (498) is a model for the introduction of the Passover laws into the play, while Nicholas Love's translation of the *Meditationes*, the *Mirrour of the Blessed Lyf of Jesu Christ*, an important source for N. Town, also alludes to the disciples standing and carrying staves at the Last Supper.¹⁵

---

12   In Lucerne the same table was used for the scenes of the meal at Simon's house and the Last Supper, even though the scenes were there separated; see Kuné '"In the Beginning"' 95 note 23.

13   Dietl '"Let Me Have the First Drink"' 8.

14   Such 'sudden' actions are 'contrived in such a way as to condition immediate after-effects': Butterworth *Functions of Medieval English Stage Directions* 144.

15   Nicholas Love *Mirrour of the Blessed Lyf of Jesu Christ* edited Michael Sargent (Exeter Medieval Texts and Studies; Exeter UP, 2005) 146. Meg Twycross discusses relationships between drama and Love's translation of 'Bonaventure' in the *Mirrour*, and notes that 'Bonaventure' tends to visualise 'the gestures of the characters and their spatial relation to each other, so that the scene could be

How does this fit with the stage direction (348 sd) indicating that Christ and the Disciples are sitting in order around a table? They have finished the Passover meal and then sat down, presumably while the stage was closed. Certainly, they seem to have finished eating the lamb – 'we alle haue etyn' (350) – and indeed we 'haue it ete' with 'swete bredys' (353); and eaten it all, the head and the feet (355). But the meal is not over. Jesus now tells them:

> Þis fygure xal sesse; anothyr xal folwe þerby,
> Weche xal be of my body, þat am ȝoure hed,
> Weche xal be shewyd to ȝow be a mystery
> Of my flesche and blood in forme of bred.   361–4

Jesus makes explicit parallels between the 'paschal lomb' that they have eaten and himself as the 'newe lomb' (365–72), and then picks up an *oblé* (communion wafer, 372 sd) and looks up to heaven, thanking His Father 'þat þu wylt shew þis mystery' (378) of Transubstantiation: 'Of þis þat was bred is mad my body' (380). He then allegorises the physical details of the ritual of the Old Law as the spiritual ones of the New: He himself is the Lamb of God – 'Ecce Agnus Dey' (392); the sweet bread is 'loue and charyté' (399); the 'byttyr sokelyng' is 'byttyr contrycyon' (404); the head and feet are his Godhead and his Humanity (406–7); the girdle is chastity (417–20); the shoes are 'exaumpyl of vertuis levyng' (422) handed down by their ancestors, with which they will follow in his footsteps (424); and the staff is a readiness to preach (428).[16] Having explained the change of focus from carnal to spiritual, Jesus then tells them 'Now I wyl fede ȝow all with awngellys mete' (438), apparently the Eucharistic wafer, the *oblé*, which Peter describes as 'gostly sustenawns' (441).

To receive this they must 'come forth seryattly' – i.e. they go up to Christ in turn, like communicants. After Judas has received he 'xal syt þer he was' (457 sd) – so presumably all the Disciples return to their places. Judas then leaves and Jesus offers the Disciples his blood:

---

transferred onto the stage almost intact'; 'Books for the Unlearned' in Twycross *The Materials of Early Theatre: Sources, Images, and Performance* edited Sarah Carpenter and Pamela King (Variorum Collected Studies; London: Routledge, 2018) 135–84 at 141.

16 This exposition follows closely Rabanus Maurus' *Commentariorum in Exodum, Liber I: PL 108* (1951) cols 48–52.

> But now in þe memory of my Passyon ...
> 3e xal drynk myn blood with gret devocyon ...
> Takyth þese chalys of þe newe testament ...
>
> *Than xal þe dysciplys com and take þe blod ...*   482–9 and sd

The stage directions for consumption through the whole sequence thus seem to require:

- Paschal Lamb, served with unleavened bread and bitter herbs (eaten by Jesus and the disciples, standing);
- Some unspecified restorative food, eaten by Jesus, sitting;

after which the scaffold is 'closed'. It is then opened for:

- The dramatic reveal of Christ and his Disciples seated in order around the table, while Christ talks about the Passover lamb but holds a Host;
- 'Angels' Meat', actually the *oblé*, to receive which the Disciples go up to Jesus in turn.

Then a pause, during which the Disciples return to their seats;

- Finally 'blood', to receive which the Disciples, apart from Judas, go up to Jesus in turn.

This is, in other words, a Passover meal, staged as a Passover meal, followed by a Eucharist, staged as a Eucharist with the communicants going up to the priest to receive the wafer and wine. The unspecified restorative food complicates the picture, as it fits the 'blocking' requirements of neither Passover nor Eucharist; it seems to be a moment of unritualised consumption, a simple dinner at Simon's house, in between the two ritual meals. Whatever Jesus eats at this moment cannot be the Passover lamb, as the stage direction specifies that he is *syttyng* (204 sd); furthermore, Mary Magdalen anoints him in this scene, and most representations in the visual arts of the anointing present Jesus sitting at a table and Mary kneeling before him.[17] It is thus confusing that when we next see Jesus he is talking again about the Passover Lamb they have eaten that night (350), though he seems to have fitted in at least a snack since then; however, the confusing snack occurs in the interpolated O quire, the contents of which were perhaps imperfectly adapted to

---

17   Kuné '"In the Beginning"' 84–5.

their new context.[18] And, although *Jesus* has been seen seated before the dramatic reveal, the disciples, perhaps, have not, and it is the ordered seating of the disciples that is visually new.

Then, the Eucharistic staging, while theologically conventional in making the connections among Passover meal, Last Supper, and Mass, might be thought a more curious choice theatrically: the audience of N. Town watch the rather repetitive scene of each communicant receiving in turn – furthermore, since the disciples do not receive the wafer and wine at the same time, each Disciple must go forward to receive twice. N. Town perhaps here requires an audience attention somewhat different from that we now expect of the theatrical audience: indeed, members of the audience observe not drama but liturgy, and therefore must accept the different rhythm of liturgical time, the different nature of liturgical action. The Eucharist is not a spectator sport but requires participation; at the same time, 'participation' in the liturgy is not the same as 'participation' in a play. Matthew Cheung-Salisbury observes that medieval liturgy is characterised by 'the *apparent* non-participation of lay people' [*italics ours*] but that 'It would be unheard of in the Middle Ages to restrict the notion of participation in the liturgy to vocalization'.[19] Nicholas Orme explains that most people in medieval England did not receive communion very often, but attended Mass to see the Elevation of the Host, the moment which became known as 'seeing God' and 'seeing one's Maker':[20] 'for most people, most of the time the Host was something to be seen, not to be consumed'.[21] As Cheung-Salisbury describes, the physical and auditory separation of the ministers in the sanctuary, the choir in the stalls, and the congregation in the nave meant that these three groups experienced the same service in different ways, but, although it was 'not very easy for one segment to see what was going on in another',[22] it was essential, according to Orme, that the Elevation be visible: hence 'the piercing of windows in the chancel screen ... and the openings of squints

---

18   See Spector *N-Town* 2: 496–7 note 27 (on lines 141–268 on the O quire).
19   *Medieval Latin Liturgy in English Translation* edited Matthew Cheung-Salisbury (Kalamazoo, MI: Medieval Institute Publications, 2017) 2.
20   Nicholas Orme *Going to Church in Medieval England* (New Haven: Yale UP, 2021) 243.
21   Eamon Duffy *The Stripping of the Altars: Traditional Religion in England 1400–1580* (New Haven: Yale UP, 1992) 95.
22   Cheung-Salisbury *Medieval Latin Liturgy* 2.

into transepts'.[23] People participated in the Mass by watching, and the blocking of N. Town as a Mass at this point would quite probably have activated, in an audience strongly accustomed to such involvement in the Mass, expectations and modes of attention more appropriate to the liturgy than to the theatre.[24]

As Kuné discusses, in many representations of the Last Supper in the visual arts 'the institution of the Eucharist is the subject'.[25] In terms of exegetical levels, this is complicated: the Mass invites us to see Christ's suffering body as the allegorical fulfilment of Old Testament prophecies of sacrifice, while also asking us to read the bread that Christ identifies as his body anagogically, as playing a role in the salvation of souls. Rosemary Woolf suggests that the N. Town *Passion Play*'s Last Supper resembles Fra Angelico's fresco in San Marco, which presents liturgical act embedded within historical or biblical Last Supper.[26]

Here Jesus offers the Host to his disciples in a scene at once domestic and liturgical: domesticity is suggested by a well, visible through an arched doorway in the background, benches and low wooden stools around a table that is covered in a white cloth, and some disciples sitting at the table;[27] a liturgical act is suggested as some of the disciples are kneeling in the foreground, away from the table; there is no food laid on the table, only a ciborium; Christ holds the Eucharistic wafer and offers it into the mouth of one disciple. Woolf writes: 'This is in fact not the historical Last Supper but a liturgical act of communion' (234), but we would suggest that it is not one or the other, but, rather, both. Christ and

---

23 Orme *Going to Church* 243.
24 Even for modern audiences and the non-devout, this staging of the Mass can be surprisingly engaging: Meg Twycross recalls a production directed by Lynette Muir in which she was absorbed by the 'total conviction' of the participants, who at this point were perhaps not 'acting' in the conventional sense but behaving as they did at church (private correspondence).
25 Kuné '"In the Beginning"' 83. This is in spite of the fact that only the Synoptic Gospels narrate the institution of the Eucharist at the Last Supper: John only describes the washing of feet.
26 Woolf *English Mystery Plays* 234.
27 Woolf states that 'the disciples are not seated at a meal, but standing or kneeling they await the Host which Christ is putting into each disciple's mouth in turn' (234). She does not mention that the majority of the disciples are arranged around a table, and indeed those on the left of the painting – perhaps those who have already received the host – are in fact clearly seated on a bench at the table.

Fig. 1. Fra Angelico *The Last Supper*. Florence: Museo San Marco, fresco 1437–46. Image online at <https://commons.wikimedia.org/wiki/File:Fra_Angelico_015.jpg>. Reproduced under the terms of the GNU Free Documentation Licence 1.3.

the disciples wear robes, not vestments, and they are gathered not in a church[28] but in an 'upper room', as suggested by the roof arches. In fact, this Last Supper looks to be taking place in a room within the Florentine monastery of San Marco on whose walls it appears – the windows depicted resemble those of the monastery, and the view through them resembles that across the cloisters of San Marco. Fra Angelico visually conflates the Last Supper and the Mass that re-enacts it, but he also conflates the time and space of Christ and the disciples with the time

---

28 Coletti argues of Joos van Gent's altarpiece painted for the Brotherhood of Corpus Domini in Urbino that the church setting 'transforms the participants in the Last Supper into the celebrant and communicants of a Eucharistic service'; Theresa Coletti 'Sacrament and Sacrifice in N-Town Passion' *Mediaevalia* 7 (1981) 239-64, at 245.

and space of the monks' domestic lives, suggesting, perhaps, Christ's immanence in the daily routine, and in the mundane meal, not only in the Mass in a church.

Does Fra Angelico's painting in fact help us to understand N. Town, as Woolf suggests? There is, unsurprisingly, no evidence that the anonymous writer of an East Anglian play was directly influenced by a fresco in a Florentine monastery: the point is perhaps that the painting realises visually a conflation of exegetical levels that the text of N. Town also reflects. And, of course, a play is not simply a text on a page but a script for performance: as we have seen, N. Town in performance appears to require both seats and a dining table, and the Mass-like blocking of the disciples, that can be seen in Fra Angelico's painting. But although the several small stages on which N. Town was staged may each in themselves have been elaborate, and indeed could create intimacy for individual scenes,[29] the place-and-scaffold requirements of the N. Town *Passion Plays* as a whole, and especially their emphasis on playing in the place, would render impossible the sense of intimate and immediate location that Fra Angelico achieves; in Fra Angelico's painting, the world beyond the Upper Room is glimpsed only through doorways and windows, where in a place and scaffold performance it is always visible, all around the scaffold.[30] Even if it were performed in some sort of dining hall (which is highly unlikely),[31] N. Town's upper room could not be mapped onto the entirety of that hall, co-terminous with it, since the playing area must also accommodate the scenes of Conspiracy in other stages; for the same reason, in the unlikely event that it were performed in a church, N. Town's Last Supper could not entirely be equated with

---

29 See, for example, the substantial staging requirements of play 31, *Satan and Pilate's Wife*, which calls for a raised scaffold with substantial scenery including a curtain and a bed: *Here shal the devyl gon to Pylatys Wyf. The corteyn drawyn as she lyth in bedde, and he shal no dene make, but she shal, sone after that he is come in, makyn a rewly noyse, coming and rennyng of the schaffald. And her shert and her kyrtyl in her hand, and sche shal come beforn Pylat leke a mad woman* (57 sd).

30 Meg Twycross discusses the sometimes distracting effect of movement in the place, or *platea*, in her review of the Toronto Passion Play in *Medieval English Theatre 3: 2* (1981) 122–31.

31 On the possibilities of indoor and outdoor staging for different sections of N. Town, see Clare Smout and Elisabeth Dutton, with Matthew Cheung-Salisbury 'Staging the N-Town Plays: Theatre and Liturgy' *Research Opportunities in Medieval and Renaissance Drama 49* (2010) 1–30.

the Masses held there at the high altar, because the space of the scaffold creates an artificial – theatrical – limit to the extent of the 'upper room'.[32]

N. Town also seems to call for a lamb, which is nowhere to be seen in Fra Angelico's painting (we will return to the question of props presently), and furthermore requires that the lamb be consumed by the Disciples standing, before they sit to eat bread. N. Town's staging of the Last Supper looks backwards, to the Old Testament roots of the Passover meal, before it looks forwards to the Mass which the Last Supper institutes. This exegetical level is missing from Fra Angelico's painting entirely, and indeed from most French, Flemish, or English medieval representations of the Last Supper: we have been unable to find any in which the disciples eat standing,[33] though there are many that present lamb on the table, as we will discuss below.

Staging the Eucharist at Huy

In the *Pèlerinage* play, the sisters draw on a fairly early section from the first book of Deguileville's allegorical narrative, in which the narrating Pilgrim character enters the house of the lady named *Grace Dieu* ('The Grace of God') and observes the preparations for a lavish meal there.[34] A table is prepared by the servants of a figure who represents, simultaneously, the Old Law and the New; he is sometimes referred to as 'Moses', and sometimes as a minister or vicar of Moses – a bishop or a pope. Grace Dieu assists the Moses-bishop by performing a miracle at

---

32   The effect of place-and-scaffold staging is in this respect very different from that of, for example, interludes played without multiple scaffolds in dining halls, where the hall can be simultaneously the hall itself and e.g. Ancient Rome; see Elisabeth Dutton 'Secular Medieval Drama' in *The Oxford Handbook to Medieval Literature* edited Elaine Treharne and Greg Walker (Oxford UP, 2010) 384–94.

33   In typological works, such as Dieric Bout's *Holy Sacrament* altarpiece at Sint Pieterskerk, Leuven, and the *Speculum Humanae Salvationis*, this is presented as a separate though adjacent image. See, for the altarpiece, the Web Gallery of Art at <https://www.wga.hu/html_m/b/bouts/dirk_e/lastsupp/index.html>; for the block book illustration, *The Mirour of Mans Saluacioune: a Middle English translation of the Speculum Humanae Salvationis* edited Avril Henry (Aldershot: Scolar Press, 1986) 104.

34   See Guillaume de Deguileville *Le pèlerinage de vie humaine* edited J.J. Stürzinger (London: Roxburghe Club, 1893) 30–2, 45–6. Medieval theology considered human beings as 'wayfarers or wanderers (*viatores*) struggling with the consequences of sin and moving toward their eternal destinies'; Marilyn McCord Adams *Some Later Medieval Theories of the Eucharist* (Oxford UP, 2010) 35.

his request: the bread laid out for the meal is transformed into living flesh, and the wine into red blood. This is, of course, much easier said (written) than done (staged): Deguileville's narrative text can describe a miracle, but a play that turns his text to theatre must struggle to realise it. However, the *Pèlerinage* script records no stage directions or rubrics, but only the lines of each character, so stage action and props must be extrapolated.[35]

The script begins with Pilgrim asking Lady Reason to teach him about *ce maingier* ('that meal', 4) and Reason complaining in reply that the transformation of bread into *char vive* ('living flesh') and of wine into blood is *Contre Nature et ses usage* ('against Nature and her laws', 14-16).[36] In Deguileville's poem, in an episode that occurs immediately before the beginning of the play, Moses wants to eat flesh and blood rather than bread and wine:

> ... nulle chose n'i avoit
> Fors pain et vin tant seulement,
> N'estoit pas mes a son talent;
> Char vouloit avoir a mengier
> Et sanc auec pour effacier
> La vieille loi qui dit auoit
> Que nul sang mengier ne deuoit.[37]

---

35 This is, of course, far from unusual in medieval drama: the script, which survives because written down, can represent only a tiny fraction of the performance and give little clue as to the accompanying spectacle. For an egregious example in medieval English drama, see Meg Twycross and Elisabeth Dutton 'Lydgate's "Mumming for the Mercers of London"' in *The Medieval Merchant: Proceedings of the 2012 Harlaxton Symposium* edited Caroline M. Barron and Anne F. Sutton (Harlaxton Medieval Studies 24; Donington: Shaun Tyas, 2014) 310-49.

36 The play is here cited from *Recueil général de moralités d'expression française, Vol 1* edited Marie Bouhaïk-Gironès, Estelle Doudet, and Alan Hindley (Bibliothèque du théâtre français 9; Paris: Classiques Garnier, 2012) 589-648. The English translation cited is that prepared by Aurélie Blanc and Olivia Robinson as part of the Medieval Convent Drama Project; this translation will be published in 2024 edited Olivia Robinson, Aurélie Blanc, Elisabeth Dutton, and Matthew Cheung-Salisbury. There is no reason to suppose the script is acephalous, and it is introduced in the manuscript as follows: *Chi comenche le jeux de pelerinage humaine et premierement parole le Pelerin a dame Rayson et dist* ('Here begins the play of the human pilgrimage, and firstly the Pilgrim speaks to Lady Reason, and says'); Chantilly: Bibliothèque et Archives du Château MS 617, fol. 24r.

37 *Le Pèlerinage* edited Stürzinger 45-6, lines 1437-41.

> 'there was nothing there [i.e. for his meal] except bread and wine only, [and] this food was not to his liking; he wanted to have meat to eat, and blood with it, in order to go against the Old Law, which had said that one must not eat blood.'

Even though ostensibly an Old Testament character, he is deliberately flouting the Old Law – 'flesh with blood ye shall not eat' – in favour of the New.[38] It also, of course, leads to a Eucharistic miracle, engineered by Grace Dieu, that apparently makes visible the mystery of Transubstantiation. We discuss below how this might have been represented.

The editors of the play propose that the deictic *ce* is accompanied by a gesture from Pilgrim towards the bread and wine of communion;[39] it certainly seems that there must be some sort of meal onstage, and one that includes bread and wine, though its Eucharistic status has only been implied by Lady Reason's lines. The editors of the play suggest that a mimed scene of the Elevation of the Host may have originally preceded the first lines of the play as it survives; the play would thus offer a 'paraliturgical meditation'.[40] We might be inclined to wonder if a mimed Eucharist would have been considered appropriate, or even possible, for a group of women religious to perform; however, this may well reveal more about our own preconceptions than about medieval conditions and practices, at least in some convents: performative Mass-like ceremonies omitting the sacrament of the Eucharist and involving pre-consecrated Hosts were certainly undertaken by nuns themselves in Spanish and

---

38 Genesis 9: 4 (God's instructions to Noah); and Leviticus 7: 26 'You shall not eat the blood of any creature whatsoever, whether of birds or beasts'; 17: 14 'You shall not eat the blood of any flesh at all, because the life of the flesh is in the blood, and whosoever eateth it, shall be cut off' (God's instructions to Moses); Douai/Rheims translation.

39 *Recueil général* edited Bouhaïk-Gironès and others, 589 note 3; see also the discussion in Olivia Robinson 'Performance-Based Research in the Medieval Convent' *European Medieval Drama 21* (2018 for 2017) 21–42, 31–3.

40 *Le démonstratif ce a un sense déictique fort: le Pèlerin fait un geste vers le pain et le vin de communion. Il est possible qu'une scène d'Élevation, réelle ou plus certainement mimée, ait précédé le début de la pièce, qui s'offre ainsi comme une méditation paraliturgique* ('The demonstrative *this* has a strong deictic force: the Pilgrim gestures towards the bread and wine of communion. It is possible that an Elevation scene, whether real, or more likely, mimed, preceded the beginning of the play, which thus would take the form of a paraliturgical meditation'; *Recueil général* 589 note 3).

Italian convents, including the royal house of Las Huelgas in Burgos.[41] It is also possible, of course, that the play began with a more literal feast that included perhaps some special stage effect for the Moses-bishop's miracle, and that Pilgrim gestures towards a banquet. Lady Reason's words, while describing the 'unnatural' act of transubstantiation, remind us of the overlap between Eucharist and courtly or lavish feast: the wine that has been turned into blood is still explicitly *son beuvrage*, his beverage or drink – for her, the blood still retains its social function as wine, the meal is still a meal, even as it is also, of course, something else.

This distinction opens up the central question of the play: what is the nature of the Eucharist? Discussion heads in a number of directions: the hierarchical relationship between Nature and Divine Grace (represented here by the character Grace Dieu); the appropriate attitude of the sinner preparing for Mass; Aristotelian natural philosophy;[42] an anatomisation of the virtues of the Christian pilgrim. As different characters debate these questions in abstract or conceptual terms, with more or less bad temper, the Moses-bishop character's opening 'meal' sometimes recedes from view, though its visual residue would presumably remain in performance, and discussion always eventually returns to it. It is first brought back into focus with the introduction of two characters who mediate access to the Eucharist: Penitence and Charity. Penitence describes *La table Moysi* ('the table of Moses', 321) as *chi* ('here', 320) signalling the moment at which the silent Eucharistic spectacle with which the play (possibly) began is integrated fully into its action, its table becoming an object with which Penitence and Charity physically interact, rather than being something that all characters observe from one side or silently watch alongside the audience.[43] Penitence and Charity situate themselves physically *Devant la table Moÿsi* ('in front of the table of Moses', 321), between it and the audience/Pilgrim; Penitence identifies herself as the *chancelier* ('chancellor', 324) of the Eucharistic

---

41 See David Catalunya 'The Customary of the Royal Convent of Las Huelgas of Burgos: Female Liturgy, Female Scribes' *Medievalia 20: 1* (2017) 91–160; downloadable from <https://www.academia.edu/27509173/The_Customary_of_the_Royal_Convent_of_Las_Huelgas_of_Burgos_Female_Liturgy_Female_Scribes>.

42 Aristotle appears as a character in the play. On the Aristotelian foundations of medieval theories of the Eucharist, see Adams *Some Later Medieval Theories* 4–28.

43 Robinson 'Performance-Based Research' 34 discusses this scene as a form of embodied or experiential learning for participants.

Host, indicating her juridical control of it,[44] and its *portier* ('porter', 325), indicating that she controls physical access to it; she then warns Pilgrim that nobody should approach it without her (*Sens moy approchier ne deveis*; 'without me, you should not approach', 326). Charity explains that she is the *almonier* ('almoner', 396) of the Host and its *dispensier* ('steward', 397) – that is, the person charged with dispensing it;[45] she then warns that she will be very offended by anyone who approaches it without *le joweal de paix* ('the jewel of peace', 409).

The blocking here seems to suggest again the action of a Mass, in which the congregation approach the altar to receive the Host. It is unlikely that Penitence or Charity actually distributes the Host: almost certainly this would be done by the priestly Moses character, as explained in Deguileville's text and demonstrated in the manuscript illustrations that accompany Deguileville.[46] These generally show at the altar a figure in a mitre, thus a bishop that could not be identified as Moses except by the text,[47] with a crowned woman, Grace Dieu: in all cases it is the

---

44 Bouhaïk-Gironès and others discuss the double sense of the term *chauncelier*: *Lié à sa fonction d'enseignante, il la désigne comme une autorité délivrant, après examen, une récompense, ici la communion. Lié à son rôle de gardienne, il lui donne le statut de responsable du sceau, de la garantie de foi que représent le droit de communier* ('Linked to her function as a teacher, the term *chauncelier* designates her as an authority who delivers, after examination, a reward, here communion. Linked to her role as guardian, the term gives her the role of the keeper of the seal, and of the guarantor of faith, represented by the right to receive communion'; 604 note 1).

45 Bouhaïk-Gironès and others explain that the double sense here parallels that of Penitence's *chancelier*: *le dispenser désigne l'intendant qui distribue la richesse; au sense spirituel, il renvoie au «dispensateur des mystères», qu'est le fidèle animé par l'esprit charitable du partage et la foi* ('the *dispenser* designates the steward who distributes riches; on a spiritual level, it is connected to the "dispenser of the mysteries": that is, the faithful who are animated by the charitable spirit of sharing and by faith'; 607 note 2). See I Corinthians 4: 1–2.

46 Having passed by Penitence and Charité, the pilgrims then *du relief se receurent | Le quel Moises leur donna | Si com Charité l'ordenna* ('received relief, which Moses gave to them, just as Charity had ordered it'); *Pèlerinage* edited Stürzinger lines 2650–52.

47 An exception is the late fifteenth-century Parisian manuscript Soissons MS BM 0208 (194), which contains a prose reworking of Deguileville's *Pèlerinage* with an extensive programme of illuminations. On fol. 30v this manuscript shows a horned Moses administering wafers across an altar to kneeling pilgrims, while Grace Dieu, also behind the altar, chats to Pilgrim on one side. See Géraldine

FIG. 2. 'Moses', accompanied by Grace Dieu, distributes wafers to kneeling pilgrims. BNF MS Français 1577 (1345–77) fol 7r detail. Guillaume de Deguileville *Pèlerinage de la vie humaine.* Image online at <https://gallica.bnf.fr/ark:/12148/btv1b10544595h/f19.item> and used in compliance with the copyright rules of the Bibliothèque nationale de France.

bishop who distributes the Host. In the mid-fourteenth-century BNF MS Français 1577, once owned by Louis XIV, fol. 7r, a bishop stands in front of the altar[48] to distribute wafers to kneeling pilgrims; beside him a haloed lady Grace Dieu (identified in the illumination's rubric) assists.[49]

> Veysseyre 'Soissons, Bibliothèque municipale, 0208 (194)' in the Jonas-IRHT/CNRS database (permalink <http://jonas.irht.cnrs.fr/manuscrit/57867>) and for manuscript images: <http://initiale.irht.cnrs.fr/codex/5113> and <https://bvmm.irht.cnrs.fr/iiif/6382/canvas/canvas-1236412/view>.

48 Between the bishop and the pilgrims what appears to be another table is more likely to be the long cloth or 'houseling towel' that was stretched along in front of communicants to avoid crumbs falling to the floor – see Duffy *Stripping of the Altars* 94.

49 On this manuscript, see Géraldine Veysseyre 'Paris, Bibliothèque nationale de France, Manuscrits, fr. 01577' in the Jonas-IRHT/CNRS database (permalink

Of course, if the nuns played all of the roles, then Moses would here by played by a woman and there is still some potential for subversion of gender roles in relation to the Mass. But what exactly are Penitence and Charity doing? Perhaps they simply lead communicants up to the altar to receive the Host. The mid-fifteenth-century BN MS Français 376, once owned by Charles VIII, fol. 14r, shows these two female figures leading a group of pilgrims towards a bishop, Moses, who receives a document from the hands of Charity.[50] This episode is included in the play: the document is presumably the Charter of Christ, read out and displayed by Charity, *le testament que Nostre Signeur faist deuant sa mort* ('the testament which our Lord made before his death', 367 rubric): the Charter, and Charity's discussion of it, explain how, through Christ's love for mankind, he bestowed upon them as an inheritance the jewel of peace: *Le dons de pais: c'est mon joweal* ('the gift of peace: it is my jewel', 374) which is necessary for access to the Host. However, neither altar nor Host appears in this manuscript illustration. Possibly, some more pointed interaction is required between communicants and Penitence and Charity. In her opening speech, Penitence explains the significance of the props she carries, namely the mallet, the broom, and the rod: *De mailhet debrise et defrosse | Par contricion et angousse Les cuer* ('with the mallet I break down human hearts with contrition and anguish', 236–8); with the broom she sweeps clean the senses (272–84); with the rod she chastises the sinner (300–14). Did the nuns, prompted by these earlier lines of Penitence and Charity, enact some wordless ceremony by which the communicants approaching the altar were first touched by the rods of Penitence and then handed a document, or possibly a jewel (*joweal*) or even a toy (*jouet*) by Charity?[51] Given the general lack of stage directions

<http://jonas.irht.cnrs.fr/manuscrit/73629>) and for manuscript image: <https://gallica.bnf.fr/ark:/12148/btv1b10544595h/f19.item>.

50 On this manuscript, see Géraldine Veysseyre 'Paris, Bibliothèque nationale de France, Manuscrits, fr. 00376' in the Jonas-IRHT/CNRS database (permalink <http://jonas.irht.cnrs.fr/manuscrit/73618>) and for manuscript image <https://gallica.bnf.fr/ark:/12148/btv1b84702013/f31.item>.

51 Deguileville offers a complicated pun on *joweal* ('jewel') and *jouet* ('toy'). The plaything of Christ as a child was also 'Peace'. It is often depicted in Deguileville manuscripts as a form of set square with the word PAX on it (Stürzinger offers a representative illustration at 79). Could this have been the form that a *joweal* took in performance?

in the play, we cannot be sure how exactly Penitence and Charity were involved in providing access to the Host.

That the Host must be approached, and that access is controlled by a porter, gives heavy significance to its location, which seems to define the space that it occupies. The realisation of the significance of the Host in spatial terms is reflected also in the evolving design of medieval churches, which, with the emergence of the Gothic style, increasingly separated congregants from the Host with altar rails and rood screens.[52] Furthermore, Pilgrim's lines here indicate the presence of a large number of people, for he explains to Grace Dieu that *point n'enteng | Coment autant de gens suffier puit | Che relief, qui est si petit* ('I can't understand at all how so many people can be satisfied by this relief, which is so tiny', 413–15). Again, this short exclamation within the script gestures obliquely to a physical activity, spectacle, or experience that is not recorded or prompted in explicit instructions to performers within the script but that does take place in the source text: in Deguileville's *Pèlerinage* a crowd of pilgrims approach the 'table of Moses' and receive the Host, and those pilgrims who pass by Charity and Penance, and carry the jewel of peace, are completely satisfied by it, while those who hide from Charity and Penance remain hungry after eating the bread. When the play was staged by the Huy nuns the communicants may have been the sisters without speaking roles, who otherwise formed part of the audience for the play and who returned to their places in the audience just as the congregation return to their places after receiving the Host. This moment, if considered as theatre, would then constitute a striking form of audience participation, blurring the lines between actor and spectator by simulating the liturgy.

These two plays, perhaps performed at broadly the same historical moment but produced in different countries, languages, and contexts, nonetheless present a similar challenge in their staging: how do you present, live on stage, a meal that is also a staged Mass? Of course, there are many dramatisations of the Last Supper that also present it as a Passover or as anticipating the Mass,[53] but these two plays seem

---

52 This is discussed in Andrew Sofer *The Stage Life of Props* (Ann Arbor: University of Michigan Press, 2003) 36–7.

53 In the English tradition, several of the Last Supper pageants seem to have been altered or censored as a result of the Reformation, and surviving dramatisations of the Eucharist are rare. The Towneley Plays present a *paske*, or Passover supper,

to create particular staging challenges through their attempt not just to allude to two things at once but actually to present them. Both plays depend heavily on the presence of a multi-referential table: in N. Town, the table of Simon of Bethany, the table of the Last Supper, and the altar used for the Eucharist; in the *Pèlerinage* play, the table of Moses and the Mass altar. In both plays, the function of the table is defined by the blocking of characters in relation to it. Those staging these plays must also decide on the nature of the props with which the table is laid.

Edible props of the Last Supper

In N. Town, what are Jesus and the Disciples actually eating and drinking at each point? What props are required? It seems clear that a lamb is involved: tempting though it might be to stage only the allegorical meaning rather than the literal, the insistence on 'the paschal lamb' of the Passover meal and the transition between it and the spiritual food of the Eucharist would make it difficult to use only bread. But how is that transition managed? When Jesus and the Disciples enter the house of Simon, they *ete þe paschal lomb* which he was specifically requested to prepare, and which, as we have seen, they eat standing. Reference to the details of the meal imply that a lamb must be presented on the table. When the scaffold is unclosed for the reveal of the iconic 'Last Supper', Jesus makes an explicit parallel between himself as the 'newe lomb' and the 'paschal lomb' that they have eaten (365–72), and then picks up the *oblé* (372 sd), a wafer. After expounding its allegorical significance, he

> but the food is unspecified as either lamb or bread and the scene is preoccupied with the Conspiracy and betrayal by Judas; see *The Towneley Plays* edited Martin Stevens and A.C. Cawley, 2 vols *EETS SS 13* and *14* (1994) Play 20, *1* 227–51. The York Play's *Last Supper* pageant is defective: it has lost a leaf (perhaps deliberately?) between lines 89 and 90, possibly losing fifty-nine lines. The remaining portion contains the Passover meal with the lamb, but the Institution of the Eucharist is missing, and the focus of what remains becomes Jesus' washing of his disciples' feet (originally a separate pageant); see *The York Plays: A Critical Edition of the York Corpus Christi Play as recorded in British Library Additional MS 35290* edited Richard Beadle, 2 vols *EETS SS 23* and *24* (2009 and 2013 for 2011) Play 27, *1* 224–9, and notes at *2* 219–25. The Chester *Last Supper* features both Passover lamb and the words of Institution over bread and wine, but the disciples do not appear to go up to Jesus to receive them: indeed, everyone still seems to be seated at dinner, as Jesus is reclining with John sleeping in his lap (*Tunc accumbet Jesus ac Johannis in gremio dormit*; 80 sd); see *The Chester Mystery Cycle* edited R.M. Lumiansky and David Mills, 2 vols *EETS SS 3* and *9* (1974 and 1986) Play 15, *1* 268–83.

tells the Disciples that he has now taught them how they shall eat their 'paschal lombe, þat is my precyous body' (438), and then offers them the *oblé*, now defined as angels' meat and 'gostly sustenawns'. It therefore seems possible that the lamb course, having been consumed 'þe hed with þe fete' (355) in the Passover meal before the opening of the stage, and now referred to only in the past tense, is no longer visible: the closing of the stage before the reveal provides the practical opportunity to substitute the wafer for the lamb. However, it is also possible that some trace of the lamb remains, since Christ refers to the lamb with the deictic 'þis' (349): this would accord with many representations in medieval art that feature wafer and lamb – or the gravy left in the lamb dish – at the same table, as we discuss below.

'This' lamb, as Christ indicates, is the lamb that *has been* eaten; the lamb 'that is his body' is what they *shall* eat, in the future. The complexity of the typological relationships between lamb and bread, Passover and Last Supper, are here caught up also with temporal questions about a changing symbol: Jesus explains that the Passover lamb *as a 'fygure'* shall 'sesse', and 'anothyr shal folwe therby' (361) which shall be 'my flesch and blood in forme of bred.' (364) Of course, the crucifixion, by which Christ became the sacrificial lamb, has not at this point in the play happened; the institution of the Eucharist has also not yet occurred, but will follow in this same scene, and Christ indicates that it is by the words that he speaks at that moment that the bread becomes his flesh (381–3). At the beginning of this scene, therefore, the bread has not yet become Christ's flesh, nor has the new 'figure' of Christ as sacrificial lamb been brought into existence: the moment seems suspended, but of course must be staged, and it is not obvious what props should be present, nor are there explicit stage directions to help. By replacing lamb with wafer, a production may anticipate the institution of the Mass; by keeping both lamb and bread in sight of the audience, a production may remind the audience that it is the 'figure' that changes, but not the spiritual truth. The blood presents no problem, for Jesus' lines specify a 'chalys' (486) which may or may not have been on the table throughout. And, of course, unless there are glass drinking vessels involved, the audience cannot see what is inside the chalice; nor would they in any case be able to differentiate between blood and wine simply by looking.

In the *Pèlerinage* play, bread becomes flesh. As we have seen, the play as it stands begins with the Pilgrim troubled about the miracle by which,

Reason explains, Grace Dieu and the Moses-priest have turned bread into living flesh and wine into blood:

> ... *char vive, de pain at fait,*
> *Et de vin, sanc, por son beuvrage,*
> *Contre Nature et ses usage* 14–16

> 'He has made living flesh out of bread, and blood out of wine, for his drink, against Nature and her laws.'

If this scene was staged as part of the play, and if we are to take it literally, this would seem to suggest some striking sleight of hand. Wine into blood would not be difficult; but how in performance does bread become living flesh? It might seem economical to represent it with the Paschal Lamb. However, one drawback in using the roast lamb as a prop here is that 'living flesh' would not have been cooked: it must have demonstrated in some way that it was alive. This seems to be the solution in the illustration in MS Soissons BM 2028 (194), which presents the prose reworking of Deguileville's text, where the scene is depicted with a nun (probably Reason) and the Pilgrim watching Grace Dieu and Moses discussing a plate of patently living lamb (fol. 17v). But in the play, as the Pilgrim later watches the distribution of the Eucharist, Grace Dieu expounds the event to him at some length, in a way that could be helpful. The *relief* which is given:

> C'est char et sanc en verité,
> Mains pain et vin est figureit,
> Et voir est que fut jadis
> En pain et vin , mais tu veis
> En char et sanc mueir de vray
> Par Moysen qu je aydaie. 428–33

> 'It is in truth flesh and blood, but in the form (figure) of bread and wine; it is true that it once was bread and wine, but you have seen it actually changed into flesh and blood by Moses, with my help.'

Although four of his senses may declare that it is merely bread and wine, she says, they are deceptive: he must depend on his hearing, by which he has been told that it is flesh, the food of angels (440–59). It would seem from Pilgrim's reference to the *si petit* ('very small') size of the *relief* that the *char vive* or 'living flesh' into which Grace Dieu and the Moses-bishop transformed the bread at the dining table is shown as a

FIG. 3. Moses and Grace Dieu at table with three others. Oxford: Bodleian Library MS Douce 300 fol. 13v. Guillaume de Deguileville *Pèlerinage de la vie humaine*. Online at <https://digital.bodleian.ox.ac.uk/objects/b891d227-826c-4db9-adc1-0165aa391511/surfaces/19f2f238-65e9-4e8e-b812-8bbe87cd2dbe/#>
© Digital Bodleian; reproduced under Creative Commons Licence CC-BY-NC 4.0.

communion wafer. This seems to be the solution adopted at this point by the artist of Bodleian MS Douce 300 (see FIG. 3). The illustration of the miracle shows Moses and Grace Dieu seated at table accompanied by three other characters. Moses is distinguished by his horns (though he is tonsured and holds a crozier), and Grace Dieu by her crown, starry halo, and didactic stance. The meal on the table is Eucharistic: four wafers and three chalices.

That the 'flesh' is 'living' is of course because it is Christ's. Since it appears that it is represented as an *oblé*, the most practical, and visually striking, way to demonstrate that this is the living flesh of Christ would be to have a wafer, possibly oversized for visibility, suddenly bleed. (We discuss below how this might have happened with the Pilgrim's scrip.) This was the traditional way in which contemporary miracles demonstrated the Real Presence. The Bleeding Host of Dijon (FIG. 4), whose cult must have reinforced if not originated the *Croxton Play of the Sacrament*, is said to have bled through the multiple stab wounds inflicted on it by a Jewish unbeliever. The many images in Books of Hours and on devotional woodcuts show a wafer impressed with the figure of Christ on the rainbow, beaded with blood. The lightness and whiteness of the wafer would reinforce the idea that the flesh of Christ, though living, was spiritual.

It is initially helpful that the *Pèlerinage* attracted such a detailed programme of illustration, since the images show us how the playwright might have envisaged the scene onstage.[54] However, there are difficulties in using static images this way. This is especially true when choosing how to portray moments of transformation, be they narrative or allegorical. Art cannot show bread becoming flesh; a painting has to show one stage or the other. The Deguileville illustrations can show bread or some version of living flesh, but not one becoming the other. Fra Angelico, similarly, shows only the wafer Christ offers to his disciples: there is no other food on the table. This is not unusual; indeed, all of the late fifteenth-century portrayals of the Last Supper discussed by Coletti present only bread on the table. This is possibly because, as Coletti argues, late medieval artists responded to 'the increasing importance of Eucharistic devotion' by visualising in Last Supper scenes 'the sacramental consecration and

---

[54] The standard reference for the programme of illustrations is still Michael Camille 'Illustrated manuscripts of Deguileville's *Pèlerinages*, 1330–1426' (PhD dissertation, Cambridge University, 1985). Rosemond Tuve first introduced the anglophone scholarly world to them in 'Guillaume's *Pilgrimage*', chapter 3 of *Allegorical Imagery: Some Medieval Books and their Posterity* (Princeton UP, 1966). However, she does not concentrate particularly on the Eucharistic images, which are understandably much more varied between manuscripts than are the more emblematic ones. See also Richard K. Emmerson 'Translating Images: Image and Poetic Reception in French, English, and Latin Versions of Guillaume de Deguileville's *Trois Pèlerinages*' in *Poetry, Place, and Gender: Studies in Medieval Culture in Honor of Helen Damico* edited Catherine E. Karkov (Kalamazoo MI: Medieval Institute Publications, 2009) 275–301.

FIG. 4. The Bleeding Host of Dijon. BNF MS lat 1156A fol. 22r; Heures de René d'Anjou (before 1480). Online at <https://gallica.bnf.fr/ark:/12148/btv1b6000466t/f55.item.r=MS%20latin%201156>. Reproduced in compliance with the copyright rules of the Bibliothèque nationale de France.

Fig. 5. The Hospitality of Abraham and the Sacrifice of Isaac. Ravenna: San Vitale (consecrated AD 547), mosaic 546–56. Photo credit: Elisabeth Dutton.

communion', by contrast with earlier medieval representations that focused on 'narrative content' such as Christ's identification of the traitor Judas and John's falling asleep on Christ's breast.[55]

Medieval systems of typology also allowed some earlier artists, by focusing on narrative content, to draw attention to the connections between bread and lamb by presenting parallel Old Testament narratives, as in the sixth-century mosaic of the Hospitality of Abraham in St Vitale, Ravenna.

In the centre of the mosaic, the three angels hosted by Abraham each have before them on the table a bread which, though not an *oblé*, is nonetheless given a symbolic appearance through its circular shape and cross-shaped marking. To the (viewer's) left Abraham also offers his guests a platter on which is a whole lamb, and to right the patriarch raises a sword to sacrifice his son Isaac. The juxtaposed scenes create clear iconographic connections among lamb, bread, and sacrifice.

Furthermore, although Coletti's examples show only bread, the lamb often also appears in later medieval representations of the Last Supper, perhaps pointing the informed viewer to the rich typological associations of the Old Testament sacrificial lamb as well as the lamb of the Passover feast. BL Add MS 24098, a Book of Hours known as 'the Golf Book', with miniatures by the Flemish Simon Bening (1483–1561), features a table with the lamb and other plates of meat, as well as bread rolls (fol. 2v, bas

55 Coletti 'Sacrament and Sacrifice' 247.

de page). However, Bening shows no wafer, and the image thus presents the Passover meal but not the Institution that follows. Another resource for artists is to combine different moments in the same image: BL Add MS 18852, produced in Bruges between 1486 and 1506 for Joanna the Mad, presents a Last Supper in which Jesus reaches across a plate with what seems to be most of the Paschal Lamb to hand an *oblé* to Judas (fol. 45r).[56] More subtly, Dieric Bouts in his Leuven Altarpiece of the Holy Sacrament (1464–7) shows the pewter platter on which the Paschal Lamb had been served empty except for gravy; there are brown rolls on the table, and he is consecrating an *oblé* over a chalice-like cup. The full-scale Passover meal is represented on a wing of the altarpiece in all its ritual detail, including the bitter herbs.[57]

In N. Town, the Paschal Lamb of the Passover feast gives way to the very specific term *oblé*, the wafer, midway through the meal. The substitution of the *oblé* for the Paschal Lamb appears to (at least partly) take place through literal *onstage* consumption by the performers: the lamb disappears gradually as the action of the play progresses and the performers ingest it. Even if the remains of the lamb were removed before the Last Supper reveal, this onstage eating makes a stronger theological point than the simple replacement of one prop by another: N. Town's Jesus, by eating the Paschal Lamb, subsumes the Old Testament image into his own body and literally becomes the fulfilment of Old Testament prophecy. This is something more complicated than simple supercession, and is distinctively possible in narrative forms such as drama, where the process of eating can be realised.

Just as the term *oblé* signals the unequivocal arrival onstage of the Eucharistic wafer in N. Town, so in the *Pèlerinage* play this arrival is marked by the term *relief*, a brilliantly oblique or polysemous word in late medieval French, which connotes salvation or help (like Modern English *relief*) but also the leftovers from a meal (as in Middle English *relefe*), and by analogy 'a small quantity of something'. Through the related term *relevement*, used in medieval French to mean something

---

56 For London: British Library Add MS 188852, see <https://www.bl.uk/manuscripts/FullDisplay.aspx?ref=Add_MS_18852>; for London: British Library Add MS 24098, see <https://www.bl.uk/manuscripts/FullDisplay.aspx?ref=Add_MS_24098>.

57 For images, see the Web Gallery of Art at <https://www.wga.hu/html_m/b/bouts/dirk_c/lastsupp/index.html>.

Fig. 6. Charity (Sylvia Wiederkehr), instructed by Wisdom (Elisa Pagliaro) prepares the *relief* for Pilgrims, in the forthcoming film of the *Pèlerinage* play by the Medieval Convent Drama Project. Photo credit Jeremy Wright.

artistically fabricated or drawn,[58] the term *relief* was also associated with construction and fabrication,[59] so the play also draws attention to the process of bread-making, which it subsequently describes at some length. This elastic term *relief* allows the verbal co-presence of all the different approaches to or embodiments of the Eucharist which the play stages or imagines, from salvation to elements of a lavish meal to a small object that is, as we learn in the course of the play, mystically baked by the allegorical character called Charity while actually, presumably, confected by a real person in this world. The term *relief* is thus much richer than the N. Town Passion's *oblé*, as it both draws attention to the on-stage

---

58 *Dictionnaire du Moyen Français* online at <http://zeus.atilf.fr/dmf/> sv *relevement* sense C.

59 *Dictionnaire du Moyen Français* online sv *relief* sense A2.

object that is or outwardly represents the Host and almost masks it with other potential readings or meanings.

The *Pèlerinage* play, a morality rather than a mystery and thus not primarily focused on the life of Christ, does not finish with the Institution of the Mass, but pushes beyond it into the life of the Early Church, and then into the anagogical New Jerusalem to which Pilgrim's journey will lead him. Pilgrim asks if he may take some of the *relief Moÿsi* ('relief of Moses', 702) to fill him up (*mon wit corps rasazier*, 'to satiate my empty body', 704) before his journey, but Grace Dieu first provides him with a pilgrim bag or scrip in which to put it: the bag is decorated with twelve bells, representing the twelve apostles, and overspread with blood: *sanc voy sur m'esckerpe espandu* ('I see blood spread across my bag', 806) which, she explains to the shocked Pilgrim, is that of the first martyr, Stephen. Thus the Eucharistic blood of Christ/wine, which is generally overshadowed in a play that tends to focus on the bread/flesh,[60] is imagistically mingled with the blood of Christian martyrs in the early church. Grace Dieu then equips Pilgrim with a staff,[61] representing hope in Christ and in the Virgin Mary, and, at his demand, armour and weapons representing virtues that will support him on the pilgrimage to the heavenly city: the helmet of Temperance, the gauntlets of Continence, and so on.[62] In a moment of farcical comedy, however, Pilgrim finds

---

60 The bread seems to have had more iconic status than the wine: seeing the Host, not the chalice, was the high point of the lay experience of Mass, and artists portraying the Eucharist tended to depict the Elevation of the Host: see Duffy *Stripping of the Altars* 96. This is possibly because the majority of believers received only bread, and not wine, at Mass; Communion in one kind for the laity developed in the twelfth century, and in England the congregation did not receive wine as well as bread until after the Reformation.

61 In Deguileville, in a passage that precedes that covered by the play, Pilgrim resolves that he must find a staff and scrip, or pilgrim bag, for his journey, and it is thus clear, as it is not in the play, that these gifts from Grace Dieu are a delayed response to Pilgrim's own wishes: *Tantost apres me pourpense | Qu'escherpe et bourdon me failloit | Et qu'avoir les me convenoit, | C'est chose mont bien avenant | A chaschun pelerin errant* ('Afterwards I thought to myself that I needed a sack and a staff, and that it would be convenient to have them, [for] they are fitting things for every wandering pilgrim', 216–20); *Pèlerinage* edited Stürzinger.

62 The whole passage, of course, recalls the 'armour of God' which St Paul urges Christians to put on in Ephesians 6: 10–15, although the precise virtues associated with each piece of armour are different: in Ephesians, the helmet is 'salvation'. The gauntlets are also called *Gaigne pain*, literally 'bread-earner'; figuratively

himself unable to move under the literal weight of the allegorical armour, and Grace Dieu has to find him a servant strong enough to be his armour bearer: Memory, who, in another potentially comical twist, is female, a *chamberier* ('chambermaid', 1193) or *mesquine* ('servant-girl', 1196).[63] It is only then that Grace Dieu deems Pilgrim ready to approach *le pain Moÿse* ('the bread of Moses', 1225) for himself, and tells him *Va, si en prens* ('Go and take some', 1226) – this is the final piece of preparation before Pilgrim sets off on his journey to *la belle cyté* ('the beautiful city', 1219).

Up to this point, Pilgrim, who is the questioner and observer and thus may be assumed to stand for the audience – an 'Everyman' figure – has not himself consumed anything; meat, bread, or wafer. The whole play may be seen as a sort of preparation for his first Communion: it has explained the nature of the Eucharist and the appropriate moral and spiritual state of the believer who would receive it. In this final scene, then, should the audience see Pilgrim, in response to Grace Dieu's command *Va, si en prens*, finally take and consume the host? The scripted words imply that this might occur, but there are as always no stage directions or rubrics and the action is nowhere described, so there is no sense of how it might have looked or what the performers wanted to achieve. There is, however, a gap in the manuscript, where a speaker marker indicates 'Pilgrim' but no dialogue is given. This perhaps marks an action, which may be the ingesting of the wafer. But it also, strangely, may not, because the focus of this final scene of the play is that of the Pilgrim's provision for a journey, and on that journey Grace Dieu has told him he should always carry the bread and his victuals in his pilgrim bag:

> the phrase signified a labourer, but also – in a very different context – a form of leather gauntlet. The *Dictionnaire du Moyen Français* online sv *gagne-pain 2 subst. masc.* speculates that the latter expression arose out of an accidental phonetic resemblance (rather than a logical or etymological connection) with the word *canepin*, a type of leather used to make gloves. Grace Dieu nonetheless elaborates on the connection which the expression *gaigne pain* enables between glove and bread: she says (1040–1) that *par el est gagnié le pain | Dont repassus sont tous cuers humains* ('by them [i.e. the gloves] is gained the bread | that satiates or fills all human hearts'). The phrase is interesting in relation to the definition of 'daily bread', discussed in the next paragraphs.

63   The gender of Memory is not necessarily marked as, indeed, all the characters apart from Pilgrim and, inevitably, Aristotle and the Moses-Priest, are female. However, in performance the contrast between Pilgrim's complaints about the weight of the armour and the fact that a female figure is chosen to carry it may have been comical.

ton pain, ossy ta vitailh | *Dois tu dedens tous jour avoir* ('your bread and also your victuals you must have inside it every day', 750–1). It thus seems at least as likely that what the audience sees is Pilgrim taking bread from the table of Moses and packing it in his bag as provisions. The Eucharistic wafer now appears as daily bread – needed *tous jour* ('every day'): it is sustenance for the traveller, perhaps also (through the association with Moses and traditional typology) analogous to the manna that sustained the Israelites in the desert. The coexistence of bread-as-wafer with bread-as-daily-bread in this scene is sharpened by the name of the Pilgrim's bag, Faith, which is established by Grace Dieu: *L'escerpe Foy est appelee* ('the bag is called Faith', 747). Faith metaphorically 'contains' or surrounds the transubstantiated Eucharist (belief in whose transubstantiation at the moment of consecration requires faith), while, at a more literal allegorical level, the Pilgrim's bag contains simultaneously the bread that offers him sustenance.

The field of association resembles that found in Jesus' comments on those who follow him after the Feeding of the Five Thousand: they follow him because they have eaten their fill, but they should seek the bread of eternal life; the manna that Moses gave the Israelites in the desert (Exodus 16) was bread from heaven that came from God (hence its prominence in biblical typology);[64] and finally, 'I am the bread of life. Whoever comes to me will never be hungry.'[65] It is important to remember that the phrase 'daily bread', familiar to us from English scriptural translation of the Paternoster, did not necessarily carry the same connotations for the Huy nuns: the New Testament Greek *epiousion* is in the Vulgate's translation of Matthew 6: 11 rendered not *cotidianum* ('daily') but *supersubstantialem* ('super-substantial'), indicating the bread of heaven or the Eucharistic bread.[66] BL Add. MS 14042, a

---

64 This is a standard late medieval type of the Eucharist. See e.g. Avril Henry *Biblia Pauperum, a Facsimile and Edition* (Aldershot: Scolar Press, 1987) 81 and 83; *Mirour of Mans Saluacioune* edited Henry, 102 and 103, lines 1811–54. Exodus 16: 31 says that the manna 'was like coriander seed white; and the taste therof like flour with honey'; Douai version.

65 See John 6: 25–35.

66 In the translation of Luke 11: 3 the same word is rendered as *cotidianum*. For the use of Matthew's version of the prayer in medieval liturgy and devotion, see Anna Edith Gottschall 'The Pater Noster and the Laity in England c.700–1560' (PhD thesis: University of Birmingham, 2014) 1–3; online at <https://core.ac.uk/download/pdf/33528933.pdf>. The Syriac tradition translates the term

Middle-Dutch prayer book from 1517–23 that was prepared for female Franciscans, presents a typological diptych of the Last Supper and the manna from heaven which, as is traditional, looks like falling wafers.[67] The nuns, who would have recited the liturgical Latin paternoster, which was based on Matthew's version, might not have primarily associated the bread needed *tous jours* with their version of the petition of the Lord's Prayer, which was rather for *super-substantial* bread: *Panem nostrum supersubstantialem da nobis hodie*. Nonetheless, it is striking that, in the *Pèlerinage* play, the final image is not the spiritualised wafer, the *oblé*, but the daily provision for the traveller. Naturalistically, a loaf rather than a wafer might seem the more appropriate prop at this point; but this would require a change of prop from the *oblé* specified earlier.

In the *Pèlerinage* play, the meal with which the play opens turns into a visual representation of Transubstantiation, however one envisages this as happening. Here, too, then, it is the comestible contents of a meal that shift and change on-stage in order to dramatise the shift from Old Testament to New Testament. When the Pilgrim goes to receive his relief the wafer seems to transform again into mealtime bread, albeit perhaps the bread of heaven, of the New Jerusalem. Rather than using possible onstage ingestion followed by explicit explanation, however – as N. Town does when Jesus explains the historical resonance of the Paschal Lamb just eaten by the Disciples, before replacing it with a wafer and inviting a new form of ingestion – the *Pèlerinage* play is intriguingly silent as to just how, when, and through whom these shifts occurred. Moments of Eucharistic consumption are at once everywhere hinted at and nowhere explicitly demanded, central to the play but also peripheral to the play's theologically and philosophically dense verbal discussion of the nature of what is to be consumed.

---

    as 'perpetual' and 'necessary', and the Coptic translation suggests the bread to come, the bread of 'tomorrow'. We are grateful to Rev. Dr Will Lamb for these observations.

67 BL Add MS 14042 fol. 274v <https://www.bl.uk/manuscripts/FullDisplay.aspx?index=11&ref=Add_MS_14042>. On this manuscript, see Hanneke Van Asperen 'Praying, Threading, and Adorning: Sewn-in Prints in a Rosary Prayer Book (London, British Library, Add. MS 14042)' in *Weaving, Veiling, and Dressing: Textiles and their Metaphors in the Late Middle Ages* edited Kathryn M. Rudy and Barbara Baert (Turnhout: Brepols, 2007) 81–121, at 83–7.

Fig. 7. Maître d'Antoine Rolin *The Bleeding Scrip* (1465). Genève, Bibliothèque de Genève, Ms. fr. 182, #1, fol. 45r. Prose adaptation of *Pèlerinage de la vie humaine* by Guillaume de Deguileville. <https://www.e-codices.unifr.ch/en/bge/fr0182/45r>

For a live performance, the special effects required by the *Pèlerinage* play are challenging.[68] In N. Town, the fact that an audience cannot really see what is in a winecup or a chalice ensures that the wine/blood of the Mass, at least, need not be a problematic prop. But in the *Pèlerinage* play blood must be visible elsewhere, on the bag that Grace Dieu gives to Pilgrim. Furthermore, it is possible that this blood should mysteriously appear on the bag while Grace Dieu and Pilgrim are talking about it; certainly, the bag and the bells upon it are discussed for sixty lines (743–804) before Pilgrim suddenly becomes distressed at the sight of blood on the bag: *mult novellement | Suy desconforté griefement. | Sanc voy sur m'esckerpe espandu* ('suddenly I am greviously upset. I see blood spattered on my bag', 804–6). In Deguileville, the Pilgrim is troubled precisely because he had not seen the stains when he looked at the bag before, suggesting that it is not simply blood-stained but actually bleeding.[69] Such an effect is challenging but not impossible on the medieval stage, and French theatre was apparently particularly expert at producing bleeding effects.[70] If the Huy nuns ever fully staged

---

68   The Medieval Convent Drama Project, based at the University of Fribourg, Switzerland, explored nuns' plays, including those of the nuns of Huy, through performance experiment. The *Pèlerinage* play was scheduled as the final production of the project, but, like the Mass itself, fell prey to COVID restrictions. By autumn 2021 assembling full casts and live audiences was still impossible, but as some restrictions lifted we were able to gather small groups of actors – two or three at a time for each scene – and film the play, often in outdoor locations. Of course, it is much easier to achieve certain special effects on film than in a live performance: for example, it was possible to make Grace Dieu suddenly disappear from Pilgrim's sight, as the lines require that she does: *Car deis maintenant je m'en pars | De la veyue a ton regarde* ('for, from this moment, I leave your sight', 1254–5). However, the film does not attempt to simulate Transubstantiation, but rather uses a loaf of bread throughout as the *relief*. The film is currently in post-production and once completed will be freely available via the project website <http://medievalconventdrama.org>.

69   *Vi gouttes de seng semees | Dessur li* [the bag] *et esbouciees | La quel chose bien me desplut | Et mon courage tout esmut | Et de ce qu'autre fois vëu | Ne l'avoie n'apercëu* ('I saw drops of blood spattered and stained on it [the bag], which I did not like at all, and which moved me greatly, and all the more because before, I had not perceived or seen this', 3575–80); *Pèlerinage* edited Stürzinger, 111.

70   See, for example, the devices for making Christ sweat blood recorded in Provence and at Ravello: 'Provencal Director's Notebook', cited in William Tydeman *The Medieval European Stage 500–1500* (Cambridge UP, 2001) 317; *The Staging of Religious Drama in Europe in the Later Middle Ages: Texts and Documents in*

the *Pèlerinage* play, their efforts may have represented a theatrical ambition perhaps surprising in convent drama: they must have dedicated considerable attention to special effects associated with the blood/wine and body/bread props of the Mass.

Conclusion

Both N. Town and the *Pèlerinage* play stage a Eucharistic meal, but one shows that meal as a Last Supper, incorporating the Institution of the Mass, and the other is an extra-biblical, eschatological dramatisation. N. Town moves its audience from the Old Testament Passover to the New Testament Last Supper and then to the liturgy – the liturgy is the end-point, as marked by the medieval language of the *Maundé*, the term which both Jesus and his disciples use to refer to the feast. The *Pèlerinage* play is more complex: the liturgy is the starting point and the play circles round it, approaching it from literal, spiritual, and ontological angles. The Huy play does not use ingestion to move from the Old Testament to the liturgy, as N. Town does; instead it uses repeated references to ingestion to punctuate a multi-voiced exploration of what the liturgy is. N. Town is explicit about the choreography and movements required to stage the liturgy, and explicit about choreographing it as a Mass; it thus raises intriguing questions about the nature of participation required from the spectator. The Huy play, on the other hand, is totally silent as to the choreography of its scenes of liturgical ingestion, leaving spaces in which its audience may have participated as the congregation at a Mass, and is also encouraged to see itself in a Pilgrim packing his daily bread. If the play were indeed performed for an audience of sisters who also received the Mass, then this is a particularly potent example of audience participation, focused on bread that is at once the eucharistic Host and a changing theatrical object. The theatrical effectiveness of N. Town, recognised by Woolf,[71] stems from its theologically informed enriching

---

    English Translation edited Peter Meredith and John Tailby (Early Drama, Art, and Music Monograph Series, 4; Kalamazoo, MI: Medieval Institute Publications, 1983) 108. These are discussed in Elisabeth Dutton '*Macbeth* and the Croxton *Play of the Sacrament*: Blood and Belief in Early English Stagecraft' in *Blood Matters: Studies in European Literature and Thought, 1400–1700* edited Bonnie Lander Johnson and Eleanor Decamp (Philadelphia PA: University of Pennsylvania Press, 2018) 183–97, at 187–9.

71 Woolf *The English Mystery Plays* 234–7.

of Last Supper imagery with evocations of the Passover, of the manna given to the Israelites in the desert, and of Mary's anointing of Christ at the house of Simon the Leper, as well as of the Mass that the Last Supper institutes. The *Pèlerinage* play may have been just as theatrically effective, though the lack of rubrics and stage directions demands scholarly guesswork; it also enriches the spectator's understanding of the Last Supper that is also the Pilgrim's First Communion through an insistent and multivalent interrogation of the nature – shifting, super-substantial, quotidian – of its central prop.

Université de Fribourg
University of Birmingham

Acknowledgements

Research for this article was funded by the Swiss National Science Foundation, project grant 100015_165887, 'Medieval Convent Drama'. We are grateful to Meg Twycross and Aurélie Blanc for additional research.

EDITORIAL BOARD (2022)

Executive Editor:
    Meg Twycross (Lancaster University)
General Editors:
    Sarah Carpenter (University of Edinburgh)
    Elisabeth Dutton (Université de Fribourg)
    Gordon Kipling (UCLA)
Advisory Board:
    Phil Butterworth (University of Leeds)
    Garrett Epp (University of Alberta, Université Catholique de Lille)
    Richard Hillman (Université de Tours)
    Pamela M. King (University of Glasgow)
    Sally-Beth MacLean (University of Toronto)
    James McBain (Green Templeton College, Oxford)
    John J. McGavin (University of Southampton)
    John McKinnell (University of Durham)
    Peter Meredith (University of Leeds)
    Tom Pettitt (University of Southern Denmark, Odense)
    Matthew Sergi (University of Toronto)
    Greg Walker (University of Edinburgh)
Latin Consultant: Alison Samuels (Oxford)
Subscriptions Editor: Clare Egan (Lancaster University)

SUBMISSION OF ARTICLES

Contributions for consideration should be sent to one of the editors:

Meg Twycross, Department of English and Creative Writing, Lancaster University, LANCASTER LA1 4YD, United Kingdom
E-mail: m.twycross@lancaster.ac.uk

Sarah Carpenter, English Literature, School of Literatures, Languages and Cultures, University of Edinburgh, 50 George Square, EDINBURGH EH8 9LH, United Kingdom.
E-mail: Sarah.Carpenter@ed.ac.uk

Elisabeth Dutton, English Department, University of Fribourg, Ave. Europe 20, CH1700 FRIBOURG, Switzerland.
E-mail: elisabeth.dutton@unifr.ch

Gordon Kipling, 3428 Park Avenue, MINNEAPOLIS, MN 55407, USA
E-mail: kipling@humnet.ucla.edu

Articles should usually be sent as e-mail attachments, preferably in a recent version of MS Word. See website for further information:
<http://www.medievalenglishtheatre.co.uk/submit.html>

Contributors are asked to follow the *METh* house-style (see website: address above). The language of publication is usually English, and translations should be supplied for quotations from all other languages, including French and Latin.

www.ingramcontent.com/pod-product-compliance
Lightning Source LLC
Chambersburg PA
CBHW070807230426
43665CB00017B/2523